CALVIN FOR THE 3RD MILLENNIUM

CALVIN FOR THE 3ʳᴰ MILLENNIUM

HANS MOL

E PRESS

Published by ANU E Press
The Australian National University
Canberra ACT 0200, Australia
Email: anuepress@anu.edu.au
This title is also available online at: http://epress.anu.edu.au/calvin_citation.html

National Library of Australia
Cataloguing-in-Publication entry

Author:	Mol, Hans, 1922-
Title:	Calvin for the third millennium / Hans Mol.
ISBN:	9781921313974 (pbk.)
	9781921313981 (web)
Subjects:	Calvin, Jean, 1509-1564.
	Presbyterianism--Sermons.
Dewey Number:	230.42092

All rights reserved. No part of this publication may be reproduced, stored in a retrieval system or transmitted in any form or by any means, electronic, mechanical, photocopying or otherwise, without the prior permission of the publisher.

Cover design by ANU E Press

Cover Illustration courtesy of the H.H. Meeter Centre for Calvin Studies, Calvin College and Seminary, Grand Rapids, Michigan.

This edition © 2008 ANU E Press

Table of Contents

PREFACE	vii
PERFECTION and RESURRECTION: PHILIPPIANS 3:10-12	1
TRINITY and TRUTH: JOHN 16:13	5
ETERNITY: FACT or FICTION?: 1 TIMOTHY I:16	11
DREAMS: DANIEL 5:12	17
A HOLY STRUGGLE for POWER: MATTHEW 20:25-26	23
AUTHORITY from within or AUTHORITY from without: MATTHEW 21:24	31
GOD and CAESAR: MATTHEW 22:21	39
COVENANT and FAITH: MATTHEW 25:10	47
The CLOAK of INTEGRITY: ISAIAH 61:10	55
SCATTERED LIKE A CROWD OF FRIGHTENED SHEEP: MATTHEW 9:36	61
RESTORING the BALANCE: JOHN 6:51	67
CALVIN'S DOGS: MARK 7:27	71
PAWNS, PUPPETS AND PIETY: JOB 42:6	77
GROWING in WISDOM: LUKE 2:52	83
RESTORED SOULS: PSALM 19:7	89
CORRUPTING POWER: 1 KINGS 21:22	95
MISPLACED MILITANCY: LUKE 17:10	103
GRATITUDE from a FOREIGNER: LUKE 17:18	111
PEACE and POWER: PSALM 72:3	119
ABUSE of RELIGION: MATTHEW 21:13	127
MARTYRDOM and SELF-DENIAL: ACTS 7:59-60	133
The GRACE of GOD: ROMANS 5:2	141
ORDER and DISORDER: JOB 25:2	149
WORK: MATTHEW 20:12	157
The VIRGIN BIRTH: LUKE 1:35	165
The LAMB OF GOD and THE TREE OF LIFE: REVELATION 22:1-2	173
THE BEGINNING and THE END: REVELATION 22:13	181
JESUS: REFUGEE or KING?: MATTHEW 2:13	189

ROOTS and ROOTLESSNESS: MATTHEW 13:6	195
FREEDOM from OPPPRESSION: ACTS 10:38	201
PREDISTINATION or ELECTION?: ROMANS 8:29	205
BEING CHRIST'S LETTER: 2 CORINTHIANS 3:3	211
JESUS in the WILDERNESS: ISAIAH 40:3	217
IMPRISONED, YET FREE: 2 CORINTHIANS 3:17	223
SACRIFICING LIFE: JOHN 15:13	229
SEPARATE, YET TOGETHER or the TRAGEDY and TRIUMPH of DIVERSITY: ACTS 15:8	235
THE SIMPLICITY of FAITH: 2 CORINTHIANS 11:3	243
AUTHORITY and MINISTRY: ISAIAH 42:3	249
The HARMONY of FAITH: 1 CORINTHIANS 1:13	255
HEAVEN, the HABITATION of ORDER: PSALM 119:89	261
ABOUT THE AUTHOR	267
OTHER BOOKS BY THE AUTHOR	269
POSTSCRIPT	271

PREFACE

There is a section of John Calvin's *Institutes of the Christian Religion* which has always stuck in my mind as central to his view of the relation between religion and the sciences. It deals with reason and faith (Book II, Chapter ii, sections 16-18). To Calvin reason is the most excellent blessing of the divine spirit and 'one of the essential properties of our nature.' God will punish those lazy believers, he says, who do not make use of the works of the ungodly in physics, symbiotics, mathematics and other similar sciences.

To Calvin there is nothing inherently wrong with reason as such. His peer is the Renaissance. And yet the reasoning about God by philosophers 'invariably savours somewhat of giddy imagination.' Some of them are 'blinder than moles', he states, and if there is any light in what they say, it is as rare and useless as a single flash of lighting in a dark night. He hints that momentary insight is lost in the enveloping darkness of the night and falls short of an enduring comprehension of the entire landscape of existence.

Yet reason and science are so precious to Calvin that in his interpretation of Genesis 1:16 he sides with the astronomers' view of creation and dismisses the Genesis account because Moses 'being an ordained teacher as well of the unlearned and rude as of the learned, could not otherwise fulfil his office than by descending to this gross method of instruction (Calvin 37 sermon).'

Calvin, following his hero St Augustine, regards God as representing order. It is rather central in his thinking. He interprets God 'placing it in the heavens … a habitation subject to no changes (exegesis of Psalm 119:89 in Calvin 40 sermon).'

However Calvin does not want that separation to be so severe as to jeopardize its relevance; God's celestial order impinges on man's disorder, he thinks. To him the prophets in general and Jesus in particular bridge the gap. For instance in his exegesis of Acts 2:17 (sermon four) he calls them accurate observers of their times who spoke figuratively 'before their time' and applied their 'style unto the capacity of their time.'

Science and reason are not comprehensive enough to Calvin's way of thinking. To achieve the state of enlightenment and comprehension of the entire landscape of existence one has to venture beyond the fleeting and vain power of the intellect and seek the foundation of truth. And to Calvin the only source of truth is God's grace without which God-given reason is vain.

These sermons delivered at St Andrew's attempt to be true to the basic meaning of the scripture passages of the lectionary for each particular Sunday and to their interpretation in Calvin's forty-odd volumes of commentary in my library.

Yet they are also strongly informed by what, I am sure, Calvin, if he were alive today, would call the social sciences of the twentieth century: ungodly. My forty years of academic writing and teaching in the social scientific study of religion will hopefully add patches of enlightenment. The sermons represent my fundamental understanding of biblical functionality. Yet they also prevent 'slothful' neglect of up-to-date scholarship in the anthropological psychological and sociological disciplines.

Hans Mol, 1 June 2008

CALVIN 01

PERFECTION and RESURRECTION

All I want to know is Christ, to experience the power of his resurrection, to share his suffering ... (but) I do not claim that I have already succeeded or have already become perfect. Philippians 3:10-12

Today (2/4/1995) is a very special day for me personally. It is exactly fifty years ago that I was liberated by the Canadian armed forces. All relatives and friends had given me up for dead. Anybody taken to Nazi Gestapo camps for 'undermining the German war machinery' was very unlikely to get out alive.

Yet here I was, liberated and still alive. That day also happened to be Easter Monday in April 1945. Since that day Easter, or the resurrection in our text, has meant freedom and liberation to me. It meant and means to me, even now, that death has been left behind.

I was twenty-one when the Gestapo picked me up and twenty-three when World War II finished. I had grown up on a bankrupt farm in a small Dutch village, where I occasionally played the organ in the mediaeval church. The minister there was a learned and powerful preacher. He would hold forth on sin and crucifixion, but it didn't mean much to me at the time. I went to church for the music. I felt that Bach's music reflected the anxieties and the turmoil of my teenage years. I attended a high school too demanding for my mediocre talents (the Gymnasium in Tiel failed thirty percent of students each year, mainly because it insisted on the mastery of six languages). Organ music to me was consolation, particularly when I could play it myself on our twelve-stop organ.

But whatever was said from the pulpit went in one ear and out the other. To me it was drivel. What I lived by was the latent ideology in both high school and university; a philosophy built on reason and Jean Paul Sartre's existentialism. That fitted with my experiences of the humanistic liberalism of secondary education in the Netherlands and not at all with Christian theology.

And then I was plunged right into the immense suffering of the Gestapo camps and prisons. It was not just physical survival I needed. It was also backbone and spine to face it all. It was then that the preaching of this learned minister came back to me. I began to realise that I could cope with all the pain and hurt and the problems that were part of living towards the end of the Second World War in German camps and prisons if I could see myself in the larger context of sin/breakdown and salvation/wholeness. Morale needed bolstering even more than ability to survive physically. Just as important, what I remembered of the sermons in the village church of Ophemert fitted better with my war experiences than French existentialism.

But I don't want to talk too long about my personal story. The excerpts of the crucifixion from Bach's St John's Passion before the sermon and of the resurrection from Handel's Messiah later are more important today. Yet this illustration of my own experiences fits in both with the music, and what St Paul says in the third chapter of the epistle to the Philippians. To him the crucifixion and the resurrection form the drama in terms of which he would find his identity and integrity. It also would lead to his becoming more perfect. To say this differently, he would fulfil his destiny, he thinks, if he were to become part and parcel of this human drama of sin and salvation or crucifixion and resurrection, it would unify him with Christ's suffering and rising again.

In the beginning of the third chapter, St Paul says that all things he relied on for his former sense of confidence and righteousness (nowadays we would call this his sense of integrity, his identity) would have to be counted as 'sheer loss, because all is far outweighed by the gain of knowing Christ Jesus my Lord, for whose sake I did in fact lose everything' (verse 8). He mentions those things that formed the essence of his former confidence in verses 5-7: circumcised on my eighth day, Israelite by race, of the tribe of Benjamin, a Hebrew born and bred by attitude to the law, being a Pharisee, pious zeal, being an early persecutor of the church. Yet all these things, so important for his former sense of self, he now declared as ever so much garbage (verse 8). They were cut from underneath him.

Calvin's commentary on these passages compares St Paul's loss of everything for the knowledge of Christ with the sailors on the verge of shipwreck. 'They throw everything overboard, that, the ship being lightened, they may reach the harbour in safety.' Justification by good works has to be jettisoned. Or as Calvin summarizes it: '(Paul) divested himself – not of works, but of that mistaken confidence in works, with which he had been puffed up.'

That was also my experience. In the Gestapo camp and in the prisons there was nothing from the past that I could rely on for security. The comfort of music, friends, relatives, status as a university student, capacity for reasoning, logical competence, confidence in man-made truth, all vanished as anchors for one's self-respect. In the Nazi prison system political prisoners who were unfortunate enough to be university students also, were at the very bottom of the pile. Unexpectedly and miraculously in that situation of rejection and despair, affinity with, understanding of, and faith in, the crucified Christ did well up as a deep surge of inner power, as an inner spring of living water (John 4:10). God's act of resurrecting a quenched spirit did become supreme reality, pivotal to a changed identity.

Both Paul and Calvin call this experience 'election', a sense of God injecting sublime order and trust at the very moment of personal chaos in an existential wasteland. Both Paul and Calvin have been accused of overdoing predestination. Yet God's order is not a cold, static, impersonal execution (as people interpret predestination to be) but an exhilarating, dynamic, personal response to human disorder.

To me the incredible complexity of the human brain, for instance, is an example of God's blueprint for existence and indeed may seem an impersonal 'given.' But there is more to God's order. Generally, and especially in Philippians chapter 3, God's ordering is a highly specific and personal act. It consists of God actively counterbalancing moral, mental and physical breakdown (sin, as epitomized in the crucifixion) with moral, mental and physical integration (salvation as epitomized in the resurrection).

Conversion experiences as well as 'rites of passage' (birth, initiation, marriage, death) always involve the stripping of an obsolete, decrepit, threadbare identity and the welding of a new, better fitting, better-suited one. To St Paul, St Augustine, Calvin and hosts of others before and since, salvation, the resurrection, Easter, represented this new, better fitting, identity, or the new life in Christ. Yet the old life (one's previous emotional attachments) had to become obsolete, decrepit and threadbare before the new one could be grafted on.

Therefore crucifixion and resurrection are not just events that one can look upon from a distance and say: 'Well that is interesting.' The perfection that Paul is talking about in verse 12 is more than a description of an event. It doesn't mean much unless you and I are part and parcel of this dynamic, the never fully completed struggle for perfection, wholeness and integrity. It is not just a scene. Unless it is part and parcel of our thinking and feeling, our inner being, our inner self, it is, as Calvin suggests at the end of his commentary on Philippians 3, not very efficacious. And by efficacy he means that the boundless power of God has to show itself in action.

Yet that very action is spiritually anchored in the deepest source of one's being. Motivation stems from this source. The survival value of any religion and Christianity in particular rests on its ability to inform and mould this inner wellspring. St Paul calls this 'experiencing the power of Christ's resurrection (verse 10).' Calvin (commenting on verse 21) calls this being 'wholly attached to Christ because this body which we carry about with us is not an everlasting abode, but a frail tabernacle, which will in a short time be reduced to nothing.' They both refer to the unifying core of one's personal identity. St Paul (Calvin's comment on verse 12) 'did nothing except under Christ's influence and guidance.'

In other words, Christ is the model, both as a blueprint for action and as a prompter and protector of basic values. The closer one's attachment to this model, the more integrated one is both within and without. Within, because it provides balance, serenity, capacity to cope. Without, because it tames one's beast or demon, provides the humility, understanding, responsibility, reliability, altruism, self-denial, honesty and discipline which any society and culture needs for its integrity. It is in this way that God the father carries out his blueprint of order, counterbalancing man's ingrained capacity for disorder, chaos, in other words, sin.

And that is the message of Paul in Philippians chapter three. It depends on God's coming to man in the form of Jesus Christ, living by the Holy Spirit as God provides it to all humans, free of charge. It is about this that we are going to celebrate because from here onwards in this service we are thinking about the great gift of God's power. The trumpet shall sound and we celebrate the fact of our delivery, of our redeemer living. Redemption is not just something to do with a dead saviour, it is the redeemer who lives … and that's what we now hear in Handel's aria 'I know that my redeemer liveth.'

CALVIN 02
TRINITY and TRUTH

The Spirit of truth will guide you into all the truth. John 16:1

Today is Trinity Sunday. Yet the readings this morning are not about the Trinity but about wisdom and understanding in Proverbs and all about truth in John 16:13. Why are there no references in the Bible about the Trinity and so many references about truth in the Gospel according to St John? And why is the Trinity so prominent in the Westminster Confession, the basis of doctrine for Presbyterianism? Isn't the Bible the real source of our faith? What does truth mean in our text? Let us answer these questions one by one.

What is the Trinity? It is an attempt by the church fathers and theologians to systematize what the Bible says about the three elements of the Godhead: God, the Father; God, the Son; God, the Holy Spirit. In other words the Trinity is solidly grounded in Scripture. It brings together what is already there separately. Yet the sum is more than the parts. Looking at the parts separately may help us to discover why they need one another to make a whole.

First: God the Father. Chapter two of the Westminster Confession is all about God. God, it says, is infinite, in being and perfection. A most pure spirit, invisible without body, parts or passions, immutable, immense, eternal, incomprehensible, almighty, most wise, most holy, most free, most absolute, working all things according to the council of his own immutable and most righteous will. And then it goes on to say that 'God is also, most loving, gracious, merciful, long-suffering, forgiving inequity, transgression and sin.'

Let me put it all in my own, sociological, terms: God represents order as distinct from existential disorder. By transcending time and place God disconnects from disorder but remains relevant through contrasting the beliefs and values which integrate man and society with the ones that diminish, even destroy integrity. He does that by encouraging those values that strengthen solidarity in its various forms, such as humility, self-denial, discipline, altruism and love. Yet he is also 'authority', who by means of reciprocal loyalty and faith reinforces stability. Thanks to his transcendence God can also insist on change, when that fits with his plan for the world.

Second: God the Son. Jesus Christ, according to the Westminster Confession, took upon himself human nature. God is all things humans are not. We are not immortal, we are not all wise, we are not omniscient, and we are not all powerful. Therefore Jesus became the bridge, or 'mediator', as the confession calls him, between the divine and the human. Jesus showed how God the Father expected humans to actually live. God's nature is expressed in Jesus.

Jesus therefore is the concretization of God who is invisible, immortal, infinite etc. Jesus showed concretely what God's intentions were for actual living in an inhospitable, imperfect, sinful world. In Jesus God showed how values and belief sustain culture and society beyond the life spans and instincts of individuals. Jesus also put his own life on the line to maintain his integrity, as God's representative, and exemplified through crucifixion and resurrection that the fullness of life is much more than physical survival.

Third: God, the Holy Spirit. Without the Holy Spirit the beliefs and values just mentioned would not be very effective. Commitment, loyalty, dedication, or as the Bible calls it, faith, are crucial for the implementation of these beliefs and values. Emotions and feeling are essential for the maintenance of social fabric. The Holy Spirit oils the social and cultural machinery. Without the Holy Spirit the relationships with God the Father and God the Son would be dull, dry and cold rather than personal, trusting and warm.

This is not all. The Holy Spirit also reconciles and restores what has to be repaired either for the sanity and health of the individual or for the relationship with one's society or one's social group. Conflicting demands may cause the kinds of stress that prayer, meditation and the Holy Spirit behind them may mitigate. Love, inspired by the Holy Spirit, binds people and groups and, above all, strengthens one's well-being and sense of identity.

The Trinity is a unity, in which God the Father, God the Son and God, the Holy Spirit is distinct. Yet together they are necessary for salvation, holiness, or whole making. Integrity is a concept close to what is meant by salvation. Calvin in his sermon on the character of Job prefers the concept of integrity to perfection. It is closer to the original Hebrew, he says. It is also a pivotal term if one wants to link theology to the social sciences.

As you may remember from the beginning of this sermon, another of today's puzzles has to do with finding an answer to our question as to what the Trinity has to do with truth. After all to us truth has little to do with feeling, loyalty and faith and a lot with thinking and thought. We are trained to associate truth with the correct analysis of reality. Certainly that is the way 'truth' is used in my sociological profession. Truth is understanding what lies behind the phenomena, what the reality is behind what appears, what the truth of it all is. Truth has a lot to do with logic, reason, evidence.

Yet that is not the way 'truth' is used in the Bible. In the Old Testament, for instance in Exodus 34:6, God is called 'true.' Psalm 31:5 calls God, the God of truth. And the Hebrew word for truth has nothing to do with the analysis of reality and almost everything to do with steadiness, reliability, stability, equilibrium, immutability, solidity, being moored, and anchored.

And it is in this sense that not just Christianity, but all religions deal with truth. By means of the truth they provide the confines, the contour, and the reliable parameter of living. To them existence is more than chaos. It lies beyond the arbitrary and the whimsical. It deals with a deep understanding, a wideness that straddles both problems and capacity to cope with them through providing contour, furnishing the context. And in this provision of context, God is number one. He is immutability, steadiness and order par excellence.

But then these values and concepts tend to become so general that they need application to be effective. And that's why, not only in our religion, but also, for instance, in Buddhism the divine is concretized. It comes to earth in the Buddha and the followers of Buddha. And in our case and particularly in the Old Testament it is concretized in the Messiah, God becoming human. Abstractions and ideals cannot be appropriated easily unless we can see and judge their effect. So in the second person of the Trinity, in Jesus Christ, the divine is personified. Or as John (14:6) has it: Jesus is the way, the truth and the life.

In Jesus Christ then we recognize the elements of salvation to make us whole. Jesus was humble, Jesus was the mediator between God and man, and above all, Jesus was self-denying. He sacrificed himself on the Cross so that we could have life everlasting, so that our sins could be forgiven. But that's not enough to fill in the context and the contour of existence. It is not enough to realise or to be aware of God's almightiness, God's majesty, God's greatness, God's creation. It's not enough just to know that Jesus was humble and that Jesus was self-sacrificing and self denying, that he died on the cross and rose again on the third day.

There is also the emotional element. There is also the element of being engaged, the element of loyalty, the element of feeling, the element of emotion and that's what the Holy Spirit is all about. That's why God sent the Holy Spirit. In the Holy Spirit the non-rational element of man is addressed. Our wholeness is better served by our commitments than by our knowledge alone. Love, loyalty and commitment add to our life an extra which plain reason, plain logical calculation or just economic security cannot provide.

Therefore the Trinity is a whole, a whole of elements that together provide us with the context of living. The emphasis is on understanding and on truth. Yet it is the Biblical sense of truth, not the one that is found through reason and logic, but through encountering Jesus, as the Holy Spirit guides us. The Holy Spirit lifts us above the rational, explains and elaborates all the elements that go into the Trinity. It connects us with all the things I have just mentioned, values and feelings.

Our society usually understands truth to mean correctness. It is the Greek influence in our culture which leads to this kind of understanding. Yet quite frankly if it hadn't been for this kind of truth, we would be all the poorer for it. We need the strictness and the logic and the consistency of Plato, for instance, or Aristotle, or Socrates. We need fifth-century BC Athens to make sure that we don't make mistakes in our practical interpretation of what life is all about, of what the earth is all about, of what the stars are all about, of what the planets are all about.

Yet we also need the other kind of truth the Bible mentions. In the Old Testament truth does not mean logical consistency, it doesn't mean proof, it doesn't mean evidence. It means strength. It means reliability. God's truth is God's reliability.

That is also true for the New Testament. Particularly in the Gospel of John there are more than fifty references to truth. John regarded himself as a Greek speaking missionary to the Greek civilisation. Therefore he used Greek words like 'alathea', the Greek word for truth. Yet he filled the concept with biblical content. He used it to mean God's reliability, God's goodness, God's steadfastness.

Next door has a dog. He is not at all disciplined. Again and again he burrows underneath the fence specially erected for him and then chases all the kangaroos on the property. His owner treats him as her child and feels that befouling our lawn and swimming in our pond is quite OK. One night I had a dream that the pond was frozen and that the dog was confidently walking on it. But at the end the ice was not thick enough to carry the dog and he fell in.

God's truth in the Bible is God helping us to walk on ice that is strong, that can hold human beings. God is never the one that lets us skate on thin ice because he protects us. Through faith we are part of God's Kingdom. He provides us with the rock rather than the sand on which we can build our integrity. God is, as it were, the rock of our foundation not the sand. Yet we may be encountered and embraced and enveloped by things that remind us more of sand than of rock, or thin ice rather than thick ice.

In today's society there are many options. We can go in many directions, adopt many fake commitments. We have the freedom to be enthusiastic about trivial little things displacing the all-encompassing, comprehensive commitment, loyalty and faith that the Bible is talking about. In this life of ours, with all the various options and various big and little commitments, the commitments to money making or to power or commitments to sex or all the other things that can make commitment so piece-meal and so partial, God directs us to something that is more stable, that is beyond the world: a direction for our commitment, a direction for our loyalty that transcends all these other loyalties.

God's truth consists in providing us with broadness of mind, broadness of vision. Our text for today implicitly contrasts the Greek emphasis on reason, on logic, or rationality with the Biblical truth of God's stability, God's reliability, God's greatness. We need both Athens and Jerusalem. The vitality of our culture is closely related to the separate and distinct contributions reason and faith make.

Our culture is held together by opposing forces, truth as interpreted by our Greek heritage and truth as interpreted by the Bible. Yet the Bible also talks about reconciliation between these opposing forces. It maintains that Jesus Christ is the reconciler, that Jesus Christ is the mediator. It maintains that through Jesus and the truth of the Holy Spirit we are made free. It is a truth that liberates because it is anchored in our emotions, in our loves, in our commitment and in our faith. And this is what makes us whole.

Jesus Christ represents salvation to those of us who are lost in the jumble and the jungle of life, lost in the many options, in the many competing commitments and loyalties. Jesus Christ single-mindedly focuses our attention on the rock of our salvation and we happily respond because we know that we can be saved only by faith as we read today in Romans 5:1.

This is the message I want to leave with you. Truth is not just logical truth; it is not just the outcome of evidence and proof, of cause and effect. Truth as it is used in our text is relying on God who in turn is reliance, immutability and eternity personified. God is beyond us and yet, in Jesus, also with us. It is the Holy Spirit that binds us to God's truth and anchors us to the rock of His salvation. Therefore we glorify God. He shelters us under His everlasting wings and does not leave us to our own devices. And in the process of glorifying His holy name we may, as a by-product, find ourselves.

CALVIN 03

ETERNITY: FACT or FICTION?

Gaining eternal life. 1 Timothy 1:1

I would like to think with you today about eternity and time. Being left in charge at St Andrew's for two weeks, I learnt how much is happening in our church during the week. On several occasions I became more than usually conscious of God's eternity and eternal life. A few days ago I stood at the death-bed of an old, very much loved gentleman, father and grandfather of the many relatives standing around. None of them were churchgoers, but the family was of Scottish origin and therefore they had asked for a Presbyterian minister.

At this time of imminent death and fleeting mortality, all felt downcast. There was a sense of resignation and surrender in the air as though all were less sure of themselves. I read Deuteronomy 33:27 about God being our refuge consoling us in his everlasting arms. Also the 23rd Psalm about God's guidance and the famous passages of Romans 8:38 where St Paul says that neither death nor life, nor angels, nor principalities, nor things present, nor things to come, nor powers of height or depth, nor anything in creation shall be able to separate us from the love of God. And in the prayer following I stressed the same themes of God's everlasting arms and his eternity transcending human time. These readings and prayers help to make us feel in touch with God. As one of the relatives said, God seemed to be actually and realistically supporting them in their distress and grief.

God seems to be closer to humans at moments like these than when self-confidence is upper most. Jesus said: 'Blessed are they that mourn: for they shall be comforted' (Matthew 5:4). There seems to be an openness for God's word when our securities are on the skids, when death intervenes in our taken for granted relations of affection. Our emptiness seemed to be suddenly filled with an understanding of God's mercy, or a vague understanding of how God's eternity impinges on our mortality.

Time is a human construct. The idea of time very likely resulted from man's mortality being put in a larger context. Survival of the fittest demanded an increasing reliance on cooperation and communication. Or to say this differently and more brutally: man had to rise above his animal nature, if the species was to dominate according to God's plan (Genesis 1:26). And that means that time had to expand beyond physical life span. It had to incorporate all knowledge, norms and values transmitted from one generation to another.

To Calvin therefore both reason (undergirding knowledge) and conscience (vital for the implementation of norms and values) had to be God-given.

Since time immemorial, time itself had to have a clearly defined purpose beyond the limits of man's organic existence. Throughout the Bible this purpose is vested in God who is not only eternal and the preserver of values, but also the guardian of each individual conscience. This guardianship comes close to what St Paul and Calvin call 'election', God's active, personal, involvement, in man's actions. Vital, however, is also man's response, commitment, surrender to, and faith in, this intimate initiative. To be at all efficacious, it has to be a strong bond, a solemn covenant, a mutual trust between both parties. I don't think there is a page in the entire Bible that does not make this abundantly clear.

To return to eternity or eternal life as a vital piece in the puzzle of life, God is eternal, because his order stretches beyond the physical order of animal and human bodies. It includes everything that nowadays we would call civilization, culture, society, all ideas and concepts which one cannot find in the Bible, because they were not part of the vocabulary in the days God's word was written down.

Yet that animal nature of man had, and still has, its own integrity. It is and was dead set on survival and therefore health and recovering of that health, if it had, or has been, put in jeopardy. But there is more. The physical nature of man is also programmed to perpetuate itself vigorously. After all each of us is the product of one sperm, which managed to outdo millions of others, in fertilizing the one egg that began your and my life. The Bible calls that desire for physical integrity 'flesh' or the carnal aspect of lustful man or our 'lower nature', as St Paul calls it in Galatians 5:16. In Ephesians he calls it our 'sensuality', obeying the 'promptings of our own instincts.'

Augustine, Thomas Aquinas, Luther and Calvin follow St Paul closely. Again and again in the *Institutes of the Christian Religion,* his commentaries and his numerous sermons Calvin views man's lustful instincts as being at war with his higher nature. He approves wholeheartedly of St Paul when in Romans 8:7 he writes about man's lower nature being at war with God. And in this war eternity is on God's side, the temporary pleasures of lust are on Satan's. Self-denial to the point of sacrifice on the cross and martyrdom are God's will, but self-indulgence is on the Devil's side.

Yet the basic instinct in all humans to survive and procreate the species has its own well-developed integrity. St Paul and Calvin may come close (very close, yet never entirely) to associating it with original sin, but that is primarily because they are in the business of propagating, promulgating and proclaiming an altogether different form of integrity. And this altogether different form of integrity or God's Spirit (Romans 8:9) is, as St Paul so well expresses, at war with the 'flesh' (or man's lower nature).

It is the intrinsic power and potency of that mundane nature or original sin, which has to be stressed so strongly, in order for that heavenly vision to come into its own. The latter (God's eternal Spirit and his everlasting arms) transcends man's mortality and human time and cannot come into its own, unless it distances itself from, and even altogether disowns, the power of the former.

St Paul and Calvin use the concept of eternity only sparingly in the *Institutes of the Christian Religion*. Calvin calls conscience 'an undoubted sign of an immortal spirit.' It is 'evidence of our immortal essence.' In other words, all values and norms that form our conscience are God's gift: they lift man above his animal instincts and discipline them for the sake of social cohesion, strengthening and improving the social system.

Expiation (the expunging, annulling of sin or reconciliation of God and man through the sacrificial death of Jesus on the cross) is also called 'eternal' by Calvin, as indeed it is called in the epistle on which his comments are based (Hebrews 9:14). The reconciliation consists of man's sinfulness or propensity for disorder countered and modified by God's whole-making or ordered plan for existence or, as Calvin, true to the Bible, keeps stressing, the way God has predestined that existence.

To Calvin and the many biblical authors, predestination was an ordered or structured blueprint, transcendentally superimposed on an obviously not so orderly existence. If nowadays 'predestination' is an idea avoided in most preaching, it is because theology has not come to grips with the fatal symbiosis between a basic human need for eternity-requiring securities and delineations on the one hand and an equally strong, but contrasting, need for a dynamic, flexible, and therefore mortal, creating of order out of potential chaos, on the other hand.

The sacrifice of Jesus on the cross is the event through which the chasm between eternity (or whatever transcends mundane existence) and time (or whatever is bound up in that existence) is bridged for the transformation of the latter. The more permanent blueprint has to prevail over an eventually dispensable, temporal, scaffold, surrounding the intended structure. Expiation as well as the incarnation is the theological solution to the need for bridging the gap between the transcendental and the imminent, the permanent and the temporal, eternity and time.

How? Incarnation is easy. In Jesus the divine and the human (immortality and mortality, eternity and limited time) were united, even though this uniting is still an ongoing process. Expiation by contrast is not so easy. Primarily because humans rather snuff out the notion of sin, particularly 'original sin', and prefer to turn a blind eye to the disorder following in its wake. They rather work towards an imagined, self-concocted, God-denying order without bothering about its antecedents, however real and inescapable. God and His order are therefore ignored in the equation.

Yet Christians maintain that expiation and annulment of sin, forgiveness in other words, is a prerequisite for restoring order. They maintain that this forgiveness cannot come from man's convincing himself about his deflationary self-salvation and capacity for self-redemption, but can much more realistically be derived from a transcendental source. Therefore the sacrifice of Jesus on the cross is among many other things a bridging of the gap between sin and salvation, time and eternity, man and God.

Yet the chasm remains. Quite plainly, as said before, one source of integrity (based on the survival instinct and our inbred propensity to propagate the race) is at odds with another form of integrity (based on all the things that transcend the bodily survival instinct, such as culture, civilization, technology, society, norms, values, beliefs, etc.). Hedonism versus mortification; animal gratification versus the discipline of appetites; momentary pleasure versus eternal life. This seems to be the stark choice the Bible, St Paul and Calvin have in mind.

And yet, however much the God/Satan contest is still obviously around us, the reconciliation between God's eternity and man's mortality, or God's universe-wide order and man's very real disorder, is also fact. The signs are all around us. Civilization, culture and society exist and flourish. Man's self-centeredness is being curtailed for the sake of the greater good of all and his instincts are disciplined in order for culture to blossom.

However much that reconciliation is imperfect in its actual effect, but humans have indeed raised themselves substantially beyond our lower nature. Reconciliation is an ongoing process, similar to rescuing order out of disorder. Humanly speaking the chasm is too deep for final resolution. Yet spiritually speaking, as St Paul does in Romans, Jesus Christ has bridged the chasm. Salvation has conquered sin. Eternity has won out over time.

The Holy Spirit remains active in human affairs. Yet the battle is ongoing. The openness to God by all those mourning the death of a beloved grandfather in a Canberra hospital was for real. So was the collection of underworld outcasts at the funeral I conducted in Queanbeyan a few years ago. Here too God's eternity impinged on man's mortality. The deceased, a young man, had died of an overdose. He was HIV positive and I understood the coroner to have been reluctant to open the body for inspection. St Stephen's was filled to overflowing with his derelict mates and their prostitute girlfriends.

The young man was a scion of an established Queanbeyan family, but his drug habits had alienated his relatives. His mates and friends who packed the little St Stephen's Presbyterian Church for his funeral were like him, addicts and as the funeral director, who was the same age as the deceased kept informing me, many had been his classmates. 'They all look at least twenty years older than they actually are', he said, and he was obviously right.

Yet there was not the faintest trace of defiance in the crowd. Not the slightest hint that anyone felt that God had given him, or her, a raw deal. Genuine humility and what Psalm (51:17) calls 'contriteness of heart' was the best way to describe the spirit of the congregation of derelicts. After the committal at the cemetery I embraced the obviously distressed, young, de-facto wife/prostitute. On both her and my part it was a genuine sharing of grief, but also a consolation of God's love and eternity.

In the mingling crowd afterwards a young man came to me and said: 'I honestly felt that God's everlasting arms embraced all of us today.' I agreed with him. Unbelievers would probably call this sentiment an illusion. Yet if the experience was an illusion, it was perceived as both real and a fact. And that seems to count for more than a cold-hearted definition neutralizing its relevance. The centrality of emotion, feeling, sympathy, love, faith was very real in this funeral of a derelict.

The text for today, however, points to more than just an isolated experience of 'come today, gone to-morrow'. It speaks about 'gaining eternal life.' St Paul advises his pupil Timothy here on the grounds of his own experience of being saved from sin by Christ Jesus (1 Timothy 1:15). Gaining eternal life in this context did not mean an after death reward for good behaviour. It meant the discovery of a security that transcended all human based securities. It meant a strong tie and link with a living God that freed him from all other loyalties. So much so that he could say in 2 Corinthians 10: 'Poor ourselves we bring wealth to many; penniless, we own the world.'

To sum up – God's eternity is fact. It is obviously fiction to the non-believer although as our illustrations show, not necessarily to those who don't go to church. It is also fiction to those who believe that man's mind can do without the illusion of extra-terrestrial communications. All I can say to the latter is that their belief amounts to a denial of large chunks of man's evolution, of his sociality and of the importance of the non-rational for his well being and integrity.

CALVIN 04

DREAMS

This same Daniel, whom the king named Belshazzar, is known to have notable spirit, with knowledge and understanding, and the gift of interpreting dreams. Daniel 5:1.

Our Old Testament reading for today (Daniel 5:10-31) is all about Daniel, a legendary figure of the Babylonian captivity who kept his faith in Yahweh while all around him people continued to worship local gods.

King Belshazzar gave a party for a thousand of his nobles using the gold and silver goblets which his father Nebuchadnezzar had taken from the temple in Jerusalem Suddenly in the middle of all the carousing the king saw human fingers writing on the plaster of the palace wall opposite. 'He turned pale, he became limp in every limb and his knees knocked together (Daniel 5:6).'

All the wise men from the realm were called in, 'but they could not read the writing or interpret it to the king (Daniel 5:8).' Then the queen came in and reminded Belshazzar that his father had appointed Daniel from the Jewish exiles as chief of the magicians, exorcists, Chaldeans and diviners and that he might be able to interpret the writing.

Daniel was summoned and the king promised that he would be 'robed in purple and honoured with a chain of gold round your neck and ranked as third in the kingdom (verse 16)', if only he could interpret the vision.

Daniel said that he would do so, but that he did not want the gifts. Before doing so, however, he reminded Belshazzar that Yahweh had given 'your father Nebuchadnezzar a kingdom and power and glory and majesty; and because of this power which he gave him, all peoples and nations of every language trembled before him and were afraid. He put to death whom he would and spared whom he would, he promoted them at will and at will degraded them (verse 19).'

However all this made Nebuchadnezzar 'haughty, stubborn and presumptuous (verse 20)' and therefore Yahweh deposed him from his royal throne. 'He was banished from the society of men, his mind became like that of a beast, he had to live like wild asses and to eat grass like oxen, and his body was drenched with the dew of heaven, until he came to know that the Most High God is sovereign over the kingdom of men and sets up over it whom He will (verse 21).'

Then boldly Daniel suggested that Belshazzar was not much better. 'You did not humble your heart, although you knew all this. You have set up yourself against the Lord of heaven. The vessels of his temple have been brought to your table; and you, your nobles, your concubines, and your courtesans have drunk from them. You have praised the gods of silver and gold, of bronze and iron, of wood and stone, which neither see nor hear nor know, and you have not given glory to God, in whose charge is your very breath and in whose hands are all your ways (verses 21-23).'

Finally after the damning speech Daniel comes to the main point, the writing on the wall. 'Mene', he says means 'God has numbered the days of your kingdom and brought it to the end (verse 27).' 'Tekel' means 'you have been weighed in the balance and found wanting (verse 28).' 'Upharsin' means 'our kingdom has been divided and given to the Medes and Persians (verse 29).'

And so it happens. Chapter five of Daniel ends as follows: 'That very night Belshazzar King of the Chaldeans was slain and Darius the Mede took the Kingdom, being then sixty-two years old (verse 30-31).' The point of the story is not to present a historical account, but to let the reader know that earthly rulers cannot escape God's justice and that particularly those who have absolute power will eventually come to nought if they abuse that power.

Calvin obviously underlines the 'humility' aspect of the story. It is his favourite theme in his all commentaries and the book of Daniel is no exception. Both Kings Nebuchadnezzar and Belshazzar have or will come to a gruesome end because they suffer from what seems to be the 'folly of all kings: to transfer the glory of divinity to themselves.' 'There is no power but of God', Calvin says. The power given to kings is 'on loan' as it were. Yet 'the royal power which they may freely exercise over their subjects does not rest on its lawfulness but on the tacit consent of all men.' 'Powerful as they are, kings must hereafter render an account to the Supreme King.' And they will be doomed, if pride prevents them from remaining constantly aware of this ultimate duty (Commentary on Daniel 5:19).

On dreams, there are essentially two kinds, according to Calvin. There are the house and garden varieties. They are produced by 'the various affections of the mind and body.' Calvin uses his meditation during daytime as an example. It recurs during sleep 'because the mind is not completely buried in slumber, but retains some seed of intelligence, although it is suffocated (commentary on Daniel 2:2).'

One ought to be careful, Calvin says, not to 'seek a divine agency or fixed reason' in those kinds of dreams. They all have natural causes. Yet he does not want to go as far as Aristotle who 'rejected all sense of divination', because he wanted to 'reduce the nature of Deity within the scope of human ingenuity.' Aristotle 'does not think it probable that dreams are divinely inspired.'

Calvin thinks otherwise. His second kind of dreams is the ones mentioned in the Book of Daniel. They are very much inspired by Yahweh, he thinks. The entire story of Daniel and the Babylonian court is proof of God's revelation in dreams and visions, according to Calvin. God here speaks to Daniel, as he has spoken before to the other prophets in the Bible.

Yet he gives the wise men (magicians, soothsayers, astrologers) credit for whatever science he can find in their efforts. Superstition to Calvin is different from astronomy which is a true and genuine 'consideration of the order of nature' (commentary on Daniel 2:27) and therefore not to be condemned. To Calvin the order of nature is God's gift to man and therefore not to be sneezed at when it comes to understanding creation.

The reason why the wise men 'could not explain the King's dream' was that 'the dream was not natural and had nothing in common with human conjectures, but was the peculiar revelation of the Spirit.' And Calvin concludes: 'the real sense of Daniel's words is this: the magicians, the astrologers and soothsayers had no power of expounding the King's dream, since it was neither natural nor human (Daniel 2:27).'

That supernatural power was only given to Daniel. 'All human sciences are included so to speak, within their own bounds and bolts.' 'Men's minds move hither and thither and thus make clever guesses; but Daniel excludes all human media and speaks of the dream as proceeding directly from God (commentary on Daniel 2:28). 'God is the 'author of the dream (commentary on Daniel 2:29).' By contrast both the king and the wise men had no means of transcending the natural and the human and therefore the writing on the wall escaped them altogether, according to Calvin.

These comments fit with the power of prophets in the Old Testament. The power of their faith in Yahweh was stronger than their fear of the earthly power of the rulers or other individuals they were addressing. In contrast with the wise men this faith allowed them to be fearless in their recriminations. To their way of thinking and believing the ruler's power was only relative to God's power. And as Yahweh reigned beyond time and place, both the past and the future were in his hands.

God's order spreads beyond time and space. Yet the prophet's efficacy did not just depend on the strength of his faith. It depended just as much on his capacity to accurately discern and interpret past and future. Daniel's success at the Babylonian court was not just founded on the rock of his faith in Yahweh's supreme power but also on his accurate interpretation of the future. If God were in charge of supreme order and the prophet the genuine and reliable mediator between heaven and earth, future outcomes would ratify his authenticity.

The Bible insists that Daniel did fit that bill. Both Nebuchadnezzar and Belshazzar succumbed to the fate Daniel as God's mouthpiece, had predicted. By contrast the wise men failed because they did not recognize a greater authority beyond the absolute power of the monarch. They therefore had no basis for interpretation even if, at best, they had valid insights in the ruler's predicament or immoral abuse of power.

In his comments on Acts 2:17 (the section in Peter's sermon on Pentecost, when he refers to the 'visions and dreams' of young and old) Calvin suggests that the prophets were accurate observers of their times and spoke figuratively to 'fit their time' and applied 'their style unto the capacity of their time.' This means that their message was adjusted to a mundane frame of reference. Or better that their local situation was reflected in what they had to say so that their audience would have no doubt as to its precise meaning.

Yet it also means that their realism and Calvin's eagerness to rationally understand what God's nature was all about (his admiration of reason as God's gift to men) led inexorably to the secularization of the very mystery and revelation that Calvin uses when he ran out of rational explanations for the phenomena he encountered, such as Nebuchadnezzar and Belshazzar's visions and dreams. For Calvin reason can logically intrude on this realm of mystery and revelation.

Calvin assumes that science, intelligence and reason (all of them God-given) exist harmoniously within God's order. To Calvin, God comes into the picture in the realm of mystery and revelation beyond what reason can discover. This realm together with the realm of reason and science provide Calvin with a more comprehensive, cosmic, view of existence overshadowing men's partial knowledge and enriching that existence with its divine aspects. Natural, house and garden dreams belong in that first realm together with the wise men. By contrast the dreams of Nebuchadnezzar and Belshazzar together with Daniel belong to the second realm.

Yet this is not the way that present-day knowledge regards dreams. Psychoanalysis sheds a different light on dreams. It relegates reason to a partisan and less than comprehensive position in the cosmic scheme of things. It promotes faith/commitment to a much more prominent position in contrast with Calvin for whom mundane dreams 'suffocated intelligence.'

This means that there is a much closer bond of all dreams (even the most mundane ones) with 'wholeness' or 'salvation' in Biblical terms than Calvin could visualize in his day and age. Psychoanalysis nowadays explains dreams as 'compensating for', and 'completing', daily experiences and events that otherwise would be left dangling in emotional limbo. The brain 'restores' and 'unifies' these experiences and events in order to integrate the memory bank.

What is more, this 'compensating' and 'completing' takes place wholly and entirely outside human reason and direction. Rather than understanding these latent forces to 'suffocate intelligence' as Calvin thought, they 'heal' and contribute to sanity and wholeness independent of the human will. There is good evidence from research that dream deprivation invariably leads to forms of insanity.

This psychoanalytical view of dreams fits better in the Biblical view of God's ordering activity in human affairs than Calvin's (and Aristotle's) assumption of the superiority of reason over feeling and emotion. Salvation by faith or wholeness through commitment is by definition a non-rational phenomenon. Even so psychology goes too far by insisting that the unconscious will have to be subject to the conscious. Ultimately it too favours reason over feeling and analysis over synthesis.

In Calvin's way of thinking, salvation or whole making by faith is not well integrated with reason. He tends to dismiss it by isolating it as an incomprehensible mystery only known by God, whereas in present day psychology the saliency and independence of commitment, loyalty, love etc. for human wellbeing as compared with purely logical/rational processes is much more in line with basic, understandable religious functioning.

Dreams figure heavily in religions and have obviously contributed impressively to the relativization of man's rational autonomy, and submission to powers beyond his conscious awareness. After all, humans discovered soon enough that they could not in any way affect their dreams and visions. The latter obviously were quite independent from what humans could control.

Dreams are closely associated with gods in native religions. In Australia the dreaming of aborigines was the centre of their system of meaning. It can best be described as primeval order, connecting parts divided by strife or wholeness juxtaposed by what the Murimbata in Arnhem Land called 'the crackedness of existence.'

The French missionaries to the Canadian Indians in the seventeenth century regarded native dreams as their main obstacle to conversion efforts. They wrote about native dreams as the gods of the country and the seal on tradition, legality and authority They complained in their letters to France that native dreams were so powerful that they determined all major decisions, such as travel, hunting, attacking, defending, curing etc.

Of course, the missionaries were unaware that the natives strong beliefs in dreams as the safest guide for appropriate action in a whimsical world were basically not that different from their own conviction that God would transfer messages and issue warnings through dreams of individuals such as Nebuchadnezzar and Belshazzar.

In both instances dreams were closely linked to central meaning systems that formed the core of motivation. In both, decisiveness and trust in action were strengthened at the expense of indecisiveness and potential dissent. In both, order was rescued from chaos and disorder. Yet both were also embedded in sharply different cultural milieus and these were essentially the cause of the conflicts and the ardent attempts to defend each separate, taken for granted, culture.

Dreams in both instances acted out, dramatized and reconciled opposites. Dreams prevented experiences and events from being meaningless and emotionally disconnected. Dreams digested those undigested experiences and events and thereby contributed to wholeness. This is often done through dramatizing conflict in daily living and through putting these conflicts in a larger context. Dreams represented symbiosis between social pressures and human instincts or the spirit and the 'flesh' as we find it in the New Testament, for instance in Galatians 5:17.

Yet it should not be forgotten that the symbiosis has merits in its own right. It is not just a means to wholeness or wellbeing or sanity as an end product. It is also a means to growth. God is not just the author of creation (the way things are). He is also creating (the way things develop). Explanation should not obscure or take the place of dramatization.

To put this differently: dreams lead to better physical integrity or personal sanity, essential for 'perfect order.' In Calvin's commentary on Psalm 72:2 this 'perfect order' is virtually synonymous to 'predestination' and 'election.' Yet simultaneously and inevitably dreams are also examples of a 'moving equilibrium.' They have a dynamic as well as a stabilizing quality.

Yet this also means that the symbiosis of reason and faith, instinct and sublimation, the mundane and the spiritual, can be mitigated and reconciled in dreams. The fact that the dreamer has no control over this reconciliation corresponds with God's superior authority and order, pardoning and forgiving. From this point of view the reconciliation between nations and cultures may be advanced through understanding the functions of dreams, myths and religion rather than through the assumption that reason is superior to commitment.

Are dreams God's messages? Yes, but not as Calvin thought they were. The interpretation of dreams has moved out of the realm of mystery and revelation and into the realm of a more inclusive understanding of salvation by faith or wholeness through commitment.

CALVIN 05

A HOLY STRUGGLE for POWER

Jesus said: 'You know that in the world, rulers lord it over their subjects, and their great men make them feel the weight of authority; but it shall not be so with you. Among you, whoever wants to be great must be your servant. ... Matthew 20:25-26

Today's Bible story (Matthew 20:10-28) looks rather familiar. Salome, the mother of disciples John and James asks Jesus for a favour (Matthew 20:21): 'I want you to give orders that in your kingdom my two sons here may sit next to you, one at your right and the other at your left.' Obviously this is not just the motherly heart speaking. In the parallel passage, in Mark 10:37, John and James themselves make the request.

Jesus explains that his kingdom means suffering rather than status. Instead of being honoured by the world he and his disciples will endure rejection. Do they still want special privileges? John and James say that they are prepared to suffer, or as it is put in verse 22, 'to drink the cup with him.' Yet this is not the end of the story.

Naturally the request upsets the other ten disciples. 'They were indignant (verse 25).' So Jesus calls them together and makes a little speech, culminating in today's text: 'You know that in the world, rulers lord it over their subjects, and their great men make them feel the weight of authority, but it shall not be so with you. Among you, whoever wants to be great must be your servant, and whoever wants to be first must be the willing slave of all – like the Son of Man; he did not come to be served, but to serve, and to give up his life as a ransom for many.' (verse 26)

The message is clear. The Kingdom of God is an altogether different kind of kingdom. Unlike a worldly kingdom it does not believe in a power hierarchy where the rulers are served by the ruled and where the distinctions are based on service rather than dominance. The spiritual order is different from the civic one. Both may represent order and as such both have God's blessing, but the former have a purer kind of authority and are therefore a blueprint for a different kind of existence. In this blueprint the impure elements have been sifted out and eliminated.

Yet that spiritual order (the Kingdom of God) is not just a pipe dream, an escape concocted to make existence somewhat less traumatic and painful. It is also a potential, yet realistic goal, provided that societies, groups in that society, or isolated individuals, manage to distance themselves from their obsession with instincts for self-preservation, self-enhancement and physical integrity. It puts natural selfishness and intrinsic narcissism on the backburner. It does not deny its importance and reality, but also puts the opposite, self-denying service, in the forefront.

In the Kingdom of God promotion of self-denying service has higher priority. The Biblical passages relating to the Kingdom of God imply its communal, family-like aspect. It is more a brotherhood where love and mutual acceptance rather than power and hierarchy are central. The Kingdom of God requires a vision beyond mere seeing, hearing and understanding (Matthew 13:15).

Jesus and his followers are steeped in the ancient tradition of Jehovah's authority subjugating all lesser authorities (Exodus 20:3). Yahweh requires obedience, self-denial for the common good, loving one's neighbour, all norms and values pointing to a just social order and all contributing to binding such a society together. If that society is corrupt, hypocritical and allows abuse of power, Jesus with a long line of prophets stretching way back to Moses does not hesitate to voice opposition.

How does Calvin interpret the story? As expected, he does not spare the followers of Jesus. 'This narrative contains a bright mirror of human vanity; for it shows that proper and holy zeal is often accompanied by ambition, or some other vice of the flesh, so that they who follow Christ have a different object in view from what they ought to have.' And then he follows it up by saying 'If this happens to two excellent disciples, with what care ought we to walk, if we do not turn from the right path. More especially, when any plausible occasion presents itself, we ought to be on our guard, lest the desire for honours corrupts the feeling of piety.'

To Calvin, holy organizations are in no way exempt from corruption. Impurity is so much part of human nature that it pervades all men's actions. God may implant the pure seed in our hearts, he says, but then 'it becomes degenerate and corrupted.' The disciples imagined 'a kingdom, which did not exist', and therefore we ought to pray for the Lord to open 'the eyes of our mind' and to keep our faith 'pure from all mixture.' In other words it is commitment to a mind-enlarging universe, foreign to the kingdoms of this world that our identification with Christ encourages and promotes.

Power, to Calvin, is a dangerous thing. Those who have power run the risk of pride; Calvin has no illusions about the motives of the powerful. He refers to kings 'who have greater delight in their power, and a stronger desire that it should be formidable, than that it should be founded in the consent of the people.'

Yet the 'uneducated men of ordinary rank' are not any better. To them too 'wicked ambition' comes 'natural.' 'Power and honours' can go to their heads 'unless the spirit of modesty, coming from heaven, extinguishes the pride which has firm hold of the nature of man.' 'Every man is carried away by a love of himself.' The solution therefore is 'that this passion should be directed to a different subject. Let the only greatness, eminence, and rank, which you desire, be, to submit to your brethren; and let this be your primacy, to be the servants of all.'

Yet power is also a necessity. 'As to the degree in which some men rise above others, it is not our business to inquire, and God did not intend that it should be revealed to us by Christ, but that it should be reserved till the latest revelation. There is not necessarily equality among the children of God … to each is promised that degree of honour to which he has been set apart by the eternal purpose of God.' Here Calvin admits that the practical order and civic administrations have their own merits, however much they fall short of God's more comprehensive vision.

Calvin could have strengthened his argument about the danger of power if he had read *The Prince* by his contemporary Nicolo Machiavelli (1469-1527), written in 1513 to get back into the graces of the Medici in Florence, but not published until after his death. In it, Machiavelli advises the prince on using any worldly means (including religion) to keep worldly power and to rely only on himself. This kind of power is the exact opposite of the power Jesus and Calvin have in mind when they refer to the Kingdom of God.

Calvin thinks that 'everyone (of the disciples) preferred himself to the rest' and has succumbed to 'the deadly plague of ambition' and that therefore Christ 'warns them that nothing is more foolish than to fight about nothing.' He stresses that the design of Christ was 'to distinguish between the spiritual government of the Church and the empires of the world.'

We are reminded here of Hans Christian Anderson's fairy tale *The Emperor's Clothes*. Some of you probably remember the story of the king who was excessively fond of new clothes. One day two swindlers visit him. They claim to be weavers and say that they can produce cloth that has the most wonderful quality of becoming invisible to every person who was not fit for the office he held or who was impossibly dull. The Emperor ordered a new costume and decided he would wear it at an important procession. He could not see it himself, but was too ashamed to admit that he was not fit to be king, because everybody else was admiring it. All bystanders pretended to see the non-existing clothes, as they could not face the thought of being unfit for their job or being a nincompoop. And then a little child said: 'But he has nothing on.' Calvin interprets Christ to be like the little child and say: 'Just look a bit closer and you will discover the nakedness behind earthly power.'

Calvin also makes it clear that the opposites of power and service need one another: 'even kings do not rule justly or lawfully, unless they serve.' In so far as the Kingdom of God is identical to the invisible church it is still bound to the mundane necessity of orderly organization with all the imperfections that this implies. 'For as God has been pleased that the communion of his Church shall be maintained in this external society, anyone who, from hatred of the ungodly, violates the bond of this society, enters on a downward course, in which he incurs great danger of cutting himself off from the communion of saints (*Inst.* IV i 16).'

Calvin finishes his comments on verse 28 (where Jesus refers to himself as the Son of Man who did not come to be served, but to serve, and to give up his life as a ransom for many) by quoting from Romans 5:15, where Paul does not speak of just a section of society, 'but embraces the whole human race.' In other words the mission of the followers of Jesus is to witness to the Kingdom of God as the transcendent reality that binds the entire world together and thereby overcomes the narrow obsessions with self-sufficiency and puny cravings for earthly power.

The other reading for today comes from Isaiah 42:1-9. It was undoubtedly in Jesus' mind when he made his little speech to his disciples about service rather than power. God, according to the prophet, will send his servant, within whom 'his spirit dwells' to 'make justice shine upon the nations (verse 1).' That justice is very encompassing. It denotes both the unifying force binding the nations together and the kind of good government that treats all its citizens with understanding and respect.

That servant is not pompous and self-indulgent, but self-giving and sensitive (verse 2-3). He will make 'justice shine on every race' and has been appointed 'to be a light to all peoples, a beacon for the nations, to open eyes that are blind, to bring captives out of prison, out of the dungeons where they lie in darkness (verse 6-7).'

To Calvin, Christ is the humble servant mentioned in Isaiah 42. 'Christ was sent in order to bring the whole world under the authority of God and obedience to him; and this showed that without him everything is confused and disordered.' Yet the kingdom he represents 'is not external, but belongs to the inner man; for it consists of a good conscience and uprightness of life, not what is so reckoned before men, but what is so reckoned before God.' Calvin finds approvingly (Romans 6:4), it is Christ who came to rescue men from perversion and corruption. He 'came with the heavenly power of the Spirit that it might change our disposition, and thus form us again to newness of life.'

Christ is 'unlike earthly princes ... he will support the weak and feeble.' Christ also represents peace because he reconciles those who were formerly separated from one another or from God. He 'was promised, not only to the Jews, but to the whole world.' Calvin then finishes his commentary on verse six as follows: 'Now, then, the blame lies solely with ourselves, if we do not become partakers of this salvation; for he calls all men to himself, without a single exception, and gives Christ to all, that we may be illuminated by him. Let us only open our eyes, he alone will dispel darkness, and illuminate our minds by the 'light' of truth.'

How relevant are today's Bible readings and Calvin's commentaries for our day and age? And how can we bring the present day social science knowledge to bear on those deliberations? After all, Calvin expressly singles out those 'lazy believers who do not make use of the works of the ungodly in physics, symbiotics, mathematics and other similar sciences' for condemnation (*Inst.* II ii 16). And if Calvin were alive today he would certainly add anthropology, psychology, sociology and particularly political science on power to 'the works of the ungodly.'

There are at least three areas in which today's readings (Isaiah 42:1-9 and Matthew 20:20-28), where Calvin's interpretation and present day social sciences are relevant. I will take each of these one by one: (1) disorder and minimization of conflict; (2) global mission; (3) organizational corruption.

(1) Disorder and conflict minimization. God's Kingdom, in contrast with an earthly kingdom the disciples had in mind represents the pure order that is constantly undone by man's propensity for disorder and conflict. Selfishness and pride endanger the social bond. By contrast, self-denial and modesty strengthen it. Yet perfect order in a perfect society requires more than self-denial and modesty. Leadership may be necessary for the smooth running of any group, community or society, but tension arises when the leader is incompetent or abuses power. Therefore justice is another vital ingredient for any society worthy the name. And God, as Calvin beautifully points out in his commentary, expects a leader to also serve. This means that to Calvin, listening to those who are led is an important characteristic of a good leader. That's why he mentions 'consent of the people' when he discusses our text for today, Matthew 20:25.

Yet human nature is anything but perfect in Calvin's book and abuse of power has proved to be a perpetual threat for civic order. And therefore Calvin assumes that 'consent of the people' is a counter-balance to this perpetual threat. By implication the democratic style of government fits this suspicion of human nature. It reduces the temptation of power abuse through a system of checks and balances, assigning the power of election to the ruled. Democracy and Calvinism have therefore tended to be associated historically.

Given this view of human nature and civic order, it is in line with Calvin's thinking to favour all international efforts to diminish both internal and external conflicts within and between nations through international organizations, such as the United Nations, its various organizations and the International Court of Justice. To superimpose on rogue nations both its democratic expectations and, if necessary, punishment for abusing power is therefore an important means for strengthening global order. This in turn means, at least to me, that Christianity should be in the forefront of supporting those secular institutions which form a democratically elected umbrella under which all nations can shelter to preserve their common global interests, such as peace and conflict resolution. This is one way in which the Christian Gospel can be true to its mandate to bring the good news to all nations (Romans 5:18). However proximate this global order may be it is in no way less so than the civic order on the national, regional, communal or individual level. God's authority extends to the entire global order, as we have read this morning in Isaiah 42:1.

(2) This brings me to the second level of relevance. It has to do with the global mission of the faith. Jesus explains that his vision of the Kingdom of God must be spread to all nations (Matthew 24:11-14). St Paul follows that injunction to the letter throughout his life (Romans 1:5). Ever since the Christian faith has extended all over the world it has done so through the extensive learning of languages of native peoples, the provision of health and educational facilities for these natives and active participation of the missionaries in the economic wellbeing of underprivileged people.

One area in which a deeper understanding may be useful is the one dealing with other religious organizations. Ultimately a sense of competition is unavoidable and even healthy. Yet in an increasingly secular society and global economy it is also important to be aware of the contribution any religion makes to the social and even global order. The latter (global) order is just as much in need of an integrative soul as the prevailing national or ethnic religions. And the more secular this global order is, the more sensible it is for Christians and others to band together for the common, global good!

Yet in their interaction with one another many religious organizations tend to articulate their differences rather than their common function. This tends to be the 'lowest common denominator of thinking', and concentration on those beliefs one has in common. To be true to Calvin's suggestion of 'mind opening' interpretations, discussions about common functions are much more appropriate and would be encouraged by Calvin if he were alive.

In other words 'interfaith dialogues and meetings' are much more useful when functions and effects rather than items of beliefs are on the table. Yet even here academic comparisons can never take the place of actual commitments. Christian conversion has rarely been the result of intellectual persuasion and almost always the outcome of evangelical or charismatic example. Therefore either agreement about the lowest common denominator, the necessity for tolerance in our loosely woven society or even an understanding of the basic functions of religious organizations, are not the best tools for the missionary enterprise. Yet living one's Christians convictions is!

However, this does not mean that deep understanding of other religions or the mind-expanding dialogue and worship with people of other faiths are to be avoided. Isolation from other believers goes against the grain of what I understand Calvin to advocate when he reinforces the universality of God's Kingdom embracing the 'entire human race' in his commentary on both Matthew 20:28 and Isaiah 42:6-7.

In the middle of the eighteenth century, the Great Awakening, a religious revival, shook the young American Colonies. It had its origins in the pietist and evangelical movements of Europe, but had a deeper impact in the fertile soil of the American frontier. Like a bush fire it swept across the boundaries of the various denominations which the English, the Scots, the German and the Dutch immigrants had brought with them, enthused broad layers of the population and unified them in spite of ethnic and linguistic barriers.

It appealed to Calvin's 'inner man', or what nowadays we would call 'basic human motivation determining and making sense of all his thoughts, beliefs and actions.' This is what Jesus has in mind when he contrasts the heavenly kingdom with the human variety in his little speech to the disciples culminating in our text for today. It is also what made the difference when missionaries to the native races of North America found that it was easy enough to entice the natives to change their amulets and prayers into Christian equivalents. Yet when it came to basic motivation only charismatic example and conversion technique could make an impact.

(3) Organizational corruption; this leads to the third item of relevance: organizations having their own agenda. Calvin regards ecclesiastical organization distinctly as a mixture of secular (and therefore not-sacred) necessity and holy (and therefore sacred) intentions. Even the invisible church has to cope with individuals, such as the disciples in Matthew 20:20-28, whose motives are anything but pure. Structural organization is the issue. In the social sciences one can read extensively about organizations bending content (or corrupting of what is supposed to be protected) to suit organizational ends thereby restricting organismic flow.

This danger is all the greater in religious organizations as they tend to naturally adopt the sacralizing power of what they are supposed to protect. This actually means that on this level the religious organizations could do with a bit more secularization. Plainly functional questions should be un-squeamishly asked about the utility of such items as women in the ministry, interfaith dialogue, denominational separation, ecclesiastical offices rather than allow these issues to ride on the coat tails of the religious ends they were supposed to serve. Heritage is not unimportant, but in this instance, it is the kind of heritage that should be scrutinized on occasion.

Good examples in the Bible are the Gospels as compared with St Paul's letters. In the Gospels Jesus is hardly concerned with organizing Christian congregations. He represents a free-floating movement of preaching and representing the Kingdom of God, as he understood it to be in line with his Hebrew heritage of ancient prophecy. The Son of Man, as he said, did not even have a place to lay his head (Matthew 8:20).

By contrast, St Paul had to again and again instruct the budding congregations in Corinth, Ephesus, Galatia, Philippi, and Thessalonica how to settle differences, how to divide labour, how to use talents effectively, how to operate as a group in the face of persecution, how to make converts, etc. all very necessary things. Yet all are adjuncts, aids, to proclaiming the message of salvation.

This is the threefold message of today's readings: The heavenly rather than the earthly kingdom that Christ represents, is inclusive rather than exclusive.

(1) It includes the alienated, the rejected, the poor and the oppressed. No society can afford to exclude the powerless and deny the power of their consent. Otherwise their resentment will be like a festering sore and will destroy the very peace of which Jesus is the prince.

(2) The heavenly kingdom targets the inner man rather than the outward appearance of being law-abiding and following outward ritual to the letter. Its inclusiveness goes right to the heart of motivation and reconciles both intranational and international conflicting elements and creates unity where there is strife and rebellion.

(3) The heavenly kingdom gives priority to its inclusive heavenly 'perfect order' over the means of organization to achieve that end. It does not allow the means of organization to dictate the end of salvation for the entire human race.

CALVIN 06

AUTHORITY from within or AUTHORITY from without

Who gave you this authority? Matthew 21:2

The readings for today are all about authority. The Old Testament reading (Exodus 17:1-7) establishes the authority of Moses, whom orthodox Hebrews call 'the father of all prophets.' The Hebrews rebelled against him ('Why have you brought us out of the land of Egypt?' (Exodus 17:3), but God restores Moses' authority by guiding him to water at Horeb which saves his people.

The New Testament reading in Matthew is quite explicit about authority. Jesus has drawn the attention of the religious leaders, 'the chief priests and the elders of the nation' (Matthew 21:23). He has aroused the enthusiasm of the people, mainly because he reminds them of the prophets of old who often protected the powerless and the weak and reprimanded the arrogant, the rich and the mighty.

More recently, John the Baptist had been their hero. But King Herod, whom the people regarded as a lackey of the occupying Roman forces, had beheaded him. They now pinned their hopes on Jesus, who, like the ancient prophets, such as Elijah, Isaiah and Jeremiah, fearlessly spoke against corruption and gave them hope of a better future.

The religious leaders were sensitive to popular opinion, but they also felt that this opinion should be shielded from charlatans and impostors. Their own authority would be at stake if just anybody could get up and proclaim to be Israel's saviour. Their leadership of a subjugated nation was precarious enough as it was, without rogues fishing in their socially troubled waters.

Hence the question of authority. Who gave Jesus the right to speak and heal as he did? Jesus counters their question with a question of his own: 'Did John the Baptist derive the authority for baptism from God or was it just a man-made invention (Matthew 21:25)?' The priests and the elders were now faced with a dilemma. If they said 'from God', Jesus would scold their lack of belief in John the Baptist and if they said that it was a mere human invention, the people would accuse them of disrespect for one whom they regarded as an authentic prophet.

The chief priest and the elders therefore decline to answer and Jesus reciprocates by not answering their question either, or at least not answering their question directly. Yet the parable he tells subsequently makes it very clear what he thinks. More than this he goes beyond the original question on authority as such and addresses himself also to the effect of authority. Are the expectations of the authority met? Or more concretely, are God's commandments obeyed? The answers Jesus gives to these questions through the parable turn the tables around. Instead of entrapping Jesus, the religious leaders entrap themselves as we shall see later.

What does Jesus say and what does the parable mean? He says (Matthew 21:28-31): a man had two sons. He went to the first and said: 'My boy, go and work today in the vineyard.' 'I will, sir', the boy replied; but he never went. The father came to the second son and said the same. 'I will not', he replied, but afterwards he changed his mind and went.

Jesus then asks the priests and the elders: 'Which of these two did as his father wished?' 'The second', they answered (Matthew 21:31) but by saying so they indirectly accused themselves of being like the first son ostensibly obeying, but actually not doing what they were asked to do. How?

The implication of the parable is that God (the father in the story) is indeed the source of Jesus' authority. Yet God is more interested in performance than in hollow promises. Jesus accuses his protractors of making hollow promises for the sake of keeping the peace with the governing authorities who regarded John the Baptist as a troublemaker and had him killed off. They are like the first son who personifies hypocrisy. He promises to work in God's vineyard while he actually does not. In other words they are in the 'does what I say rather than what I do' category of religious officials, or those who preach, but not perform. They recognize God's authority, but God is only façade. They do the opposite of what God wants them to be and do recognize John the Baptist as in line with authentic prophecy.

By hinting at a basic truth through a parable Jesus puts the problem of authority in the larger context. The issue is not authority per se, he seems to say, but whether or not that authority is adhered to or just used as a means for more mundane motives. Jesus turns the tables around. Instead of defending himself by elaborating his relationship with God as source of authority, he contrasts their fraudulent use of religion with the genuine repentance of the despised.

The tax-gatherers and prostitutes (Matthew 21:31) are obviously at odds with God's intentions for living, he says, yet finish up meeting God's request. They repent, go to work in God's vineyard and thereby enter the Kingdom of Heaven ahead of hypocritical clerics. And Jesus insists on making his position on God's authority abundantly clear by observing that the despised tax-gatherers and prostitutes were also the ones who believed in John the Baptist (in contrast with the clerics who did not, Matthew 21:32) and therefore accepted God's authority and finished doing his will.

This is also Calvin's position. In his commentary on the parable he accuses the clerics of being ministers of God who only pretend to be godly, but are actually ungodly and impious, motivated by 'ambition, pride, cruelty and avarice.' They 'falsely allege to be anxious about the order of the Church, as if they are its faithful and honest guardians.' They are like the first son, appearing to obey, but are really 'hunters after popular applause' instead of being 'disposed to good for its own sake (*Inst*. III vii 2).'

By contrast the tax-collectors and the prostitutes, despised by the people, were genuinely repentant and humble rather than spoiled by applause and therefore, Calvin suggests, ranked above the priests and the elders, because 'they do not continue to the end in their vices, but on the contrary, submit gently and obediently to the yoke they had fiercely rejected.' The design of Christ, Calvin adds, is to strip the clerics 'of the honour of which they were unworthy, because their ungodliness was worse than the lasciviousness of the harlots.'

From the social scientific point of view the parable contributes to communal solidarity in two ways. It not only reinforces the prevailing values of that community by disapproving of the vices of publicans and harlots, but also by reabsorbing them in that community through their repentance. In other words it rescues them from total rejection and marginalisation and thereby contributes to the cohesion of that community. The parable restores the despised and the marginal to legitimate position.

But there is more. Calvin distinguishes between the invisible church and the visible one. The first one consists of the saints and the elect. The second one harbours 'a very large mixture of hypocrites, who have nothing of Christ but the name and outward appearance: of ambitious, avaricious, envious, evil-speaking men, some also of impure lives, who are tolerated for a time … (*Inst*. IV i 7).'

From the sociological angle we may take this to mean that the church is both a divine and a human institution. In so far as it is the latter, it is embedded in social functions and psychological needs. Its functionaries respond to these functions and needs and in doing so, allow religion to reinforce prevailing structures of order. In this way religion reflects rather than redeems its environment. The genius of biblical religion is its capacity to also reinforce the non-priestly, prophetic and change-promoting side of religion. This is what Jesus represented in the episode of Matthew 21:23-31.

The authority of both John the Baptist and Jesus was grounded in that prophetic tradition allowing for a breakthrough of the encrusted priestly, conservative pattern. The mutual critique of Jesus and the Hebrew priests was grounded in the strands of both priestly and prophetic tradition. As Jesus was quite familiar with the history of Hebrew prophecy, it is understandable that he assumed his authority to rest on that very foundation.

But there is more. Authority was vested in both traditionsis r. Yet the priests assumed that it was particularly vested in the religious organisation, of necessity protecting religious beliefs and ritual. Yet at least some of the prophets, for instance Hosea, (6:6), diminished authority of religious practice as compared with loyalty to Yahweh. The relevance of this distinction is rather significant. Loyalty to denominational and religious boundaries rather than to content of the beliefs being protected seems to be at the core of all so-called 'religious conflict', whether in the Sudan, Indonesia, Northern Ireland or Afghanistan. The confusion of means and ends seems to be closely linked to the bitterness of these conflicts. It is rather sad that the more ephemeral/constantly reconciling authority of religion/denomination is almost always weaker than loyalty to boundaries that divide and separate.

The problem crops up again and again both in the Bible and in actual life. All universal religions struggle with the greater accessibility and therefore believability of the material as compared with the spiritual, the concrete as compared with the abstract, or to use St Paul's language, the 'flesh' compared with the spirit, or to keep humans focused on their physical integrity rather than on what lifts them beyond ego and self. Certainly a great deal of theological writings and concern hinges on this conflict. The solution of the conflict is of profound concern for the shape of society, culture and civilization. Even scientists who describe themselves as religiously 'unmusical' (Max Weber) or as atheists (such as Auguste Comte, Emile Durkheim, and Sigmund Freud) would agree with this point of view.

Freud is a good example. Towards the end of his life Sigmund Freud wrote a little book 'Civilization and its Discontents' in which he advances the idea that civilization would have been impossible without restricting human instincts. To him ego is a compromise between the Id (human instinct) and the Superego (social conscience). Yet his belief in individual rationalism prevents Freud from detecting that very process of reconciliation and compromise in all religions.

All surviving religions have focused their attention on the issue of transcending man's raw instinct for physical survival even now coursing in everyone's blood. One could put all this more strongly: there is not a single religion, whether primitive or sophisticated, which has not invested its major efforts and energy in widening the gap between the physical/spiritual, the material/immaterial, the real/ideal, the concrete/abstract, the tangible /intangible or the corporeal/ethereal. The most effective of these religions (particularly the universal ones) have always been those who have managed to increase the authority of the first at the expense of the second.

This is not just a matter of historical insight. As mentioned above, it is the essence of the bitter, so called 'religious conflicts' in the Sudan, Northern Ireland, Indonesia, India, Afghanistan. 'Religion' in those countries always refers to concrete, organizational boundaries around the beliefs and the values they promote rather than the more intangible, spiritual elements the organization is supposed to protect. Here too the authority of the visible seems to outweigh the authority of the invisible.

Yet one's eyes may be open to the effects and the quality of commitment to the authority of the invisible rather than its intrinsic, narrow, truth content. Sociologists stress the consequence of beliefs rather than their rational truth so beloved by philosophers and theologians.

The last reading for the day is Philippians 2:1-13. Here there is not the slightest doubt as to what is the all-embracing authority of both St Paul and the community of Christians in Philippi. It is decidedly not an authority from within. The core source of motivation is not physical survival or celebration of the self and its instincts. By contrast it is a firm denial of anything that could even hint of self-satisfaction, self-sufficiency or self-indulgence. St Paul more than hints (Philippians 2:7) that in the same way Jesus emptied himself ('made himself into nothing') so he himself and the Christian community should also maximize room in one's existence for God's authority.

It is a celebration of authority from without. The Christians in Philippi had been receptive to Paul's message. They were Jews whom Paul had persuaded that with Christ as their central authority their lives would not only become more meaningful, but would also lift them above their mundane concerns. And this included a capacity to even cope with martyrdom and death for their faith. Jesus' death on the cross and Paul's own imprisonment (the letter was written from prison) were ever so many instances of what humans could endure under the most trying of circumstances.

It would have been fascinating if there had been more clues about the status of these first Christians on European soil. Were they well-to-do Jews who felt alienated from a decaying society surrounding them? Had they found in St Paul and the Christian fellowship formed as a result of his missionary enthusiasm an exemplary communal alternative? Was St Paul's charismatic leadership the bridge to a saner and better blueprint of existence? And had their Christian response to his call and radiant authority become the lodestar for other citizens of Philippi? There are only a few clues in the story to provide a positive answer to these hunches, apart from their relative wealth, their exemplary morality, the existence of opponents and their suffering as a result. As an aside, that first Christian community on European soil apparently consisted of more women than men. St Paul also exhorts them to share the Holy Spirit and have a 'common care for unity (Philippians 2:1, 2).'

He also expects them to 'humbly reckon others better than yourselves (verse 3)', and to have these values 'arise out of your life in Christ Jesus (verse 5)' In other words the authority for motivation and action rests not within, but without.

St Paul stresses the authority from without even more in verse 12, when he says that unfortunately he cannot physically be with them and that therefore they have to rely exclusively on the heavenly source for their authority, unity and motivation.

Calvin devotes nineteen pages of commentary to this section of St Paul's letter to the Philippians. He obviously regards it as important. He deals prominently with the theme of humility always close to his heart. This theme in turn is linked to the authority of Christ. Unless Christ is the cardinal point of reference, Calvin says, the Philippians run the risk of disagreement thereby opening the door for imposters; false prophets and Satan.

It is Christ's emptying himself (Philippians 2:7) which fosters a similar spirit of self-denial in his followers, thereby paving the way for communal harmony, as 'everyone esteems himself less than others.' And this in turn, Calvin says, is a definition of true humility. In other words faith in authority from without (Christ) has important, practical, consequences for the Christian unity in Philippi.

Still on Christ's emptying himself, Calvin relates this act to the cross. 'Paul speaks to Christ simply; as he was God manifested in the flesh but nevertheless this emptying is applicable exclusively to his humanity … he became obedient to his Father, even so far as to endure death.' In the same way 'every one therefore who humbles himself will in like manner be exalted (1 Timothy 3:16).'

To Calvin, Christ's 'whole life is as a mirror set before us.' The purpose of a mirror is to be 'advantageous and profitable to others, so Christ did not seek or receive anything for himself, but everything for us.' That is also what Paul expects of the Christian community in Philippi: to be consistently obedient whether he is with them personally or far away in prison and not to be hypocrites and chameleons who act differently according to other people's expectations.

Yet that authority is not dictatorially imposed. It is gently and humbly suggested and therefore all the more effective. '(Paul) knew how to exercise authority when it was necessary, but at present he prefers to use entreaties, because he knew that these would be better fitted to gain an entrance into their affections.'

Authority within or without? Our readings for today are quite explicit about the answer. If the authority around which our private life, communal existence or national identity is structured originates from within, it is conceived too narrowly and is likely to hinder the very universal order it seeks. By contrast, if it is both perceived, and more importantly, if it is believed to originate from without, it advances that order as something still to be achieved and to be rescued from the disorder (or sin) all around. Of course this is not a very colourful way of interpreting our Bible passages.

It is much more satisfactory to let the Bible speak for itself and then our summary goes as follows: God's authority is founded on his eternal blueprint for man's existence. It has both priestly (consolidating) as well as prophetic (change-promoting) aspects. Jesus combined both aspects and lifted his followers and disciples beyond the mundane level of self-sufficiency, local power and organizational boundaries. Salvation is bound up with acceptance of God's authority particularly as it has been concretized in Jesus.

The first Christians on the European continent (in Philippi) were encouraged by St Paul to fit in (obey) this pattern of Christian beliefs and values. They thereby became the prototype and lodestar for Christian civilization as it spread all over Europe in subsequent centuries. Their missionary success flows from their infectious belief that, as Calvin puts it in his commentary on Philippians 2:13 '… distrust in ourselves leads us to lean more confidently upon the mercy of God.' In other words, authority from within must make room for authority from without if we are to live life to the full.

CALVIN 07

GOD and CAESAR

(Or: the SACRED and the SECULAR)

Then pay Caesar what is due to Caesar, and God what is due to God. Matthew 22:21

The readings for today, Matthew 22:21 and Exodus 32:12-25, have a common theme: rebellion against God. I will take them one by one and discuss Calvin's perspective and explain why I think this.

Exodus 33:12-23 follows the story of Moses returning from Mount Sinai with the Ten Commandments and discovering that in his absence the Israelites have made themselves a golden calf to worship. Moses is thoroughly disgusted and demolishes the tablets. God is very angry too and smites 'the people for worshipping the bull-calf (Exodus 32:35).' The Israelites are now very sorry and God decides to give them a second chance.

Moses returns to Mount Sinai for a second set of Ten Commandments, but then complains to God that it would be helpful if He were a bit more visible, implying that the whole golden calf episode would have never occurred if He (God) had been better known. How do the Israelites know that they are now returned in his favour unless there is some evidence?

Moreover, says Moses, (and now we are back at our reading for today), I too am personally in a bit of a quandary. You may have put me in charge of leading this Nation into the Promised Land, but you have not taught me 'to know thy way (Exodus 33:13).' And the Lord then assures him: 'I will go with you in person and set your mind at rest (Exodus 33:14).'

Moses is still not satisfied. 'Show me thy glory', he says (Exodus 33:18).' God again assures him: 'I will be gracious to whom I will be gracious, and I will have compassion on whom I will have compassion (Exodus 33:19).' That still does not cut any ice with Moses, particularly when God then adds: 'My face you cannot see, for no mortal man may see me and live (Exodus 33:20).'

Obviously things are at a standstill, but God is ready for some give and take. All right, he says, I will 'cover you with my hand until I have passed by. Then I will take away my hand, and you shall see my back, but my face shall not be seen (Exodus 33:22-23).' And so it happens. Subsequently God reveals his proper name, Jehovah, and tells Moses that he is 'compassionate and gracious, long-suffering, ever constant and true, maintaining constancy to thousands, forgiving inequity, rebellion and sin (Exodus 34:6-7).' He also makes a solemn covenant with the Israelites (Exodus 34:10).

Even to the present day, Jews, substitute 'adonai' (Lord) whenever they come across God's name, Jehovah. In year five at high school in the Netherlands a few of us took Hebrew taught by a Jewish rabbi. I vividly remember the first lesson, when he implored us to never pronounce JHV when we read it in the Hebrew text, as this would upset him and instead say 'adonai.'

In other words, God represents red-hot majesty to Moses as well as to our rabbi in year five. God may remain a mystery who can never be fully known, but he is also concretely present in the love, compassion, the faith and order of his people, his tribe or nation. That faith and that order may have a human element, but it is also divine and therefore pure. It is safeguarded through its separation from man's disorderly existence.

Man's rebellion against God consists primarily in his desire to possess, hog and command the very purity which can only be God's, because man lost this purity in the fall, or in the inevitable mixture of good and evil, perfection and imperfection, self-seeking and self-denial part and parcel of his existence. The Bible calls this 'original sin.'

The Bible also insists that the only way out of this dilemma is to recognize the distance between God's purity and man's impurity, or God's holiness ands man's sinfulness. There is a bridge between God and man, but it does not consist in God's surrender to man, but in man's surrender to God. It does not consist in man's usurping God's place, but in letting God be Himself. And in today's story it is made clear that totally knowing God is just another word for possessing Him. There is a distance between God and man and it has to remain that way for the good of man. Consequently Moses is only allowed to see Jehovah's back.

Therefore the Bible uses words like 'repentance', 'forgiveness', 'pardon', 'remission of sin' as often as it does. It is the vital bridge between God and man. Without it humans would have no intimate experience of perfection, integrity and purity. However with it, God and the transcendental vision of goodness, compassion and love are accessible, because man now realistically confesses his true state of imperfection and submission in a broken existence.

In his commentary on Exodus 33 Calvin almost exclusively stresses 'humility.' I wondered why, until I realized that Calvin rightfully insists that God can only be partially understood and comprehended and that man's pride and his instinctive need to be master of his own destiny leads him to usurp God's place in the scheme of things. The Bible and the Westminster Confession call that 'original sin.' It is the essential recognition of the distance between God's perfection, purity and compassion and man's imperfection, impurity and selfishness.

God assures Moses that He will be with him and the Israelites through thick and thin. Yet He also safeguards His independence by protecting the mystery of His being and preventing corrosion of the treasures of heaven by moth and rust (Matthew 6:19). Repentance, remission of sin and humility are all the practical means to accomplish that goal.

How does our New Testament reading (Matthew 22:15-22) fit this goal? You remember the story. Jesus' reputation had been established far and wide in the population. The people had accepted him as an authentic mouthpiece of God in line with the prophets of old such as Nathan, Elijah, Isaiah, Jeremiah and others. They too had spoken fearlessly. They too had not been afraid to say whatever was politically unwelcome to the rulers.

Yet the religious establishment had not been happy with the way things were going. And so it had combined with the opposition (the Herodians, the followers of King Herod who were collaborating with the Roman occupation) to entangle him and ask: 'Should we pay tax (tribute) to the Romans (as the Herodians wanted them to do) or to God (as the Pharisees thought should happen) (Matthew 22:17).'

Jesus sees through their game. If he says 'Caesar' the religious establishment and the people will brand him a traitor and if he says 'God' the occupying forces will be on his back as a dangerous rebel. He therefore begins by calling them hypocrites but then realizes that the issue is genuine, requests a coin and asks (Matthew 22:20): 'Whose is this image and superscription?' They answer: 'Caesar', upon which Jesus replies with the words of our text for today: 'Then pay Caesar what is due to Caesar, and God what is due to God.'

If nothing else Jesus' reply to the Pharisee is a highly political, yet also clever response to what is an attempt to entrap him. Jesus separates the secular from the sacred to avoid conflict between the separate functions of religion reinforcing the solidarity of the subjugated nation (as the Pharisees want him to insist upon) and reinforcing the function of subjugating the nation (as the Herodians want him to do).

Both the Herodians and the Pharisees rebel against God by squeezing Him into the narrow mould of local patronage. King Herod was the stooge for the real power. He was put on the throne to pacify the recalcitrant nation by providing it with a token self-government. By contrast the Pharisees wanted Jesus to bless and therefore strengthen their resistance to the foreigners occupying Israel. Jesus refuses to do either. Both are attempts to use God for conflicting purposes and therefore implicit acts of rebellion. None allows God to be God and to be worshipped for what God is in God's own right rather than what others want God to be.

But Jesus also has to be practical. God has a unique relation with Israel, so much so, that the latter claims God to be their special protector. What is more natural than expecting Jehovah to exert God's cosmic authority and safeguard their political independence? Yet the real power seems to be with the Romans and

King Herod who is only partly of Israelite stock. Perhaps God is impotent to liberate Israel? Or do priest and prophets misread His purpose for its existence? And more important, does God's authority not actually have to bow to man's authority?

Jesus' answer to these questions is to practically separate heavenly and mundane authority, as has happened ever since when religion and education, or religion and welfare provisions, were separated during the twentieth century. Jesus suggests that God's and Caesar's authorities have different functions. God's authority deals with a purified kind of order distilled from the actual situation in which humans find themselves. It is the ideal separated and yet linked to the real. It functions to bolster the confidence in, and commitment to, an underlying order eclipsed by the more obvious conflict and disorder of human existence, or original sin as the Bible calls it. It is the heavenly blueprint or the heavenly treasures as Jesus calls them in Matthew 6:19.

By contrast the mundane authority, as exercised by Caesar and his henchmen, such as King Herod and Pontius Pilate, is geared to perpetuate itself and strengthen the very subjugation to which the Israelites object so strongly. It is pure human power. Its owners will use anything to strengthen the latter, including religious authority. Yet it is also order and therefore Jesus (and Calvin following him) claims that with some reservation it also has God's blessing. The reservation is that this kind of civic order may have its own potential for disorder and injustice.

Using God's heavenly authority for justifying either an Israeli uprising or Roman subjugation may be blasphemy, the Gospel story suggests. God's intent and God's heavenly authority may be falsely used for narrow human ends. Yet the separation does not mean that God's authority is irrelevant to Israelite resentment or human power. Heavenly authority consoles through elaborating the peace and serenity transcending the deep conflicts ravaging the country. It also relativizes, and strenuously warns about, the dangers of overindulgence in mundane authority however much order is a plus for a sane society.

Given due consideration Calvin's comments on Matthew 22:21 are downright conservative. Jews obeying the Romans, he says, do not violate God's authority. In the same way as children obey their parents and servants their masters, so citizens should obey their rulers. He goes so far as equating destruction of political order with rebellion against God.

So far so good. But then Calvin creates quite a loophole for his conservative view. God, he says, is the only governor of our souls and if princes and magistrates claim 'any part of God's authority' one has the right not to obey them any further. God is offended, he says, if one usurps His power. Furthermore outward subjection (to civil authorities) 'does not prevent us from having a free conscience.' And that conscience, as Calvin keeps pointing out in numerous other places in his voluminous writings, is God's gift to man.

Unfortunately for Calvin, this loophole is so large that it effectively negates his statement that humans who do not obey their rulers are rebels against God. Many rulers are godless and have no qualms in claiming divine powers. And men's consciences are conditioned by upbringing, socialization and the changing norms and values of one's community. If therefore one's social environment, as obviously was the case in Jesus' time in Israel, unanimously despises the Roman occupation, people's consciences would be clearly anti-Roman and pro-Jehovah.

Jesus was therefore quite astute in separating the spiritual and the civil order. Yet Calvin's introduction of the private conscience in the debate was less fortunate in the light of present day scientific thinking about formation and changing content of consciences. It makes more sense to think about the separate functions of God and Caesar: God epitomizes fairness and spiritual order in human affairs, Caesar concretely looks after the civil order hopefully judged in terms congenial to the larger context in which God has placed the human race.

Yet separation does not mean a complete break. The mundane political order may now be separate, but its independence is only relative. It is still subject to God's expectations as to what is fair and not corrupt. It still has to meet rules of order, and reconciliation. The chaos of man's war, cruelty and conflicts is still subject to God's condemnation. God continues to promote order out of man's chaos.

In other words there is a symbiosis between God's order and civil order, similar to the symbiosis between Calvin's faith and law. The more complex a culture and society, the more differentiation or division of labour progresses, the more stress has to be put on 'symbiosis' rather than 'separation.' The relationship changes rather than disappears. Evolution works via superimposition rather than elimination.

Caesar and God may now have separate functions, but the civic order still needs the sacred one. The power of the first is finite. Not just because individuals possessing or usurping that power have to die like all other humans, but because absolute power corrupts absolutely. God does not just legitimate any power and is thereby relegated to a tool of human manipulations. Making God a victim of what man wants God to be is tantamount to rebelling against man's essential being.

God is authority. Or to be more specific: God's authority and being are closely linked to an order counterbalancing existential disorder. Abuse of power is part of disorder because it denies justice to its victims. God's authority is anchored above all in his compassion, understanding, justice and fairness: all elements necessary for a balanced society or balanced individual.

The prophetic strain in the Biblical tradition insists on God's compassion and justice. Kings who abuse their power are clearly and utterly denounced. The prophet Nathan condemns King David for his successful attempt to do away with Bathsheba's husband so that he can possess her (2 Samuel 12:7) and King Ahab is similarly censured by the prophet Elijah for having Naboth killed so that he can appropriate his vineyard (1 Kings 21:21). In other words, powerless individuals have rights surpassing the power of absolute monarchs.

Yet this also means that we should have a second look at Calvin's individual conscience. After all conscience is more than the seat of moral principles affected by time and place which as 'laws' have their own symbiotic relations with faith and commitment. Conscience also has an individual right's aspect that Calvin assumes and the Bible clearly adopts. It is directly linked to God's eternal being transcending time and place.

This may also explain why Calvin puts so much emphasis on individualism. Not only does he start the *Institutes* with a clearly unbiblical, Greek principle of self knowledge, but he elevates both conscience and individual reason as God given.

And this is rather remarkable because Calvin following scripture is very (I feel almost like saying 'extremely') voluble on man's sin which is anything but God given.

A good ruler therefore should take into account individual conscience. If he upsets too many, not only will his acceptance by the ruled suffer, but God's blessing is likely to become precarious as well. After all man's individual conscience has divine origins in Calvin's mind and abuse of power denies this very aspect of God's gift!

There is extensive literature on the effect of the Calvinist ethic on rational capitalism, science and democracy. Calvin has been accused of not being particularly democratic in actual practice. Under his guidance Geneva was more an oligarchy than a democracy. And indeed Calvin was worried that too much individual freedom might lead to chaos. He wrote in his commentaries: 'If everyone has a right to judge and arbiter in this matter nothing can be set down as certain and our whole religion will be filled with uncertainty.'

Yet both the Renaissance and Lutheran ('salvation by faith') thinking formed Calvin's intellectual climate. Furthermore the Reformers made the marginal individual central in their writings, rather than an intervening church institution. That the individual might be a sinner, at the margin of God's holy enterprise, but his salvation or whole making was just as central in the cosmic intentions of the biblical drama. Coping with his marginality, standing aside from the comforts of the economic, political and scientific establishments was therefore an enhanced possibility for those affected by Calvin's teaching. And there were many thus affected in the sixteenth and seventeenth century.

Democracy is therefore the political institution least likely to fit unimpeded power abuse which Calvinist realism designates as a real possibility given man's sinful nature. It protects the powerless not only by limiting the time the rulers can rule, but also by giving the powerless a vote in the election of government. Often democratic constitutions in the West mention the supremacy of God for the nation. These counterbalance the discontinuity of the ruling bodies in the same way as a hereditary, yet powerless monarchy or a representative system of governors-general provides the continuity or fixed point of reference for some nations.

By separating civil from religious power, as Jesus did in our text, justice for all has been promoted. What started out as an insoluble national conflict in Israel (ruled by foreigners rather than by natives), Jesus made into a practical solution. Yet it did not suspend the pain of occupation. It may have rescued God's power and the religious relevance for order. It also implicitly warned against usurping God's power by using him for parochial patronage.

Through our bond with God rather than through our possession of God can the power of the positive, the pure, love, compassion and kindness be enhanced in human affairs. Certainly that is what the Bible insists on. However, if we refuse to expect it solely from human efforts, but from God alone, it can still exist (and flourish) independent from human interference.

CALVIN 08
COVENANT and FAITH

Those who were ready went in with him to the wedding. Matthew 25:10

Covenant is another word for contract, mutual agreement, pact or alliance. In the Bible it means contract between God and man. Each provides the other with something they both need. God provides protection, guidance and order. Humans promise obedience and faith. Even when the covenant is sealed with a solemn oath, it may become null and void, unless it is kept alive with mutual goodwill. Both a handshake and a 20 page legal document depend on mutual willingness, trust and faith.

This is what today readings are about: covenant and faith, or about problems with the covenant when the link with faith has become threadbare. Both Old and New Testament reading can be summed up as the erratic relation between God and men. Another summary of both readings may be 'the precariousness of faith.' Joshua 24:14-25 is about the people's lapse in idolatry until Joshua manages to persuade them to re-new their pact with Yahweh. Similarly, the parable of the ten virgins (Matthew 25:1-13) is about those maidens whose faith in God is not strong enough to last their waiting for Him.

What is the message of Joshua 24? It is the story of Israel's conquest of Canaan and the pivotal importance of their leader Joshua. He is the successor of Moses and like Moses he knows that it is the faith that kept the Israelites together as a disciplined army. Faith is part and parcel of the covenant or pact that unites them with God. They promise to unconditionally obey in return for God's protection and guidance.

Yet God's covenant is more than a human contract. It deals with the deepest and most solemn emotions. It transcends the mortality and failures of even the best and most successful leader. After all, the most charismatic general, such as Joshua's predecessor, Moses, eventually dies before he can savour the fruit of the goal, the conquest of Canaan. And human shortcomings are apparent even in the most successful of managers. By contrast God's leadership is not bound by death. Nor is it flawed by personal deficiency.

Furthermore, the covenant between God and man also directs social order, something mere mortals can only do imperfectly. It seals the norms and values that oil the machinery of social relations. It condemns whatever mars those relations, such as envy, greed, anger, hypocrisy, dishonesty, stealing etc. and encourages those values and norms, such as altruism, humility, generosity, honesty, kindness, love, understanding etc., that strengthen those relations.

Yet above all, the covenant or pact concentrates all emotions in one supreme focal point, God. It jealously rejects idols and other usurpers of its authority over the minds and loyalties of people. Division and dissipation detract from this focal point. They destroy unanimity and thereby diminish solidarity and concerted action. And therefore Joshua strongly insists on renewal and on putting new life in the covenant at Shechem.

It was time for the renewal. Yahweh had been closely associated with a nomadic tribe. But now the Israelites had settled in Canaan and the local gods of the Amorites, sensitively geared to settled living had intrigued a considerable number of them. And so Joshua felt it his duty to remind them that Yahweh was more than a nomadic god for an army on the march and that He could quite adequately deal with the new situation. Yahweh to Joshua was as relevant for the nomadic as for the settled life style.

Common faith in Yahweh had made the conquering Israelites into a formidable fighting-fit force. Their faith was so strong that the Israelites began to think about it as super-human. They did not think about it any longer as a human product, or as their responsibility in the contract, but as Yahweh's gift. The remarkable conquests of the Islamic armies in the seventh century AD are rather similar. Faith in Allah and the fanatic conviction of the followers that they were carrying out his work, made them as formidable as the Israelites were in the conquest of Canaan.

Calvin interprets Joshua 24 as an example of astute psychology. Joshua, he says, badly wanted the covenant with Yahweh to be renewed, but he also wanted it to be the people's decision rather than his own. It would make the covenant all the stronger, he felt, if they were to decide for themselves. And so he gives them two options: either you follow 'the gods of the Amorites in whose land you dwell (verse 15)' or you follow Yahweh. He stacks the cards by adding that whatever they do, he and his house will worship the Lord. Calvin then says: '… (Joshua) gives them freedom of choice that, they may not afterwards pretend to have been under compulsion, when they bound themselves by their own consent.'

But before we get too far involved in Calvin, let us look at our other reading, the parable of the ten virgins. Life is waiting for a final climax, a fulfilment, Jesus tells us here. And that climax has something to do with completion, being unified. The wedding party is a good metaphor for the covenant between God and man. It is a joyous occasion and yet it is the waiting and anticipation that is almost as satisfying as the arrival itself.

As in Joshua 24, the strength of faith is the cardinal issue. The five virgins who did not provide for a long wait were excluded from the wedding party. Jesus implies that one has to be well prepared for the wedding party or man's final destination, the Kingdom of God. What is more, one cannot borrow what is both very personal and part of maturing, a growing in faith.

Therefore our text says that one has to be ready to enter the wedding party or the Kingdom. It cannot just be a minor option or a minor interlude. It has to do with basic meaning. It is serious business. It needs careful preparation. And even with the most careful preparation, things can go wrong. Satan may interfere even with the best intentions and tempt with the attraction of the immediate and pleasurable rather than the long term and eternal. That was also the message of Joshua 24: God is more than the immediately relevant. He is beyond all that.

And in all this faith is the glue that binds to what is long term and eternal. Faith connects with a vision of final destination. It is basic commitment transcending all lesser commitments, or actually infusing those lesser commitments with an overarching, umbrella-like glow of understanding. Faith is the emotion-laden link with God's embattled order that Christians have solemnly adopted in preference to the many sources of disorder impinging on existence.

The glue of faith binding Yahweh and Israel is central in both readings. What is different is the understanding of what God is about. In the book of Joshua, God is regarded as the exclusive possession of the Israelites alone, nothing more than a god of a nomadic tribe. He is still an exclusive God, for the Israelites alone. The quality and the sincerity of faith in God affect the cohesion of one ethnic group. Yet, in Jesus' parable of the ten virgins, that cohesion is now universal. The Kingdom of God now spans all humans and societies. Salvation and fulfilment relate to both individual integrity and communal solidarity.

One can say all this somewhat differently: the new covenant has burst the ethnic boundaries of the old covenant. Even now Judaism is an exclusive, ethnic religion. In sharp contrast with Christians, Jews are not very comfortable with making converts of non-Jews. This strengthening of ethnic identity has certainly contributed to their survival as a nation in spite of dispersion, pogroms and persecution, but it has also restricted their appeal to non-Jews.

Yet the new covenant has its own boundaries. The community of the faithful in the New Testament replaces the Israel of the Old Testament. The boundary here is between the elect within and the non-elect without, those who accept God's authority as central in their lives and those who do not, those who are saved and those who are not.

How does Calvin see the link between election and faith? To him election is primary and faith secondary. Election and predestination are conjoined with faith, he says, 'provided the latter holds second place.' In the same section (*Inst.* III xxii 10) he actually calls 'election the mother of faith.' He quotes John 10:29, where Jesus says that his own sheep know his voice and that 'no one shall snatch them from my care', explaining that 'our salvation will always be sure and certain' because 'it is guarded by the invincible power of God.' At the end of the section Calvin insists that this and other biblical passages are 'attestations to the inflexible constancy of election.' Yet these passages can just as well be interpreted as trust in God's invincible power of order over chaos and thereby thinking of the believers as allies in an ongoing battle rather than wooden puppets without inherent power of their own.

Election in this section is sharply contrasted with chance. Chance is not a favourite in Calvin's books and for that matter in the entire Bible. Election and chance are opposites. Chance is a spoiler of security and delineation. In the above section Calvin quotes from Amos (4:7; 8:11) that drought in one city and rain in another is not accidental. It is God's will, he says, assuming all along that anything that happens must fit in Yahweh's preference for order, security, and delineation.

One way to undermine that order is rebellion against God and thwarting rules of morality. But other sources of disorder, such as accidents, death, droughts, famine, floods etc. have nothing to do with moral order. They are sometimes called acts of God, as the existence of pure chance is too hard to contemplate. They are therefore ascribed to God in order to minimize their power and their assault on security. Yet it makes more sense to think of them as events which God actively and lovingly uses to help humans rise above traumas by putting them in a larger perspective.

To Calvin, election and predestination are a natural and necessary counterbalance to chance and its potential for disorder. They are an assertion of God's superiority and faith in that superiority, in the face of very real moral and natural disorder. The renewal of the covenant both in Joshua and entering the wedding party or the Kingdom of God are an implicit vote for, and fundamental commitment to God's authority, negating all that injures, wrecks, demolishes or destroys that authority.

One can understand both God's gift of faith and God's blueprint of order better, if one optimizes God's authority as a counter to the inevitable disorder resulting from man's self-will. Calvin stresses this point again and again, if only because he had to replace on good scriptural grounds the pillar of the institutional church with man's direct relationship with God.

This bothers Calvin's logical, clear, mind. He asks in the section on covenant and faith (*Inst.* III xxii 10) whether God is not actually inconsistent, when on the one hand he invites everyone to his Kingdom, but then elects only few. How does scripture reconcile, he asks, 'that by external preaching all are called to faith and repentance, and that yet the Spirit of faith and repentance is not given to all?'

If salvation is by faith, as Paul insists and Luther reiterates so strongly, Calvin appears to be on slippery ground when he makes faith secondary to election. If election means to be found by God, Calvin has solid scriptural grounds. Actually, in his commentary on 1 Peter 1:2 Calvin says so: 'election is not to be separated from calling.' However if it means that anything that happens (accidents, death, earthquakes, floods) or anything that humans do, is fore-ordained, it smacks too much of the unscriptural, exclusively structural god of Aristotle, who wound up the clock of existence and let it run its prescribed path without any further interference. Yet Calvin rejects Aristotle on this point.

Calvin, strongly influenced as he was by the Renaissance and its renewed interest in the classics, seems overly keen to reconcile Athens with Jerusalem. The consequence is that the large gulf separating the two (God's creation – a noun – versus God's ongoing creating order – a verb) is prematurely closed. Yet this attempt also leads to Calvin's poor solution of the determination versus chance problem (*Inst.* III xxii 10), although in his correspondence he strongly objects to those who accuse him of attributing authorship of sin to God.

To him, God's authority is absolute and therefore God must also be the author of disorder. He rejects those whose faith is not up to standard rather than treats them as unfortunates whom he has lost in the battle for their soul with Satan.

There is something appealing about absolute rather than relative authority. The first is rocklike, the second flexible. Faith in whatever concretely represents order tends to be preferred by humans over the moving equilibrium represented by chance impinging on that rocklike order. Yet our readings for today suggest that both Joshua and Jesus assume the latter. God may represent rock-like authority, but the relationship with him is active, evolving, growing, maturing rather than passive and predetermined. The covenant is not one-sided. It actually is a sham unless there is room for at least some human freedom.

Dostoyevsky's 'The Grand Inquisitor' from *The Brothers Karamazov* describes this dilemma of the human need for order and authority versus God's leaving humans with the freedom to choose well. It is the story of Christ's Second Coming in the town of Seville, Spain, during the burning at the stake of hundreds of heretics by the cardinal, The Grand Inquisitor. Christ radiates compassion, heals the blind and raises the dead. He is instantly recognized and followed by everyone, but the Grand Inquisitor has him arrested and thrown in prison, where in the pitch darkness of the night he visits Jesus.

'Why hast thou come to hinder us?' he asks. 'We have completed and corrected the work Thou hast begun. We have taken the people's fearful burden of free choice, appeased their conscience and given them the earthly bread they desired instead of the heavenly one Thou didst promise. We have protected them against the uncertainty of believing in the vague, enigmatic and unseen. I will burn thee at the stake tomorrow.' But Jesus does not say a word. And the story finishes with Jesus softly kissing the old man on his bloodless lips, upon which The Grand Inquisitor opens the cell door and says: 'Go, and come no more … come not at all, never, never!'

The intrinsic need for authority and security, Dostoyevsky seems to say, leads directly to rejection of the unbelievers and their gruesome death. By contrast, Christ's love for all creatures and tolerance of even the unbelievers is a worm in the woodpile.

The story also warns us not to throw the baby away with the bath water. A good case can be made out for both the link of religion with social solidarity and for Calvin's stress on the indisputable authority of God. In both instances religion anchors the constancy and continuity of order in an existence marked by change, chance and chaos. But that disorder is a given and should be presented as an ever present symbiosis and drama rather than squeezed in the logical mould of Calvin's deep reverence for reason and neat thinking. Both the dramas of Joshua 24 and Matthew 25 should stand on their own rather than squeezed into an elegant mould of priorities.

There are, of course, other sections of the Bible where such events as Job's afflictions or the captivity (Nehemiah 1:9) are attributed to Satan or sin, but usually breakdown of the natural or moral order are Yahweh's way of punishing individuals or nations. The faith in God's order has to be maintained and strengthened through thick and thin. God's authority has to be defended at any price. It is the only antidote the Bible knows to breakdown and chaos. Particularly at times of change and upheaval God's superiority must be re-asserted.

The problem with this strong emphasis on God's authority both in Calvin and the Bible is that man's authority may correspondingly be weakened and diminished. It may actually unbalance the covenant, as actually happened, when the Israelites intermarried with the people they had conquered (Joshua 23:12) and began to worship foreign gods (Joshua 24:23). Joshua's long speech towards the end of his long life had the single purpose of restoring the covenant and thereby Yahweh's authority. Anything that takes away some of God's authority he calls rebellion and sin (Joshua 24:20).

On good scriptural grounds one could expect the answer to be that moral and natural disorder of any kind are all around us, that chance and change are the order of the day and that therefore God's call is not heeded by everyone. Not everyone can see God's triumph of order and salvation over disorder and sin. The seeds of God's word can fall among the thorns or in stony places rather than on fertile grounds (Luke 8:4-15) and therefore not produce the faith, the prerequisite for salvation and wholeness.

Calvin is disinclined to let go of anything that takes away from God's authority and that makes room for man's part in the covenant, as Joshua does in his speech and Jesus implies in the parable of the ten virgins when he blames five of them for not making sufficient provisions. Freedom to choose and freedom to build faith on the part of man are implied here and in the concept of covenant.

Our readings for today assume that God actively rescues, saves, those that actively take a stance for him, renewing their faith or preparing for union with him. Those people who, by contrast, follow other gods or who are not adequately prepared are obviously the rejected or as Calvin calls them, the reprobate. These are the people who have heard the call, but have rejected it. It is a matter of believers versus unbelievers or sheep versus goats. To assume that humans have nothing to do with this separation is going too far.

Calvin's section on faith (*Inst*. III ii 24) calls Satan the destroyer of the certainty of faith. Obviously the devil is the prince of disorder, the arch rebel against God, ultimately defeated by Yahweh. Understandably Calvin feels that rebellion is inconsistent with God's omnipotence. More importantly, Calvin also feels on good scriptural grounds, that nothing should stand in the way of God's authority, the more so as he has also, again on good scriptural grounds, insisted that 'faith consists in the knowledge of God and Christ, not in a reverence for the Church (*Inst*. III ii 3).'

The dilemma for Calvin, of course, is that by kicking the stud of the Church as mediator from underneath the covenant and by restricting it to Christ and the believer, he has to cling all the more to God's authority instead of the more visible Church as an institution. Calvin is fond of quoting Hebrews 11:1 ('Faith makes us certain of realities we do not see'), for instance in *Inst*. III ii 41. This may be because it is the only stud remaining after diminishing the authority of a mediating institution.

We can put all this in sociological terms. In the same way as four centuries later another Frenchman, the famous sociologist Emile Durkheim, oversimplified and overemphasized the link between religion and social solidarity at the expense of personal identity, so Calvin tends to oversimplify and overemphasize God's authority at the expense of man's freedom of choice, however limited that freedom may be.

Actually, Calvin comes close to admitting the mutuality of the covenant rather than God's one-sided determination. In *Inst*. III ii 41 he says that humans can transcend the reach of their own intellect and 'be wholly inflamed with love to God' after God has engendered His love for them. In other words humans are not just wooden puppets, but act in response to God's initiative.

This leads to other Biblical statements about God, Jesus or the Holy Spirit being the author of the faith or faith as a super-human phenomenon. Or as something that made Joshua's army feel capable of superhuman feats in the conquest of Canaan. Faith as a gift from God is also mentioned in the New Testament where Jesus is called 'the author and finisher of our faith (Hebrews 12:2).' It is the authority of God, rather than man's responsibility that has to be optimized, if unity is to prevail.

To Calvin, the burden of the covenant therefore has to be based on individual man rather than on Israel's ethnic identity in the Old Testament. Calvin was thoroughly steeped in, and influenced by the Renaissance with its admiration of rational individualism it inherited from ancient Greece.

Conclusion: there are always two parties in a covenant. Yet the power and responsibility of either should never obliterate the power and responsibility of the other. If for good scriptural reasons Calvin puts a great deal of emphasis on God's authority, initiative and power by stressing his election, predestination and authorship of faith, this power should not eliminate man's responsibility. As our readings for today showed, it was up to the Israelites to reject Yahweh or to obey him and the five excluded virgins failed in their responsibility to provide for a long wait. In other words rejection and responsibility by man are still part of the equation.

Inner motivation and solid commitment or faith on man's part is crucial for both the Kingdom of God and a sane society. God's authority is not to be diminished. Yet neither should it be blown out of proportion, leaving man's responsibility for the covenant irrelevant and insignificant. Nor will the opposite do, enhancing man's authority so much that there is nothing left for God. One cannot reduce Yahweh to just a figment of man's imagination. This too will lead to disaster. Mutuality and balance are essential for a viable culture and society.

CALVIN 09
The CLOAK of INTEGRITY

God has robed me in salvation as a garment and clothed me in integrity as a cloak.
Isaiah 61:10

Like me, some of you may have affectionate grandchildren or children. Their love seems unconditional. It is always spontaneous. They don't worry about old age, charm or ugliness. They don't consider merit. They don't even know what 'merit' means. I suppose that's why we like Christmas and the story of the baby Jesus born in a manger. It reminds us of the innocent, spontaneous affection for, and of, babies and little children and God's unconditional love for young and old, the ugly and the beautiful, the poor and the rich, the successful and the losers.

But then on the day after Christmas we are brought back to reality. And so today's reading from Luke 2 is about Simeon blessing the little baby Jesus. He recognizes the Messiah, but then predicts that men will reject Christ and tells Mary that she 'too shall be pierced to the heart.' In other words, salvation is not a sugar-coating of existence, an airy-fairy projection of goodness, affection and order in the sky. It is part of a drama intertwining good and evil, heaven and hell, God and Satan right here on earth.

But let us first look at our Old Testament reading from Isaiah 61, where the prophet proclaims good news to his people exiled in Babylon. The humble, the broken-hearted, the captives, the mourners shall be released and redeemed (verses 1-3). The ruined cities of Israel shall be restored (verse 4). Foreigners shall shepherd the flocks and tend the vineyards (verse 5). The Israelites, now returned from exile, shall enjoy the wealth of other nations (verse 6). God will doubly compensate them for their suffering in a foreign land (verse 7), make a covenant with them and bless them and their offspring (verses 8-9).

Then follows our text: 'God has robed me in salvation and clothed me in integrity as a garment (verse 10).'

By 'me' Isaiah means not just his personal self but other Israelites as well, so that 'righteousness and praise' can 'blossom before all the nations (verse 11).'

Obviously salvation, righteousness and integrity are the key words in our text and are central to what God's intention is for both individual members and the nation as a whole. What do these concepts mean and why are they so important in the total scheme of things? Are these ideas the heart of God's blueprint for Israel in particular and mankind in general?

Actually all three key words, concepts and ideas have much in common. They all refer to 'wholeness.' In point of fact, the last of the three words, 'integrity', sums up what the other two are all about. It denotes completion, unity, inclusion, totality, identity, sameness. Integrity (the *New English Bible*) is used instead of righteousness (the King James and Revised Standard versions) and the reason for adopting it here is its better fit in present day vocabulary. Righteousness is almost exclusively used in religious literature and reminds people of self-righteousness; by contrast integrity is something we admire in others and strive to have ourselves.

More important, however, is that the word 'integrity' comes close to the original Hebrew word. Righteousness in the Bible meant 'what God regarded as right behaviour.' Right behaviour is whatever contributes to the integrity of society or person, or what makes the wholeness of that society or person more solid. By contrast wrong behaviour takes away from that wholeness or integrity and makes for 'unrighteousness', dissipation, disintegration.

In Isaiah 61 salvation means rescue from disintegration or restoration to integrity. The exile to Babylon almost destroyed Israel, but God came to the rescue and restored Israel to its rightful place amongst the nations by letting them return to their land. To the prophets and the priests God was definitely and uniquely an ethnic God. God's covenant is with Israel alone. Other nations and foreigners (verse 51) are inferior and destined to serve Israel and to make it wealthier. Only much later does the concept of God burst out of narrow ethnic bounds.

Yet the centrality of integrity, salvation and righteousness remains. It now expands to all mankind. Now God comes to be seen as the vital, living, epitome of whatever contributes to order generally on a variety of sometimes conflicting levels. Personal disobedience, private sins correspond with whatever diminishes the strength of the social fabric or social order. Yet that social fabric or social order as a whole can also destroy its own inner integrity, irrespective of individuals, such as the prophets, maintaining their personal integrity.

Calvin uses 'righteousness' or 'integrity' often. In the *Institutes* (III xiv 1) he distinguishes four categories or degrees of integrity. The first, lowest, category consists of individuals who Calvin calls 'idolaters.' The second category is formed by the 'profane.' The third consists of 'hypocrites.' Only the fourth and last have perfect integrity.

Calvin starts with the last category, but right from the start admits that it is impossible for humans to achieve. Only Christ possesses perfect integrity, he says (III xiv 12). Humans can obtain it through proxy, through faith in Christ as mediator. The road to that perfect integrity is not via 'good works' or scrupulously performing whatever society expects of a good citizen (according to Calvin and also, of course, St Paul), but only through humble confessions of sin and obedience to the will of God.

Translating this in sociological terms – perfect order on any level is impossible. Yet humans strive towards it, if only because God who is order personified, will never surrender to the prince of disorder, Satan. Yet scrupulous adherence to the laws governing good behaviour is not enough in itself. Commitment, faith, love (the unconditional kind I mentioned at the beginning of this sermon) are essential for whole making or for progress on this path to personal integrity.

Calvin comes back to this theme of inner motivation, sincere faith as against outward compliance and fake religion in his discourse about the other 'kinds' of righteousness or integrity. True integrity, he says, is 'estimated not by acts, but by motives (III xiv 4).' And this is what his first category of humans lacks. They have no integrity whatsoever. They are the 'idolaters', who have made an idol of 'the flesh.' And by flesh, following St Paul, he means a long list of sins: 'adultery, fornication, uncleanness, lasciviousness, idolatry, witchcraft, hatred, variance, emulation, wrath, strife, seditions, heresies, envies, murders, drunkenness, revels and all kinds of pollution and abomination which it is possible to imagine (III xiv 1).'

Nowadays we would be a bit more careful with our use of 'integrity.' The world is immensely more diverse and complex than it was in either Biblical or Calvin's days. The idolaters do not so much lack integrity as derive their integrity from 'the flesh.' The 'flesh' has its own satisfactions and promises of integrity. They may not have the lofty, comprehensive and fundamental intent of the Christian variety, but they certainly attempt to be staging points on the road to integration and wholeness. Satan is certainly not beyond using human longings for his own distorted ends.

Calvin's second and third categories are not much better. They are the 'profane' and the 'hypocrites' and are equally condemned. They may not be as obvious as the idolaters who openly flaunt their misdeeds. They may actually be within the Christian fold. Yet their God-given consciences are 'impure.' 'They lack faith and are not yet reconciled and justified.' They may falsely claim 'some degree of righteousness', but their 'impurity of heart nullifies that claim (III xiv 7).'

Honest convictions, sincere faith and unblemished motives are to Calvin prerequisites of salvation. If they are not present, integrity does not exist. Calvin preserves 'integrity' for an exclusive group of believers. But by doing so, he also makes the process of becoming saved, or being made whole, more elusive. God may separate the sheep from the goats, but he also creates order out of chaos. Definitiveness may tend to subvert process as equally real and necessary for integrity formation.

This brings us back to Simeon's blessing of the baby Jesus. As I said at the beginning: Simeon predicted that the promised redeemer, the righteous one, the Messiah, would be rejected by his own people and that 'because of him … the secret thoughts of many will be laid bare (Luke 2:35).' Here too God as personified in Jesus is not interested in appearance, but in actual motives. God is interested in the heart and action rather than in what people say, in mere words.

And that is where the rub lies. A viable, sane society is not served by fake conformity, by façade decency, by bad faith, by lip service, by sham. It needs real faith, actual decency and honest conformity. Mutual trust can only be assured if individuals have faith in one another and can communicate on a common wavelength of understanding and implicit confidence. Above all there must be enough openness for others to savour the actual source of motives of the other. That's why Calvin's interpretation of Luke 2:35 stresses the capacity of the light of Christ 'to disclose every artifice and unmask hypocrisy.'

In other words, the cloak of integrity of which our text speaks has a lot to do with not just the Christian, but any human being discovering his real self and opening his heart to God. The problem is invariably that being honest with oneself also means confronting one's imperfections and shortcomings rather than hiding oneself behind a façade of make-belief and sham confidence. That's why the forgiveness of sin is tied so closely with salvation and integrity.

Yet the cloak of integrity is not just confined to the resolution of conflict within the human soul. It is more than the outcome of the struggle between the honesty and dishonesty about our basic motives. Integrity is also hammered out on the anvil of social appeasement and condoning of injustice, abuse, oppression and corruption.

When St Paul equates Jesus with the personification of righteousness or integrity (2 Corinthians 6:15) and regards him alone as such, it is because Jesus saw himself as part of a long line of prophets who were often marginal to (and therefore severe critics of) the community in which they found themselves. Their integrity was hammered out on the anvil of communal pressure to conform. It often sustained itself solely because their faith in Yahweh was stronger than communal loyalty.

Integrity therefore is often strengthened by conflict rather than conformity. Israel's integrity was reinforced by setting itself off from other nations as we have seen in Isaiah 61. Jesus was rejected and eventually crucified because his loyalty to God the father was stronger than his loyalty to Israel, dominated by pharisaic priests.

Integrity is also sometimes hammered out on the anvil of adversity. I vividly remember the despair my friends and I felt of ever surviving the Nazi holocaust in 1944. Gnawing hunger, severe under nourishment, deteriorating health, the odour of death in Gestapo camps and German prisons had taken their toll. We kept dreaming of escaping in spite of the executions of those who tried and had been caught.

Three times we were tempted to join the Waffen SS. Our reasoning was that greater freedom would improve our chances to escape. The first time the invitation had come from a fellow prisoner in the Rothensee Gestapo Camp. The commandant had given him a list for signatures of volunteers. We had made fun of him at the time.

The second time was much more serious. It happened in the Magdeburg Prison. I had been summoned by the examining magistrate who noticed my acute agony. He said: 'If I were in your shoes I would join the Waffen SS. This would prove to the court that you are not Deutschfeindlich, hostile to the German cause. You would be freed almost immediately. The trial would be advanced and your sentence reduced, more likely cancelled.' Joining the Waffen SS was now linked to our court case: it was proof that we were not hostile to the German war effort and not joining was proof that we were!

Integrity versus opportunism seemed to be the choice. The entire Nazi world surrounding me encouraged the brutal principle of means serving ends. Why not be as Machiavellian as the Nazis were? In June 1944 the warden himself invited me to join the Waffen SS. On this occasion I was even more emaciated and in a correspondingly poor frame of mind. I also had to avoid having a sentence added for continued hostility to the German war effort. Similarly, I had to avoid the risk of being sent to a concentration camp after the prison term. I had been coughing blood, and so I used that as an excuse for being less than interested. Hopefully the Waffen SS was not so hard up that it pressured young people with tuberculosis to join up!

Integrity versus opportunism. I was brought up to use opportunities well. The Great Depression had seen to that! The imprisonment had made us even more expert in taking advantage of any chance for an extra ounce of bread or an easier job. From the vantage point of today the school of hard knocks had made us more adroit at exploiting potential than our children and grandchildren will ever be.

Yet there was a limit. Instinctively I had stopped at opportunism as a mainspring of action, as the underlying motive for surviving. Mastery and survival at any price offended something within me that had been part of my upbringing. Yet it was unarticulated, vague and tantalisingly elusive. I was slowly and painfully discovering that integrity was crucial, but how could it become both strengthened and more focused?

It was later in life that I slowly discovered that in Jesus Christ I had the answer to that question. He was the forerunner (Hebrews 6:20) on the path to clearer and stronger integrity. To Jesus, death on the cross was his choice for integrity (as represented in God's destiny for him) rather than for survival through conforming to the sham world of hypocritical clerics and Machiavellian conquerors.

God spreads the cloak of integrity over his followers from the ancient prophets, such as Isaiah, his son Jesus, St Paul, and Calvin to the millions of believers in our day and age. It has given backbone to numerous individuals. It has warmed the cockles of many hearts. It has healed societies and cultures. It has rescued order from chaos. It has reconciled humans, families and nations, one to another. It has united what once was divided. Thanks be to God!

CALVIN 10

SCATTERED like a CROWD of FRIGHTENED SHEEP

The sight of the people moved Jesus to pity: they were scattered like sheep without a shepherd. Matthew 9:36

Wherever Jesus went large crowds would gather. The people before him reminded him of what he knew from the prophets, such as Jeremiah who compared Israel with scattered sheep (Jeremiah 50:17) and who also took pity on flocks without a shepherd.

The crowds, however, had not just gathered to be inspired. Jesus' fame was also based on something more mundane and practical. He was known to be a successful faith healer. Chapter nine of St Matthew's Gospel mentions many instances of his curing 'every kind of illness and disease (Matthew 9:35).' In those days medicine as we know it did not exist. By contrast faith healers were much in demand. People loved miracles and Jesus performed many of them.

Alternative medicine has taken a closer look at these miracles. It is interested in the body's inner pharmacy and the release of natural healing chemicals in our physical make-up. Much modern research has gone, and is going, into the so-called 'placebo effect.' That is the effect not of the drugs as such, but of the expectation of their effect.

Researchers have found that depression, for instance, has been lessened by a placebo, a harmless pill without bio-medical value. They compare the psychosomatic, or mind-body effect of those placebos with the proven healing ingredients of medicine and think that these placebos have symbolic significance. Other researchers think that the expectations of the mind release endorphins, natural chemicals in the brain which reduce pain and provide marathon runners, for instance, with a sense of elation.

Yet something has to trigger the power of mind over body. And this trigger, usually the authority of the healer, is vital for the outcome. People felt that Jesus had the very charismatic authority to produce not only the healing of their ailing bodies, but even more, to provide the spiritual leadership to unite them and to be their shepherd, as today's text has it. It was this ability to change them from a crowd of scattered sheep into an effective body of believers, which was the main reason for large crowds gathering wherever Jesus went. People craved charismatic authority.

Charismatic authority is in demand particularly in times of rapid social change. Our Old Testament reading of Genesis 1:1-5 points to God as such a charismatic authority, creating order out of chaos, or light out of darkness. Genesis 1:2 describes the situation before God took it in hand as 'formless and void.' The Hebrew words mean empty and confused or vain and worthless. Without God's intervention and ordering spirit, the earth would return to shapeless chaos.

Calvin comments that the world was an 'indigested mass' before God had a chance to perfect it. And the Spirit (charismatic authority?) was his means for creating order out of chaos. He rendered the disorderly heap 'stable' and prevented dissolution. In other words, like the author of Genesis, Calvin assumes that there was something he called 'shapeless chaos' before God changed it into something that had shape. Or to say it with our text, God the shepherd gathered the scattered sheep and made it into a united, responsive flock.

The value of the first five verses of the Bible lies in the picture of God's actual, personal, involvement. God is not an aloof initiator of a self-maintaining universe. Ceaseless participation rather than cold neutrality is the password, the clue to an understanding of what the millions of words following are all about. God's authority is charismatic, unruffled and serene rather than passive, unfeeling and insensible.

This has both an advantage and a disadvantage. The advantage is that man's emotional, whole-making, commitment/faith/loyalty requiring, and therefore ordering equipment is not only aroused, but also permitted to take centre-stage. It is housed usually in the right hemisphere of our brain. It balances the usually dominant left hemisphere of our mental equipment, the analytic side, which might otherwise make humans into rational automatons.

The problem is that this capacity for emotional fusion rather than fission, focusing rather than fragmenting, can be misdirected. Instead of contributing to healing it contributes to disparity. Or to stay with our text it can scatter rather than unite, disperse rather than gather. And that's where the concept of sin comes in.

All through history men's intrinsic commitments and loyalties have been directed not to the centre stage where God dwells, but to countless other causes, desires and objects. They have become attached to a golden calf (Exodus 32:4), and may worship material objects, precious metals, readily available, desirable, man-made symbols of self-enhancing power. They have limited man's vision away from God and made humanity into a crowd of frightened sheep without a shepherd.

That is essentially why sin is so central in the Bible. It is best translated as rebellion against God, or refusal to accept His authority. Sin is having a preference to go one's own way. Yet the inclination to make the self occupy centre stage invariably leads to the chaos of a scattered crowd with no ultimate purpose and goal. The advantage of order and discipline for society, culture and civilization must be crystal clear by now.

Yet there is also a disadvantage and that is that we have to take God's omnipotence, or him being almighty with a grain of salt. God's blueprint for existence may indeed be ultimately victorious, but of necessity it has to remain vague and has to forever remain in the 'becoming' rather than 'being' mode. God's blueprint is a continuous, never-ending, creation of order out of chaos, or salvation out of sin.

But if 'order' is something to be accomplished perpetually, it cannot also be something already there. One cannot logically overlook the difference between the transient and the enduring, the dynamic and the stable, the temporary and the eternal, creating and creation, ordering and order. Maybe therefore we should think about God's blueprint for existence as vague rather than specific, as something ultimate rather than concrete. Or to put this differently: maybe we should be less concerned about logical reconciliation than about the dramatization of the symbiosis between sin and salvation, chaos and order, reason and faith.

Actually the value of Genesis 1:1-5 lies not only in reconciliation, but also in dramatization at the heart of human existence. An exclusive emphasis on reconciliation may underestimate the function of the right hemisphere of our brains, even when one has to hasten adding that God's creating order out of chaos is indeed a rescuing of logical meaning from shapeless meaninglessness. Yet by resolving the tension prematurely, rather than leaving room for an ongoing battle right up to the present day between chaos and order we may unknowingly squeeze the comprehensive intent out of God's blueprint for existence. Dramatization does as much justice, if not more, than logical reconciliation to that blueprint!

Our second reading for today fits like hand and glove, or key and lock, with our first reading, even though it was written many, many centuries later. It is the story of John the Baptist in Mark 1:4-11. He is 'the voice crying aloud in the wilderness' that Isaiah 40:3 is speaking about according to Mark 1:3. The wilderness represents the chaos of man's sin, the repentance for which is the prerequisite, the essential element, the sine qua non, for order and salvation (Mark 1:4).

Yet the wilderness here is also the simple place to which John (and later Jesus. Mark 1:12), retired to find his soul and his calling. It is a place, shorn of all earthly, tempting comforts, where humans can rediscover their real self. It is nature where people can come to themselves. And so we read (Mark 1:6), about John being 'dressed in a rough coat of camel's hair' and feeding himself on nature's products, 'locusts and wild honey.' It was the place where John's inner being was strengthened to accomplish his task for which he was later beheaded.

Nature is also, however, devoid of the structures that humans need to keep the wolf of chaos from the door.

Still the wilderness in which John the Baptist appeared (Mark 1:4) is here not pristine nature anymore, but a society in which people resemble scattered sheep without a shepherd. Calvin in his commentary on Mark 1:4 associates Jerusalem at the time with 'a wilderness: for all had been reduced to wild and frightful confusion' a term which Calvin also uses when he explains what is meant in Genesis 1:2 by chaos. It is this 'state of death' which 'stupid and hardened men' attempt to avoid and makes them flock to hear John the Baptist's message of salvation. To Calvin it is also the place where hypocrites, such as the Sadducees and Pharisees, reign.

Repentance for, and confession of, sins is to John the Baptist the key to salvation and the key to rescue from the human wilderness to the Kingdom of God and baptism with the water of the river Jordan (Mark 1:5). And the sins that John the Baptist is speaking about are not just the trespasses of the Ten Commandments, or the individual sins of pride, lust, envy, gluttony, covetousness, anger and sloth but also corporate sin and the corruption of human nature.

John the Baptist, like Jesus after him, was thoroughly steeped in Israelite piety, central to which was the story of the fall in Genesis 3. The focus of sin was therefore man's physical/sexual mortality as the centre of meaning. Escaping from the human wilderness into the wideness of God's spiritual/immortality was only possible through breaking out of the narrow bond of physical survival. And in order for this to happen, John the Baptist insisted, repentance for, and confession of, sin was a prerequisite.

God was at the heart of this wider centre of meaning. To be part of the larger context was not opposition and self-will but participation and surrender. Calvin correctly interprets the story of the fall and original sin to be the clash of man's physical and God's spiritual integrity. The 'desire for knowledge is naturally inherent' in man's essential being. It is in this desire that the source of 'happiness is supposed to reside.' Yet the path to it is not competing with God, but obeying, Calvin insists. Only then can the curse of original sin (its seizure of 'the very seat of reason and the heart') be suspended.

The reading of Mark 1:4-11 finishes with Jesus being baptized in the Jordan River 'and the Spirit like a dove, descending upon him.' In other words, through baptism Jesus has become God's concretization. Concretely, in human form, he represents God's blueprint for order. Jesus rescues order from chaos. As a pitying shepherd he gathers the scattered sheep into a functioning flock.

Both the readings from Genesis (1:1-5) and Mark (1:4-11) fit like a hand in a glove or a key in a lock, I have said, although they were written many centuries apart. Does this also apply to our days? Are the images of rescuing order from chaos and frightened sheep being gathered by a shepherd applicable to our day and age? Hasn't our advanced technology and incredible progress in medicine, hygiene, genetics, transportation, communication, astronomy, and other research over the last century made those images irrelevant?

Maybe the answer lies in another question. Has all this technical and scientific progress improved our personal and social integrity? Has it helped you to put your mind at ease? Has it promoted a safer and more secure society? Has the high standard of living in the West provided the cushion of stability, which we apparently need as much, if not more, than our independence from the vagaries of nature and the economic wellbeing of our nation? Is our present world actually so different from the world of Jesus, John the Baptist, Calvin, where individual selfishness also tended to undermine social responsibility?

The answer to all these questions is likely to be an emphatic 'No!' particularly from the older generation. The original sin the Bible talks about may have a somewhat different form, but underneath it all is a disconcerting similarity. Memories may often be selective: we remember the good and pleasant aspects and forget, and even repress, the more ugly parts. I still remember the stable village community and family bond surrounding me when I grew up, but the hardship of no electricity, the poverty of the depression, early death of relatives from diphtheria tend to be forgotten.

Still the younger generations are not any less aware of a crisis of confidence and trust or the frustration with a fast changing society in which there is precious little left to hold onto. Or the loneliness of losers, the non-caring ambitions of colleagues on a power kick, the hardness and ruthlessness in the business world, a devil-may-care survival syndrome in peer groups, the abuses of the strong in both small and large groups, the injustices and tyrannies perpetrated by the dictatorships still flourishing in many parts of our planet, the deceptive illusions in the advertising industry. They all contribute to a cynical, yet realistic, view of the nature of man.

We could add much to this list. I am thinking about the trauma and bitterness of divorce in so many families here in Australia, or how romantic love changed into hatred and the children of the union are baffled at the conflict between their parents, both of whom they love. How divorce often destroys the sense of the stable belonging in younger children.

I am also thinking about the adversarial culture prevailing in many corners of the public service here in Canberra and how a façade of amiability sometimes hides the dagger of cunning, knavery and intrigue. Adversarial culture may advance desirable efficiency. Yet it can also destroy trust, cooperation and mutual respect.

I am also thinking about the lack of balance between permissiveness and discipline in many homes, leaving children with a truncated, poorly developed, sense of communal responsibility. Centring the world around the self often results in treating the outside world as something to be used and manipulated rather than to fit in and comply with.

Does not all this sound familiar when the Bible speaks about original sin crying out for salvation, or chaos needing to be subdued by order, or the crowd of scattered sheep looking for a shepherd to guide it?

To Christians the Bible is the rule of faith and life. Its writing has been conditioned by the language and setting of its time, but its relevance has not been in any way affected by our technical and scientific progress. Today's text and readings are good examples. If anything, our times cry out even more for salvation from chaos and mustering a frightened crowd of scattered sheep.

Yet the Bible is not just convicting Christians of original sin and the chaotic wilderness of existence. It also speaks specifically and triumphantly about the victory over chaos and sin. It says that God is constantly ordering and bridling what otherwise would succumb to disintegration, depravity, corruption and confusion. It also says that the Holy Spirit, God's love, God's mercy, God's kindness and God's forgiveness are firmly established extending beyond the grave and that the crucifixion is followed by the resurrection.

All this has been aptly summed up in Frederick William Faber's Hymn 72 in the Australian Hymnbook, particularly verses one, two and four as follows:

> Souls of men, why do you scatter
> like a crowd of frightened sheep?
> foolish hearts, why do you wander
> from a love so true and deep?

> There is a wideness in God's mercy
> like the wideness of the sea,
> and forgiveness in his justice
> sealed for us on Calvary.

> For the love of God is broader
> than the measures of man's mind;
> and the heart of the Eternal
> is most wonderfully kind.

CALVIN 11

RESTORING the BALANCE

I am that living bread which has come down from heaven. John 6:51

Our Old Testament reading this morning, Psalm 130, is a famous poem. It deals with the desperate cry of a believer who cannot get it all together. 'Out of the depths have I called to thee, O Lord; Lord hear my cry.'

Why is he so desperate? He is overwhelmed by a sense of sin. Not just his own, but all the sins of Israel.

What is meant by all this sinning? It is not just any moral aberration, stealing, lying, lusting, hating, rebelling etc. It is any form of disorder, a fundamental characteristic of the entire created world, failure to fit the divine order; it is being out of kilter, out of sorts. It is like a scar, a severe depression. It is what the Westminster Confession calls 'original sin.' One could sum it up by living and experiencing the story of The Fall in the book of Genesis.

Yet all this misery, confusion, guilt and pain are not the end says the psalmist. God restores the balance. He forgives. 'For in the Lord there is love unfailing', he liberates the believer and frees him from his sin. And the Psalm ends with the psalmist eagerly waiting for restoration and regaining lost confidence.

Our second reading from the New Testament, Ephesians 4:25–5:2, is also about 'restoring balance.' The apostle Paul, writing from his prison in Rome, has heard about the backbiting, displays of anger, bad feelings in the Christian assembly in Ephesus and is obviously worried about it. It gives a bad example, he thinks. If you have to be angry with one another, he observes practically, 'don't let sunset find you still nursing your anger.'

Nursing bad feelings to Paul is a loophole through which the devil destroys Christian fellowship. To restore the balance you have to 'be generous to one another, tender-hearted, forgiving one another as God in Christ forgave you (verse32).' '… live in love as Christ loved you, and gave himself up on your behalf as an offering and sacrifice … (5:1-2).' After all, the Holy Spirit should not be grieved. It has sealed the Christians in Ephesus off from the devil's reach and liberated them from his clutches.

I want to spend a bit more time with the third reading from John 6:30–51. Here too God's heavenly bread restores the balance through providing a vantage point of transcendental order beyond the brutal instinct for survival of the individual creature. And I want to illustrate this with an insignificant event that happened 58 years ago, but has been engraved in my memory ever since.

In the autumn of 1944, I was transferred to another cell in the prison with hard labour (Zuchthaus) in Halle, Germany where I was doing time for what the Nazis called 'undermining the war machinery.' There were two others in that cell, who had just squabbled about a slice of bread. The first one was a bow-legged Norwegian sailor, who had been caught in a boat ferrying escapees to England. He only spoke Norwegian and a bit of broken German. All he had was primary school education. He had a wife and three children somewhere on the rugged coast of Norway, but he had lost track of them and they of him.

The other was a highly sophisticated German with two doctorates. His career had been meteoric. From prison official he had risen to warden, then to judge of a court in Dessau. But he had fallen as hard as he had risen. He was sentenced, he said, because he had taken his money out of Germany and invested it in a Swiss bank. Of course he failed to mention, as I learnt later, that this money had been milked from an orphan fund he administered.

Now the general rule in each cell was for prisoners to take turns with whatever had to be distributed. Usually there was not much difference, but sometimes one piece was slightly larger. The judge had ignored this rule and had put himself in charge of distribution. Invariably he had kept the better piece for himself. The sailor had given him a withering look, but had kept his cool. The story repeated itself that same night, but the next morning I happened to be closest to the trusty handing out the bread and I let the sailor have first choice which earned me a withering look from the judge.

This insignificant event was a little link in a much larger chain of events that taught me to value moral integrity and spiritual backbone above material survival, or to say it with our text, to search for the living heavenly bread more than the earthly variety. My schooling and upbringing had trained me to believe that man's reason was the glorious capping stone of creation. Yet here was a very intelligent person with a sharp logical mind who somehow failed as a moral being. He was good-looking, authoritative, the kind who automatically attracted people when entering a gathering. He was a clear, quick thinker, a genius in debates and yet he would cheat this sailor with his broken German out of his due, a slightly larger crust of bread.

The judge was not an original Nazi. He had joined the Party when membership had become advantageous. But then the Party had taken over and like a leech had sucked his native intelligence for its own twisted purpose. His intelligence had become a whore dancing to the tune of whoever paid the price. Yet, I began to suspect, wasn't that usually the case? Wasn't intelligence on its own a monster or a marvel according to the basic commitments it served? But if this were the case, which commitment could make it a marvel, and which a monster?

The sailor by contrast did not sparkle at all. He was incomparably worse off and yet he never lost a sort of instinctive steadfastness and dignity. He was polite and yet natural as though he owed all other beings, even Nazis, at least token respect. He was clean and reliable. He was not moody, but affected the morale of the cell with a ready smile and the whistling of a Norwegian tune if he felt like it.

The judge was always talking about himself, his accomplishments, his predicaments, as though he was desperate for someone to allay his anxieties by admiration. He was sorry for himself, basically because the world, even the Nazi world, had not let him get away with self-aggrandisement and self-enrichment. I felt drawn to the Norwegian, because he seemed to be the wisest of us all. All three of us were hungry, undernourished and underweight. Yet he had managed to rise above it all and not let it get to him.

It was this balance of mind, this equanimity, serenity, mental calmness which proved to be more precious than a thicker piece of bread. Slowly it began to dawn on me that if I were to survive the holocaust, trust in the heavenly bread represented in Christ was more essential than a desperate obsession with a slightly larger crust. Survival had more to do with belief in death-transcending eternity than in spasmodic, tenacious grasping of the ephemeral and transitory.

Slowly, but unerringly the squabble about bread in the cell in Halle Zuchthaus helped me to find an answer to the question I put earlier: 'which commitment can make intelligence and reason a marvel and which a monster?' It was the commitment to the living, heavenly bread, which is Christ that could do the trick of turning a potential monster into an actual marvel!

In his commentary on this section of John, Calvin makes additional observations. Earthly bread is what the brute beasts need to fill their belly (John 6:31, 32). But the followers of Christ are different. They can receive God's bread (Jesus) and thereby can live the true life and have their souls immortalized. All this corresponds with modern sociological views of religion as reinforcer of values which restrain rather than sustain the instincts and in so doing strengthen the social good beyond the mortal life of individuals.

As Calvin does in Genesis 1:2 (where God creates order out of chaos and nothingness), so here too Calvin links predestination and election to God creating order and salvation where man's sin and disobedience have created disorder. Sin is 'beholding Christ with carnal eyes' (John 6:42). In other words not seeing Him as the living heavenly bread, but in earthly form, as the Jews did who murmured amongst themselves: 'Is not this Jesus, the son of Joseph whose father and mother we know?' Here Calvin reminds himself of Philippians 2:7 where Christ is depicted as taking on the flesh of mortal man and emptying himself (becoming 'nothing') in order to be one with fallen humanity and save it from self-destruction. Sociological correspondence here lies in the necessity of any viable group, tribe or society to transcend the self and derive its vitality from man's capacity to fill the emptied self with commitment to social cohesion, sacrificing, if necessary, his own integrity.

Yet the heavenly bread (Jesus) also restores the balance between God's order and man's perpetual breakdown of that order (sin). The offer of salvation (wholeness) is quite practically the point where transcendence, the sacred, immortality meet immanence, the mundane, mortality. It provides the meaning and purpose where otherwise only self-destroying chaos would reign. Or to put the same differently: man's capacity for self-giving, altruism, sacrifice and self-discipline are crucial for the viability of a precarious culture and civilization. God's bread in turn is the guarantee for this viability.

And this is God's message for today as I perceive it through the Bible readings. It links the ancient past with the present. It is just as relevant today as it was 2500 years ago. Losing one's bearings was just as much an issue then as it is today. God's work of salvation in Jesus Christ has restored the balance for untold generations before us and is doing so for all of us.

CALVIN 12

CALVIN'S DOGS

... it is not fair to take the children's bread and throw it to the dogs. Mark 7:27

I am sure that like me, you are intrigued by Biblical puzzles. Well, today's reading of Mark 7:24-37 presents us with a real 'corker.' Doesn't Jesus here say that foreigners are dogs? And if so, isn't that sheer racism? But let's look first at the story and the slightly different version in Matthew 15:21-28.

In both Mark and Matthew the chapter starts with the Pharisees and 'some doctors of law' accusing Jesus of undermining tradition and disregarding rules about food. Jesus then calls them hypocrites and the disciples report back to Jesus that he has greatly offended the Pharisees. Next we read that Jesus leaves the country altogether and travels north to Phoenicia. Maybe the ground has become too hot under his feet. Maybe the popular demands on his faith healing have become too much. Phoenicia was the place where he hoped to remain unrecognized as we read in verse Mark 7:24. But no such luck. Here too his fame has preceded him. A Syrian woman begged him to help her daughter who was tormented by a demon.

Jesus refuses: 'I was sent to the lost sheep of Israel and to them alone.' But the woman does not give up. She fell at his feet and again cried for help. Then follows Jesus enigmatic response: 'Let the children be satisfied first; it is not fair to take the children's bread and throw it to the dogs', meaning 'my mission is to Israel and not inferiors, such as you people here in Phoenicia.'

It is obvious that when Jesus uses the word 'dogs' he does not mean the nice affectionate dog we used to have on the farm in Holland while I grew up. I still remember my mother crying when Henny died of old age. I remember it so well, because it was the only time I ever saw my mother cry. Nor did Jesus have in mind the kind of pet dog one has nowadays in retirement villages and nursing homes as companions. Or the lovable Dalmatian who sits under the table at my daughter's place, in Niagara-on-the-Lake, hoping that my grandchildren who are messy eaters will be more messy than usual.

No, Jesus meant it in the sense of 'inferior.' Calvin certainly interprets it that way and uses the opportunity in his commentary on this verse to spill his gall about another 'dog' he has it in for, a Spanish doctor and theologian, Servitus, with whom he thoroughly disagrees. Usually, however, he reserves 'dogs' for Catholics who of course made his life so miserable that in 1533, when only 24, he had to flee for his life from Paris. The church authorities there utterly condemned the presidential/vice-chancellor's inaugural address at the university, which Calvin had helped to write. It was on the theme of Jesus statement 'Blessed are the poor in spirit, for theirs is the Kingdom of God' and reflected Reformation ideas which the Catholic Church had strongly rejected.

Nowadays, of course, we frown on calling anyone of another religion a 'dog.' And justifiably so. I may disagree with some Catholic doctrines, but nowadays I am sure that like me all of you regard Catholics as allies in an increasingly secularized society. I certainly hope you do. Yet I can also understand why Calvin said what he did.

He grew up in a strict Catholic home in Noyon in Northern France. His family soon discovered that they had a prodigy on their hands and let him have the best available education. It did not take long for him to be established as the outstanding scholar of his age. Already in his early twenties he was acknowledged as the brightest star in the intellectual firmament. Yet the Catholic hierarchy feared anything Martin Luther and he stood for, such as his scriptural approach to doctrine and his emphasis on the community of believers.

Another cleric who used 'dog' in the derogatory sense was Pope Pius IX who lived from 1792-1878, and was the longest reigning pope (32 years) in papal history. I have a lot of respect for Pio Nono. Through his opposition to the liberalism of his age and the creation of the Catholic school system he doubled Catholic Church attendance worldwide. Yet in the recent process of his beatification he was reported as having called Jews 'dogs' and this certainly does not sit well in this ecumenical age.

Where does all this take us? Am I trying to argue that like Pius IX and Calvin, Jesus lived in a different age, when tolerance for other races and religions was not as fashionable as it is nowadays? The argument may have some merit. After all in Jesus' time slavery was generally accepted. Yet times have changed and we have now become more civilized. Foreign slaves could be kept for the term of their natural life, but Hebrew slaves had to be liberated after seven years. To the Jews foreigners or Gentiles, as they were generally called, were a lesser breed. They were regarded as a political menace, a threat to racial purity and religious integrity. Could we therefore blame Jesus for calling them 'dogs' as obviously all other Jews did?

Yet there is a much better solution to our puzzle and to discover that we have to go back to scripture. Here we read in Mark 7:28 that the Phoenician woman answered Jesus with the following words: 'Sir, even the dogs under the table eat the children's scraps', meaning that Gentiles too need salvation and healing, even when they are regarded as a lesser breed.

In verse Mark 7:29 Jesus buys this argument. He says: 'For saying that, you may go home content; the unclean spirit has gone out of your daughter.' Mark 7:30

provides the happy ending. When she returned home, she found the child lying in bed; the spirit (in Greek it is actually called a demon) had left her.

Jesus obviously has a change of heart. He now praises the woman because of her faith, suggesting that she has the kind of trust and faith similar to the one he had come to instil in 'the lost sheep of the house of Israel and to them alone (Matthew 15:24)'. Calvin in his commentary argues that this was the beginning of Christ's mission beyond the boundary of the Hebrew nation, as it was so strongly advanced by St Paul in the book of Acts.

Yet looking beyond national boundaries was well established particularly in the prophetic strain of the Hebrew heritage, long before Jesus appeared on the scene. The prophets generally challenged the encrusted pattern of tradition which the priests and the powerful establishment defended so vehemently. The prophet Isaiah (49:6) portrays God as the One who does not just restore the tribes of Jacob but makes his descendants 'a light to the nations, to be my salvation to earth's farthest bounds.' Malachi (1:11) rebukes Israel and contrasts it with the Gentiles where His 'name shall be great.'

Where does all this leave us? Aren't we tinkering with the Bible as the rule of faith and life and the standard of all doctrine if we let tolerance prevail? Shouldn't we heed Dean Inge's remark that he who marries the spirit of the age and its fashions will soon find himself a widower? Yet God, Jesus, the Holy Spirit, our Biblical heritage are not just fossils of the past. They are alive. Through the prophets God rebuked Israel's ethnocentricity. Jesus changed his mind about healing the daughter of a foreigner. The Holy Spirit guides us into a deeper understanding of others. In other words, God's order is dynamic. It continues to confront man's sin and disorder.

And this disorder is not just confined to our individual nature as it rebels against God and the constraints of society which requires humility and self-denial of individuals for its survival and sanity. We discussed that a few weeks ago from this pulpit. Disorder and suspicion also exists in the hatred between nations and groups within nations or between religious organizations, Catholics versus Protestants, Christians versus Jews and Muslims. And God has something to say also about this kind of disorder. It goes against the grain of his blueprint of order on our planet.

Jesus widened the horizons. The new covenant, the New Testament, is a blueprint for salvation of all mankind. By contrast the old covenant or the Old Testament is a blueprint for salvation of one ethnic group or nation, Israel, although the seeds for globalization or internationalization were already present in the prophetic rather than the priestly strand. Yet that also meant and means that the brotherhood of nations, a deep understanding of, and concern for, other parts of the world is in God's plan. God frowns on us regarding other individuals, groups and societies as ever so many dogs, inferior to ourselves.

Yet we can be more positive than this. Or to say it with our Old Testament reading of Proverbs 1:22, things are not as simple as they seem. Loyalty, commitment, understanding, love are all positives in our Christian lexicon. Yet too great a commitment and loyalty to our own nation may go at the expense of our international concern for the rights of other nations. The unconditional love and all-absorbing commitment of Germans for their nation during World War II meant that they had to put my friends and me behind bars for regarding the allies as angels of liberation rather than despicable dogs. Loyalty and commitment to one nation may exclude the salvation of another.

Wars are anathema to God. They destroy rather than build up. Yet there is room for pride in national accomplishments. God does not object to us hoping for Australia to do well in the Olympics and being very pleased, if Matthew Dunn, grandson of one of our elders, manages to get a medal in the 200 or 400 individual medley. After all competition in any sport is subject to an impressive number of rules and regulations promoting international order in the same way as we are slowly moving to global acceptance of democracy and natural individual rights. God is with us on that score. Personal integrity, social order as well as order between nations are part of God's blueprint.

Those of you who saw the impressive opening of the Olympic Games in Sydney two days ago may remember the colossal tarpaulin coming down from the stands and slowly spreading over the entire playing field. It had at its centre an enormous dove of peace with an olive branch in its beak. Speakers and commentators referred again and again to the contribution the Games made to the unity of nations. Correctly so. Here in Canberra the interdenominational organization Awakening 2000 organized giant screenings of the opening night, as if to say: 'participants and Christians have something very valuable in common, living together in peace.'

Yet living in peace together does not mean that we cannot be proud of individual national achievements. It is not necessary to give up our individual, local or national identity to make room for an international, global sense of identity. It is excessive commitments to one of these to the exclusion of other identities that is likely to put a spanner in the wheel.

The specifically Christian contribution to global unity is its insistence on Jesus Christ as the prototype of man, capable of self-sacrifice, self-denial and humility, yet also one who denounces injustice, ill-treatment of the powerless, hypocrisy and dishonesty. It is this kind of man who sows the seed of peace amongst all nations and provides the foundation for global equitable existence.

Next Sunday we will celebrate the sixty-seventh birthday of this church. We can be proud of this beautiful church and its dedicated, hard-working membership. In the same way as we will be proud of those Australians who earned an Olympic medal because of their self-discipline and long training. Yet all this training, self-discipline and hard work are in vain, if the church does not also produce Johnny Kirkwoods. By this I mean the elder in my American congregation who had died long ago, but was still remembered as the outstanding elder who represented Christ wherever he went in his actions, thoughts and behaviour.

To summarize: the story of the Phoenician woman is the story of God extending His covenant with a single nation to all Gentiles. They were not 'dogs' anymore. God does not discriminate. Salvation by faith is available to all individuals, groups, denominations and nations. God creates order out of chaos globally. In the same way as Jesus changed his mind about outsiders, so should we too go out of our way to understand, appreciate and love other individuals, groups, religious organizations, and nations. If this means tolerance, so be it! Yet our tolerance should never be wishy-washy or lack backbone. After all we believe with the story of Mark 7 in faith as a prerequisite. Or as we will sing in our final hymn: All our hope on God is founded…God alone calls our heart to be his own. … Christ does call one and all: ye who follow shall not fall.

CALVIN 13
PAWNS, PUPPETS and PIETY

I knew of thee only by report, but now I see thee with my own eyes. Job 42:6

The story of Job starts with a celestial bet. God is proud of Job, his prize exhibit. He characterizes him as 'a man of blameless and upright life, who fears God and sets his face against wrongdoing (Job 1:8).' But Satan puts a spanner in the wheel and says: 'No wonder, you protect him and bless him with a wonderful family and much wealth. Take all that away and he will curse you to your face (Job 1:11).' In other words Job's integrity and piety will disappear if calamity strikes. Prosperity wins out over faith any time in Satan's books.

God then allows Satan to afflict Job, but the latter remains faithful and God wins the bet. Satan, however, does not give up: 'Touch his bone and his flesh, and see if he will not curse you to his face (Job 2:5).' God accepts this second bet too and the helpless victim in the celestial game is disfigured within an inch of his life. Yet again Job 'did not utter one sinful word (Job 2:10).' God wins again. Or does he?

On the surface the story seems nothing but an entertaining tale. Yet there is a rather serious assumption underneath it all. It assumes that Job's deprivations and suffering are caused by a celestial bet between God and Satan. It assumes that both God and Satan treat humans as puppets and pawns in a game that has no further meaning and no moral intent. These assumptions are denied in what follows in the bulk of the book. Job's friends insist that the cataclysmic events are caused by Job's sin (Job 4:7-9). His piety is hypocrisy (Job 8:13). Or character is made in conflict; suffering has disciplinary value (Job 33:19).

Job's friends are not fair weather friends, abandoning him when the weather gets rough. No, they cover great distances to be with him, to console and comfort him (Job 2:11). They sit with him for days without saying anything. They understand how he feels after all the calamities that have befallen him. And as true friends they suffer with him. Their religious and moral arguments are their way of making sense of it all, hoping that it will mitigate the pain and hurt. The friends seem to come close to agreeing with God here.

Job, however, does not accept their interpretations. Suffering is not God's punishment for sin. The wicked do prosper (Job 21:7-9). Job actually appears to deny that there is a moral order in the universe. 'When a sudden flood brings death, (God) mocks the plight of the innocent (Job 9:23).' 'If humans can get peace and prosperity without God, they will refute him (Job 21:13, 14).' 'The rod of God's justice does not reach (the wicked) (Job 21:9).' Job comes very close to agreeing with Satan here. He feels that God has treated him badly.

Yet his friends continue to argue that God is good and just. Therefore Job had to have some hidden faults, such as being cruel to his fellow men, giving no water to the weary, refusing bread to the hungry, sending widows away empty-handed, striking defenceless orphans (Job 22:9). Job denies it all vehemently and does not hide his resentment of God's treatment (Job 23:2). God 'has denied me justice and … has filled me with bitterness (Job 27:2).' 'God is aloof, has cruelly turned against me and has pursued me in hatred (Job 30:21), for no reason, in spite of all my many good deeds (Job 31:5-22).' If only he could 'plead the whole record of my life and present that in court as my defence (Job 31:37)', he would be vindicated. But unfortunately, as Job says (Job 9:32): '(God) is not a man as I am, that I can answer him, or that we can confront one another in court.'

Well, as Job had been hoping so desperately, God finally appears on the scene (Chapters 38-41). But instead of answering Job's questions he disregards them. Is God too much of a despot to care about the suffering of his underlings? Is God, like Hitler or Stalin only interested in the larger picture, even if it goes against the grain of what is nowadays called human rights? Or is God nothing but the aloof starter of the universe leaving it alone once it was set in motion, as He was represented in Greek philosophy?

God turns the tables and directs a barrage of questions to Job, such as: 'Who is this whose ignorant words cloud my design in darkness (Job 38:1)?' 'Where were you when I laid the earth's foundations (Job 38:4)?' 'Have you comprehended the vast expanse of the world (Job 38:18)?' To top it all, God challenges Job: 'OK Job, you can save yourself (Job 40:14), if you can also manage to humble the proud and the wicked.' And this, of course, is not humanly possible. God does a real number on Job.

And now comes the astonishing part. Instead of getting his back up even more, Job succumbs entirely to God's majesty and power. He says: 'I knew of thee only by report, but now I see with my own eyes. Therefore I melt away; I repent in dust and ashes (Job 42:5, 6).' Has Job altogether lost his marbles and turned from lion into lamb?

There are at least three answers to this major question.

(1) The first one is that Job has asked the wrong questions. They all centre round the injustice done to Job, as though his justification is the only and major problem. By contrast God's questions all lead to what lies beyond the self, the order of nature and society. God's questions imply that the larger context is more important than the tiny place occupied by mortals. God extends horizons. That's where God dwells. Job repents in dust and ashes, because he has judged

God instead of allowing God to judge him. He now understands that self-justification is an implicit rebellion against God.

Job also begins to understand that God is not and could never be, 'a man as I am, whom he could confront in a court (Job 9:32).' God is altogether different. Job realizes that there are aspects of God way beyond human understanding. But in so far as humans can comprehend God, He sums up in His very being those elements that make for perfection, order and integrity. That's why Job's friends naturally expected God to punish the wicked and to reward the godly. And Job was quite correct in pointing out that reality is different: the wicked do not always get punished. In other words, man's disorder and sin are very real. The law does its best, but is not perfect in its execution, however much God is on the side of the just and the righteous.

In other words conflict is inevitable when the real does not reflect the ideal. Often what is good for a person's self-assertion is much less so for a smoothly running society. Humility is a prime source of social and religious approval because it makes the individual receptive to others. Instead of putting him or herself forward, a humble person is more likely to make others feel comfortable and understood. That's why in our other reading for today (Mark 10:35-45) Jesus rebukes James and John for requesting a privileged position on his left and right side. It would have created a pecking, rather than an equalizing order amongst the twelve disciples. 'For the son of man did not come to be served, but to serve and to give up his life as a ransom for many (Mark 10:45).'

A well-integrated society will approve and reward those who prefer serving to being served, giving rather than receiving. Certainly in Christian circles and organizations, but also in society at large, authority is often given to those who are least likely to threaten others. Invariably they are those who are secure enough in themselves not to need self-aggrandizement. Of course other factors, such as leadership and competence etc. are also important, but everything else being the same, the humble individual will prevail over the arrogant one.

Calvin preached as many as 159 sermons on the Book of Job, all available on the Internet in French. The word 'humility' keeps cropping up remarkably often in all sermons and commentaries. In the sermon he preached on Job 38:1-4 (the beginning of God's reply) he takes the view that adversity is sometimes God's way of making us humble enough to obey him more. Glorifying ourselves, he says, is man's way to shut God out, whereas being emptied of all pride teaches us to serve him and become more acceptable in his sight.

There is then a strong correspondence between God's insistence on more humility and society's reward to the contrite of heart. A viable culture will always encourage members to fit in well and discourage those who are puffed up and arrogant. Australian society is certainly not an exception. If anything it goes further. To be self-effacing, telling jokes at one's own expense are important ways to be accepted. By contrast to brag about one's achievements is politely regarded as not the done thing. Australian identity has in no small way been affected by the Anzac myth, which in turn is characterized by resistance to all pretensions and is woven around much self-denigrating humour.

(2) But there is a second important answer to our question why Job succumbed so quickly to God's power and majesty, or why he turned from an accuser to a worshipper. Job 42:6 shows this rather clearly. Job apologizes: 'In the past I heard of thee only by report, but now I see thee.' In other words academic knowledge is not enough. Job's integrity (so well recognized by Job's wife, when she said (2:6): 'Are you still unshaken in your integrity? Curse God and die!' has little to do with academic reports and a lot with actually meeting God.

The logic of God's long and detailed speech impresses Job less than now seeing God rather than relying on second hand reports (Job 42:5). It is the personal contact and the experience of God's Spirit that cements and enriches his integrity. So he repents in dust and ashes (Job 42:6), presumably because he had never fully understood and had underestimated God's majesty. Now the simple tale of the prologue becomes pregnant with meaning. What appears to us as a celestial game played altogether outside our world, has all of a sudden touched the core of Job's identity, or as the author of the book has it, Job's integrity. God communicates with man and did so supremely in Jesus Christ, who is precisely what Job said he needed so badly (Job 9:32): another human rather than a towering, austere figure beyond the world of suffering and injustice.

It is the personal, binding, element of God's presence with us through the Holy Spirit which Calvin also stresses very much in his commentaries and sermons. He contrasts 'self-will' with 'election' or 'predestination.' A sense of being linked with or even 'one' with God (seeing, experiencing God's presence in Job 42:6) puts the self on the back burner. Self-will and self-seeking retreat into the background and self-denial and a sense of being elected by God take their place. It now appears as though one has found one's destiny, as though this has always been in the cards, as though it has been 'predestined' to be found by God and to have finally been set on the path of fulfilling one's life. It delineates the past as leading up to the event; it delineates the present as its fulfilment and the future as its now clearly visualized destiny.

Again there is a correspondence here with social expectations. To feel at one with God invariably includes having a glimpse of immortality or whatever transcends the 'id' as Sigmund Freud has it, the life of the instincts, physical survival. It is the realm of social order, transcending the 'flesh' as St Paul called it, that contains such God-approved values of justice, kindness, love, consideration for the poor, the weak and the destitute, honesty, sobriety, responsibility, reliability etc. They meet social expectations and are reinforced by law and even more traditionally by religion. It is Job's integrity that is fed and strengthened by his communion with God, but which also forms the point of balance between the requirements of his mortal body and of being in tune with the social expectations of the perfect human being.

But this integrity, strengthened by the Holy Spirit, has a great deal to do with feeling, emotion, love, loyalty, and faith. The academic literature on the importance of emotion rather than reason as the deepest foundation of our mind is increasing exponentially. This is also true for the social scientific study of religion where I had to write a separate chapter on commitment to do justice to the increasing amount of material available. Job's integrity was enhanced by his faith, increased by God's very presence.

To Satan it is this very integrity that has to be fatally destroyed, if he is to win the celestial battle. It is the crux of the story. Integrity, salvation, sinlessness are in God's realm. Or as Calvin has it in his sermon on the very passage we are considering here, God does not reverse or pervert order, by for instance changing heaven into earth. By contrast, disorder, destruction and sin are Satan's essential prerogatives. Like Job we are not pawns and puppets any more. Through our piety we are participants in God's order competing with Satan's disorder. Our integrity is constantly in jeopardy. Yet God has won both the bet and the battle and therefore also our identity is now secure.

(3) There is a third possible answer to our question as to why Job makes a 180 degree turn from critic to worshipper. Remember, Job with all his wealth gone, was still badly afflicted with sores when he met God, or better, when God met him. He felt so miserable, that he wanted to die: 'Why did I not die, when I came out of the womb (Job 3:11)?' and later: 'My sighing is all my food, and groans pour out from me in a torrent (Job 3:24).' Everything that made his life secure had gone. The question had become: 'How can I cope when there is nothing left to live for?' And then God came into his life, not as he had heard about him or as he imagined him to be, but as a living presence.

Miraculously the very situation of having all one's earthly securities kicked from underneath one-self can also be a pre-condition for being receptive to discovering and experiencing God's presence. It is as though all the other attractions of this world have prevented individuals hearing God's still, small voice. St Paul speaks about this when in his letter to the Philippians (2:7) he depicts Jesus as making 'himself nothing, assuming the nature of a slave', yet by humbling himself and accepting the ultimate horror of the cross, to be raised by God and 'bestowed on him the name above all names (Phil. 2:10).'

And in Mark 10:35–45 Jesus expects the same of his disciples. Not just humility to be acceptable to one's peers, but more actively to serve and to give one's life for others. Let us never forget that the Christian Church as we have it today has been built on the blood of the martyrs of all the preceding ages, not just the first four centuries. It is in the experience of being deprived of all earthly attachments and even one's life, that God has met many Christians in the past and the present.

Actually I doubt whether I would have ever become a Christian, if it had not been for a similar experience. Being a guest of the Gestapo in 1944 I had begun to doubt whether I would survive the ordeal. I felt rudderless and the sense of having all studs kicked from underneath was bewildering. Family, friends, books, music, freedom, all sources of my security, had been taken away. Instead I was relegated to the bottom of a prison hierarchy, despised both as a university student, and even more as someone 'who had undermined the Nazi war machinery.' And then when I had convinced myself that I was dying of typhus, I remember being flooded with a sudden sense of consolation from reading one of the Psalms describing God as the mainstay in times of trouble, a refuge in disaster, a stronghold against the enemy.

Job almost lost his integrity when everything of value was taken away from him. Are our possessions, our securities, our luxuries, our comforts, and our earthly attachments so valuable to us that we would lose our integrity, if we had to do without? I guess that each of us would have to answer that question for his or her self. If you are honest with yourself and you have to admit that under those circumstances you would lose your equanimity, serenity and sense of self, let me assure you that God is very likely waiting for you, if you distance yourself from what are after all only the accoutrements of life.

Because of Job's confession, God forgives him. He restored his 'fortunes, and doubled all his possessions (Job 42:10).' Job's friends are rebuked 'because you have not spoken as you ought about me, as my servant Job has done.' They have to make it up to Job through gifts of sheep and cattle. Conceiving God as the one, who metes out suffering according to the gravity of one's individual sins, is their main mistake.

What can we learn from Job's story? Are we, like Job, pawns and puppets in a celestial game of God versus Satan? The answer seems to be that indeed mortals are inextricably, and on all levels, bound to the symbiosis between order, represented by God, and disorder, represented by Satan. And yet through our piety and personal faith we are lifted up beyond these mortal bounds and original sin to God's sphere of immortality where nothing can separate us from his mercy and love and where our equanimity, integrity and serenity are strengthened beyond our ken.

Calvin finished all his sermons as follows: 'Now we shall bow in humble reverence before the face of our God.' Let us do that very thing!

CALVIN 14

GROWING in WISDOM

As Jesus grew up he advanced in wisdom and in favour with God and men. Luke 2:52

There is an underlying theme in our readings for today. Guided by Eli in Shiloh (1 Samuel 2:18-26) the adolescent Samuel slowly develops into a worthy prophet of Israel. As the Old Testament says '… the young Samuel, as he grew up, commended himself to the Lord and to men (verse 26).' This is in sharp contrast with Eli's own sons, who were spoilt brats and are called 'scoundrels.'

And then in Luke 2:41-52 we read a similar story about the twelve year old Jesus who was found by his parents in the temple in Jerusalem, 'surrounded by the teachers, listening to them and putting questions; and all who heard him were amazed at his intelligence and the answers he gave (Luke 2: 46-47).' Luke sums it up as follows: 'As Jesus grew up he advanced in wisdom and in favour with God and men (Luke 2:52).'

The final reading (Colossians 3:12-17) elaborates what St Paul expects of those who follow the Lord and have advanced in wisdom: 'compassion, kindness, humility, gentleness, patience, forbearing of one another, and forgiving (verse 13).' 'To crown all, there must be love, to bind all together and complete the whole (Colossians 3:14, 15).' 'Instruct and admonish each other with the utmost wisdom (Colossians 3:16).'

Growing in wisdom. That is obviously what the Bible regards as God's intention for our lives. It is our earthly pilgrimage to salvation. We may never get there completely, but we may slowly accumulate more frequent flyer points and so get closer to the final prize when God says: 'Well done. You are a good servant. You have shown yourself to be trustworthy. Here is your reward (Luke 19:17).' In other words, God expects us to go forwards and not to be stagnant or miss the point altogether. That option leads to utter condemnation: as the parable of the talents clearly tells us (Luke 19:27).

I assume that is what we expect our children and grandchildren to do: grow in wisdom. We would like our offspring to be more secure than we are ourselves. A good job, good education, good health, fitness, success in their earthly pursuits, we think, are the means to that security. Safeguarding, Teflon coating our children against the inevitable shocks and hurts of existence has always been a basic motive in our upbringing of offspring.

Well the Bible appears to support this very practical view of wisdom. Wisdom in Proverbs means success. And to be successful one has to have tact, respect for one's superiors and be trustworthy. 'Do not keep company with drunkards or those who are greedy for the fleshpots, for drink and greed will end in poverty, and drunken stupor goes in rags (Proverbs 23:20-23).' Or 'wisdom builds the house, good judgment makes it secure, knowledge furnishes the rooms with all the precious and pleasant things that wealth can buy (Proverbs 24:3-4).'

A wise man is not proud, or a hypocrite. He is not a false witness, or one who stirs up quarrels (Proverbs 6:19). He is not an adulterer or haughty. He is prudent, just, virtuous, honest and understanding (Proverbs 8:9). The best means to security is to be blameless (Proverbs 10:9). But 'the first step to wisdom is the fear of the Lord (Proverbs 9:10).'

Here the Old Testament goes beyond this rather practical view of wisdom. Job (28:28) also defines wisdom as 'fear of the Lord' by which is meant that reverence for God is the essence of wisdom. Solomon's wisdom is called 'the wisdom of God (1 Kings 3:28)', because his sound judgment was perceived to be not just an application of bits of practical advice but founded in a transcendental frame of reference, a fundamental order underlying all existence.

The New Testament builds on this Old Testament foundation. The parables are powerful illustrations of profound wisdom. Jesus depicts God as the loving, forgiving father of a wayward son who finally finds his way home again after discovering that when he got what he wanted he did not want any more what he got. The prodigal son slowly matures. His experiences have made him wiser and culminate in returning to the father.

This is the same with the parable of the Good Samaritan. It is a powerful illustration of practical help being higher on the scale of human values than theological convictions of the religious establishment. Jesus is saying the wise man acts in close accordance with basic principles. And these principles in turn are based on what restores and aids fellow human beings rather than on intellectual convictions about life that do not issue in practical action. The despised Samaritan therefore lives up to social expectations in contrast with the priest and the Levite who leave the robbed individual on the side of the road. Wisdom here consists in abandoning fear for one's security in order to aid a fellow human being in his hour of need. Helping the robbed Israelite overrides ethnic belonging.

For Paul, Jesus was personified wisdom. 'Jesus is the power of God and the wisdom of God (1 Corinthians 1:24).' And by this St Paul meant that Jesus practiced what he preached. Jesus represented convictions about destiny being synonymous with the way he actually lived and died. To Paul he was wisdom, because he preached through his life without even a hint of hypocrisy. Preaching with one's life rather than with one's words was to Paul reaching human perfection or achieving salvation. Jesus to him not only embodied wisdom, but also 'righteousness', that is to say, 'integrity' and 'wholeness' (1 Corinthians 1:30).

What does Calvin have to say about wisdom? At the very beginning of the *Institutes of the Christian Religion* (I ii) he defines true wisdom as knowing oneself, an idea which one does not find in the Bible, but is close to the heart of Socrates and Plato's philosophy of life. And therefore Calvin hastens to say that one cannot know oneself unless one also knows God, 'for in Him we live and move, in him we exist (Acts 17:28).'

God, to Calvin, is the fountainhead from which all our talents and endowments spring. Without God we are nothing but an unmitigated disaster. Humans are innately disposed 'to rest in themselves', but they arrive at true wisdom only by humbly accepting God's gifts of 'solid virtue and exuberant goodness.' If we don't, we remain in the cesspool of 'ignorance, vanity, want, weakness, in short depravity and corruption (*Inst.* I i 1).'

All this is typically Calvin. Basically humans are animals acting on their instincts alone. This conviction plus the necessary humility to get out of this miserable animal state of living are everywhere in Calvin's voluminous writings. It is God who changes humans from beasts into valuable co-workers in the Kingdom. Calvin has learnt from St Paul that the Holy Spirit makes all the difference. It is superimposed on a corrupted physical existence and therefore the pivotal source of salvation.

Yet God is not just acting in history and in the lives of individuals in the present. To Calvin God's wisdom is evident in all past creation, in medicine, astronomy, the physical sciences. An example is the human body; its connections, symmetry and beauty 'proclaim the admirable wisdom of its Maker (*Inst.* I v 2).' But that does not mean that one can equate God with nature. Calvin has it in for those who replace God with nature (*Inst.* I iv 5). They draw a curtain between God and themselves, usurping God's place.

God's wisdom also shows in that he has implanted a conscience in our immortal souls (*Inst.* I xv 2). God is the carer, perpetual keeper of our immortal souls. Our capacity for reason, justice, honesty etc. lifts us above our animal nature and allows us to rise above our bodily instincts, thereby ascending to an understanding of God's order and wisdom.

The social sciences (anthropology, psychology, and sociology) did not exist in Calvin's days. If they had, Calvin would undoubtedly have treated their findings as ever so many proofs of God's wisdom. Very likely he would have pointed to the intricate social connections as very similar in nature to the physical ones. All the values that we have come across so far contribute to a saner and healthier society.

Let us delve somewhat deeper into some of these contributions. Our reading from Colossians 3:12-17 mentions compassion, kindness, humility, gentleness, and patience as a hallmark of God's people or the community of Christians in Colossae in what is now the western half of Turkey. Being compassionate, kind, humble, gentle and patient the members create a sense of belonging which Paul says 'binds all together and complete the whole (Colossians 3:15).' And all this is a counterfoil to selfish individualism, self-assertion, pride, hostility, cruelty and aggression that break up the sense of belonging and security.

And this is just as true for the tiny group of Christians in Colossae as it is for all citizens of the town, many of whom condemned the Christians for introducing a new religion. Paul assumes that by being compassionate, kind, humble, gentle, and patient the Christians would set a pattern of wholesomeness for the entire community. The best of its citizens would be impressed with the exemplary behaviour of the Christians. By being models of virtue and decency, Paul assumes that Christians would automatically attract potential converts to the cause.

And if the concept of wisdom sums up all these characteristics then growing up in wisdom means that young and old who are on this path of maturation and good citizenship will contribute to a better, healthier society. The Old and New Testament, Calvin and all Christians, ancient or modern, agree on this point. If distrust of motives, aggressive techniques, excessive careerism, and selfish consumerism pervades present day Australia, Christians must counter these values and norms with their age-old concept of wisdom: understanding, kindness, humility, gentleness and patience.

There is much to be critical about in modern society. To this some editorials in last weekend's papers testify. *The Australian* complains about the vanishing of a moral substratum providing the foundation for our social relations, our forms of justice, our political life. It is critical of the current philosophy of choosing our own individual values without much reference to others, often masking 'intense selfishness.' It speaks about moral decline, but then expresses the hope that the younger, better-educated generation may reach some core values by which to strengthen society.

I doubt it! The 'me'-generation of the 1990s does not seem to be looking for those institutions in our culture which perpetuate the very heritage which has traditionally reinforced these basic values. Paul's letter to the Colossians admirably summed them up. And however much Athens differed from Jerusalem, they both agreed that 'hubris' (or pride) was a basic flaw in any society only to be relieved by more humility. And neither humility nor concern for the social good seems to be very high on the list of priorities of the 'me'-generation.

Religion is often rejected by the very generation that is searching for new ground. It is usually rejected because it has not taken the trouble to understand what it rejects. But some of the criticism of Christianity may be justified. Do we in the church practice what we preach? Are we like Jesus whose entire life was a sermon? Who represented wisdom and integrity personified?

At The Australian National University here in Canberra in the 1960s we researched the state of religion in a large number of countries. We discovered that church attendance varied widely according to whether or not a particular church was a state church or not. Wherever a church had a monopoly, attendance was much poorer than when there was competition. That is still the case. Maybe that religious vitality correlates with such mundane factors as organisational competition. Wisdom requires that we balance obedience to God's word with listening to those who ignore our message. God may speak through them as well!

And while on balance, growing in wisdom implies that we also grow in our ability to juggle the numerous contrasting elements of living. It means that we can juggle both the demands of the mind and the demands of the heart, reason and affection without letting the one completely overshadow the other. Or that we find the right balance between overestimation and underestimation of ourselves, that we juggle the demands of career and family, job and responsibility for wife, children or parents. It means that we do not let rational economics, competition, and an exaggerated faith in the market mechanism, overshadow our concern for the neighbour in need of our practical assistance.

Tomorrow we celebrate the centenary of the Australian Federation. The future of our country may well hinge on our cooperation with, rather than on our cynical suspicion of, the political arena, or more generally on forbearing and forgiving rather than on hostility and opposition. We will become a lonely world if animalistic instincts of aggression and attack are allowed to prevail over charity, understanding and love. Growing in wisdom means strengthening Christian integrity rather than secular antagonism.

It also means that fitting in and meeting expectations rather than aloofness and destructive criticism lead to increasing wisdom. Often stress and depression relate to withdrawal from meaningful social participation. Certainly feeling rejected or cold-shouldered by a harsh world does not improve our mental health. Wisdom requires that we make our contribution to the wellbeing of others through sharing our material as well as our spiritual resources with those worse off than we are.

And this is our message for today. Like Samuel and Jesus, or the Christians in Colossae, we owe it to God to grow in wisdom, to live the very values we profess to believe in. Or to say it with Calvin, to transcend the selfishness of animal survival instincts and to ascend to God's order and be true to our immortal soul, of which he is the carer and guardian.

CALVIN 15
RESTORED SOULS

The law of the Lord is perfect and restores the soul. Psalm 19:7

On the central coast of British Columbia in Canada lives an Indian tribe, the Bella Coola. Like other Indians in Canada they link insanity, or socially unacceptable conduct to the soul and social order. They equate the disintegration of personality with the loss of the soul. And so they say of a person who has taken leave of his senses that his soul has departed. At such an occasion the shaman (or witchdoctor) is called in. He searches for the departed soul and, if he can locate it, catches it in his cloak which is then placed around the madman. Other Indians, such as the Ojibwa, account for the anti-social conduct of a drunk as a temporary leave of his soul.

In other words they believe that the soul can be restored to its rightful owner. What do they mean by 'soul?'

It often stands for the essence of personality, the stable core of an individual, the real person behind superficial trappings, or the anchor of security of the inner self. The soul is also immortal, unless it refers purely and exclusively to the physical integrity of a person. Then the mortal soul dies with physical death. However when it is linked to beliefs, values and social expectations which transcend a life span, it is called 'immortal' and justifiably so. Then it is part of a heritage of customs and rules that form a stable frame of reference for meaning, passed on from generation to generation.

What about the Bible? Does the restoration of the soul in our text similarly refer to a strengthening of the inner self? It does. I can't think of any religion, whether ancient or modern, primitive or sophisticated, that does not refer to souls and spirits as closely associated with a particular personality, yet also as surviving physical death. And the Bible is not an exception.

In the Old Testament the soul is created by God (Genesis 1:27) and is generally regarded as immortal. In the Gospels Jesus contrasts the soul with the body. The former is eternal, precious, source of wholeness and integrity. The body, by contrast, is mortal and bound to the earth and the material. 'Anyone who wishes to be a follower of mine must leave self behind (Mark 8:34).' And Jesus follows this by asking: 'What does a man gain by winning the whole world at the cost of his soul (his 'true self' in other translations, Mark 8:36)?'

It is even clearer what Jesus meant by the soul ('psyche' in Greek) in the parable of the rich man who built bigger barns for his abundant harvest and continued accumulating wealth in order to be secure 'enough for many years (so that he could have an easy life, eat, drink and enjoy himself (Luke 12:20).' But God calls him a fool: 'this very night your soul is required' and Jesus comments that all that amassing of wealth for himself has shrivelled his soul and made him 'a pauper in the sight of God (Luke 12:21).'

To Jesus, a shrivelled soul is overly focussed on the self and material treasures. It needs re-focussing and restoring. And therefore in his explanation to the disciples he stresses the 'never-failing treasures in heaven, where no thief can get near it, no moth destroy it. For where your treasure is, there will your heart be also (Luke 12:33, 34).'

This is different from the Bella Coola madman. His insanity was a threat to community. Madness always is. It upsets taken for granted behaviour. And so is any other kind of social disorder, such as drunkenness. A drunk has lost his soul temporarily, according to Ojibwa beliefs. In Central Australia natives ceremoniously send the souls of the departed away in order to prevent their disruption of social relations.

Jesus goes further. Obviously the rich man did what was regarded as prudent. Given the chance everyone would have safeguarded well-earned possessions. People might have envied his wealth, but no one would have regarded being well off as immoral. Yet for Jesus the soul reflects the true values, loyalties and commitments of the individual. And in the case of the rich man his soul had shrivelled because his fundamental loyalties were too narrowly based on the material rather than the spiritual.

To Jesus, therefore, restoration of the soul is, more positively, being guided by God's order and that order is different from and beyond man's mundane order. For David, who is thought to be the author of Psalm 19, for the prophets of the Old Testament and for Jesus there is a world beyond the immediately accessible world of culture and society. And, precisely because this world is out of human reach, neither moth nor rust can destroy it. The true self, or a fully-grown soul (not the shrivelled one which cannot see beyond its narrow horizons) is strongly anchored in that other world, or what Jesus called 'the never-failing treasure in heaven (Luke 12:33).'

The trouble is that humans are perpetually tempted to take the easy way out and to confine themselves to the here and now, as though that is the only guarantee for survival in a cruel, dog-eat-dog world where all that matters is to stay alive physically. No, Jesus resolutely relativizes the mundane, down-to-earth world. It is a world desperately in need of redemption, not a self-concocted one, but provided by God who is beyond time and space and dwells in the highest heaven.

Moreover, Jesus does not advocate pie-in-the-sky idealism. The narrow view of the rich fool with the shrivelled soul did not represent 'realism' as opposed to 'religious idealism.' After all the fertility of the soil, the steady rainfall, the sunshine ripening his grain were not his and to claim that they were (he speaks in the parable about 'my grain and my goods') was claiming too much. After all he did not own the rain, the sunshine and the fertility of the soil. And this is probably another reason that Jesus calls him a 'fool.'

Also he owed much to society rather than individual achievement. The taken for granted rules and morality, the context of honest dealing, the reliability, loyalty and sense of responsibility of his workers were not his doing, but passed by a previous generation to the present one. He would not have been able to reap a rich harvest, if there had been civil unrest and tension in his region. Yet instead of making him grateful and humble, his wealth had made him proud.

Still, pride is not the only sin narrowing the rich man's vision, but also our own. There are six other deadly sins: covetousness, lust, anger, envy, gluttony and sloth. Each of them shrivels our souls. Each of them diminishes the cohesion or the perfection of the social good. Each of them makes the restoration of the soul all the more urgent. Each of them makes forgiveness a prerequisite for that restoration. And most important of all, each of them is basically rebellion against God and his ordained order. After all the best definition of sin is still alienation from God.

We really fool ourselves if we think that our enormous technical progress since biblical times has liberated us from the pangs of the imperfection of our souls. The equally enormous progress in our biological, medical, genetic and astronomical knowledge has not freed us from mental anguish, depression, loneliness, a sense of feeling alienated from the harsh work place, the adversary game playing in our political and administrative arenas, the crime-ridden slums, and the injustice of the power hungry.

To single out just one of these many imperfections: the rampant consumerism of our age is not that different from the rich man in Luke 12:13-24, who had convinced himself that his basic security was in his wealth, so that he could eat, drink and be merry until the end of his life. He must have gotten a nasty shock when God required his soul and all he could present was a bedraggled rag.

No, consumerism in our age is as the love of the 'goods' for the rich fool. An escape from what God expects of the soul which, after all, we have on loan from him. We know it and God knows it. Has the excitement of more and more acquisitions, our frantic buying sprees, surrounding ourselves with the latest status symbols and the latest car models made any difference to the health of our souls? A few weeks ago, when my grandchildren were unpacking their over-abundant heap of Christmas presents, I had the uncanny feeling that the two onions our starving carcasses received from prison management in 1944 Germany made us more appreciative (or did more for our souls) than my grandchildren could possibly feel now.

What does Calvin have to say about the parable of the wealthy individual whose soul was obviously not up to standard?

Christ, he says, does not condemn him for being a careful householder, storing produce for leaner days. No, he is condemned for putting up a 'brazen rampart against death' and imagining that the fortress of his riches can protect life. His confidence was shut up in his barns and he ignored his dependence on God's providence. Therefore he damaged his soul, 'the seat of all the affections' and suffered the penalty of his own folly.

Calvin has more to say about the soul and its deficiencies in other places. It is not just the seat of affections (or 'will', 'appetites', 'desires' as he calls them in the *Institutes*) but it is also the source of the intellect. It is this part that does the guiding and the ruling, the approving and disapproving. Seeing that the soul is created by God, so its constituent parts (reason and faith) are similarly God-given, Calvin thinks.

But whether emotional or rational, the soul, or our true self, is also corrupted compared with human nature as God originally intended it to be. Calvin, true to his understanding and admiration of classic philosophy is too impressed with reason to give it much of a negative report card. All he says (*Inst*. III ii 14) is that the certainty of faith cannot be reached by reason.

Nowhere does Calvin go as far as Pascal does, when he unhesitatingly calls reason as such 'corrupt', or Eastern scholars when they regard logic as a whore serving anyone who can pay the price. I assume that Calvin would have been more outspoken, if the extensive psychological literature on rationalisation had existed in his days. It would certainly have persuaded him that reason and rationality can be used for the loftiest as well as the basest purposes.

By contrast, Calvin is very voluble on the 'will' or 'appetite' part of the soul. He comes back to it again and again, in the *Institutes*, in his sermons and commentaries. He sees that part of the soul as closely linked to man's animal nature or as we would say nowadays, man's origin. Here the words 'corrupt' and 'original sin' flow naturally and frequently into his argument. He does not hesitate to use such words as 'depraved souls', 'hereditary corruption.' And, of course, his argument is always true to scripture and loaded with biblical references.

Lust to Calvin (and to Paul who refers to it as 'the flesh') is part of natural man. He goes so far as to say that 'everything which is in man, from the intellect to the will, from the soul even to the flesh, is defiled and pervaded with libido; or to express it more briefly, ... the whole man is in himself nothing else than lust (*Inst*. I ii 8).' And this in turn, he says, leads to the perversity of adultery, fornication, theft, murder, hatred, high jinks, debauchery instead of the righteousness (being right with God), innocence and purity God expects. Atheists, such as Sigmund Freud, agree that civilization necessitates the repression of instincts in general and the diversion of libido in particular.

Pride, lust, greed, covetousness, envy, sloth, anger, gluttony, they are all participants in the battle of the soul. It is an unending battle. It apparently lasts until the end of our days here on earth. Yet it is also a necessary battle. Has it ever occurred to you that each and all these items of 'original sin' contribute to the deterioration of our community, our culture and our society? And that their opposites, such as humility, discipline, kindness, gentleness, understanding, altruism, generosity, self-denial contribute to the amelioration, improvement and restoration of our communal, cultural, and social environment?

In other words, Calvin's view of man's nature hinges on the body/soul contrast. Yet even the soul can be corrupted. To Calvin, following Jesus, restoring the soul means strengthening spiritual authority and power over the mundane material, physical existence. This may not be easy or attractive. It does not fit with the choice we have now of rejecting what is uncongenial and only accepting what gratifies the senses.

This of course makes the topic of original sin and our inadequate souls rather unpopular. Yet, it would be quite unrealistic not to see the link with the personal and social disorder all around us. Do not all the sins that the Bible present to us in great detail ring a bell? Or have we been so much conditioned by modern advertising that we open our ears only to what is pleasant to hear rather than real? Actually what is pleasant to hear, read and see nowadays in the paper, radio and television or the porno shops in Fyshwick falls in the 'corruption' category of Jesus, Paul and Calvin.

What are we to conclude from all this? That our souls need constant restoring and repairing? That the battle for our souls will continue until the end of our days? That sin is all around and within us? That our communities, our churches, our Australian culture, our entire society, our personal identity and integrity are constantly in jeopardy because of human shortcomings, such as pride, lust, greed, envy, anger, etc? And that their amelioration is hampered by a shortage of responsibility, sobriety, reliability, understanding, kindness, humility, generosity etc.?

I do not want to make the mistake that was made the night before last in a play that my wife and I went to see here in Theatre 3, Ellery Crescent, Canberra. The play is called 'The Burning.' It is written by a young Canberra playwright, Duncan Ley, who also acts the main character, Francis Schiller. The play is all about the witch hunts and the heresy trials in the town of Bamberg, Germany, in the year 1626. The performance was impressive with excellent acting and very appropriate background music. The entire play is an illustration of the corruption of man's nature as has been so much part of today's sermon. The injustice perpetrated on the innocent by the intellectual, spiritual and political elite of the town is grippingly and graphically portrayed.

On the way home, my wife and I discussed whether there had been any redeeming features in the ideas of the script and the performance which had kept us on the edge of our seat. All we could come up with was how lucky we were to live in more enlightened days, the example of human love binding young Francis and his innocent wife Madeline who was dreadfully tortured and burnt at the stake, and a smattering of courageous tolerance shown by one of the older, minor, and ultimately defeated characters.

Well that is not the way I want this sermon to finish. The gospel is after all good news. And if a sermon is true to scripture it should never finish with a despairing realistic note of man's decrepitude and depravity.

And there is no reason to. As always, returning to scripture allows for a happy ending. After all our text says quite explicitly that the soul can be restored and that the law of the Lord is perfect and actually restores the soul.

If the law is narrowly interpreted as a set of mundane rules to live by, it is doubtful that it can restore the soul. But the law is usually interpreted in a much broader sense as the entire first five books of the Old Testament. And even if we confine ourselves to the Ten Commandments (Exodus 20:1-17), it is God himself who keeps faith with those who love Him (Exodus 20:6) and therefore salvation and the restoration of our souls are secure. The perfection of the law lies in this guarantee and in God's subsequent revealing himself in Jesus Christ and in the Holy Spirit as our guide and comforter. God forgives, even if we do not deserve it and therefore our souls will be restored to the full through the sacrifice of Jesus on the cross for those who repent.

Forgiveness is a way to restore the soul and to become acceptable to God. Forgiveness in the context of the story of the rich property owner would have been for putting the self and its possessions ahead of God. Forgiveness is also the means for a community to heal tension and to promote cohesion and solidarity.

God restores both the order without and the order within. And it is about this that we will shortly sing. Hymn 556:

'Be still my soul: the Lord is on thy side' is a promise that God restores our soul for us, provided that we trust him, listen to him and let him. The hymn also assures us that we can leave it to God to order and provide and to guide our future as well as our past and that therefore nothing can shake our hope and our confidence.

CALVIN 16
CORRUPTING POWER

… you have provoked my anger and led Israel into sin (God speaking to King Ahab through the prophet Elijah). 1 Kings 21:22

I wonder whether of late any of you have had a sense that something is exploding in our culture and society, a sense of the world changing so fast that one cannot keep up with it. Hardly a week goes by without reports of new technical developments, advances in information technology, discoveries about therapeutic cloning and improved cancer treatments.

We also seem to be going in all directions at once while the communication between the parts becomes increasingly smaller like the separating waves of fire works or like the ever expanding universe with whole galaxies moving away from one another at an incredible rate.

That is certainly true on the personal level. We appear to divide ourselves in ever so many parts isolated from one another. At work we behave and talk differently from the ways we do at home or at school. We have learnt to be chameleons adopting the colour of our environment. Yet in our age of information overload we cannot handle an infinite number of interruptions from e-mail, phones, companions and co-workers without falling apart. And more and more people have to resort to anti-depressants or other kinds of medicine to ward off debilitating mental disorders.

Our society too does not seem to hang together as well as some of us older types remember from the past, in spite of the increasing security of our increasingly higher standard of living. Yet our material improvements do not seem to have any effect on our serenity, our piece of mind, our integrity. If anything the reverse seems to be true: the better off we are financially, the worse our sense of happiness and tranquillity appears to become.

There are an increasing number of individuals whose tastes, values and norms differ radically from most others. Rampant individualism some academics call it. Society is losing its cohesion and reminds one of loose sand, individuals feeling alienated from one another with only a loose and fragile blanket of tolerance covering it superficially.

My reason for starting this as an introduction to the interpretation of our readings for today is a fragment from an interview I heard on radio the other day. It was the late Douglas Adams, author of *The Hitch Hikers Guide to the Galaxy* remarking on the narrow insights of religion in the light of the exponential increase of knowledge of the universe. Now I belong to a group of specialists in the social scientific study of religion that hold exactly the opposite point of view. We feel that any religion has always attempted and still attempts to present the most comprehensive view of existence and all of what a culture and society are essentially about. Yet their views are not known because in this exploding overload of information their voices are just not heard. These views are amply available, but the competition within the avalanche of information directed to any one with access to the Internet, are lost in a sea of data. Fortunately, the less informed or frankly misinformed sources similarly suffer from being lost in a sea of data floating around our exploding world of knowledge.

Our readings for today are a very timely example of the relevance and comprehensiveness of religion in our day and age. They may have been written thousands of years ago, but they are just as applicable now as they were then. The human condition may change, but there are age-old characteristics of existence that have remained unchanged and are as relevant as ever. And one of them has to do with absolute power corrupting absolutely.

This issue is at the centre of today's readings. We keep thinking that democracy in our present form is a rather recent invention and that anything before the seventeenth century was anything but democracy as we know it now. Those of you interested in history remember the absolute power of the monarchy and ancient dictators and similar kinds of rulers before that era. And yet today's story about Naboth and King Ahab goes back at least 2850 years and the rebuke of the Pharisee about Jesus' acceptance of a lady of ill-repute at least 1970 years.

In both instances it is those who speak on behalf of God (the prophet Elijah and Jesus) who set the record straight and in no uncertain terms condemn the injustice done to the powerless by the powerful, as our text from 1 Kings 21:22 shows. In other words God is the one who makes it clear that in his Kingdom there is no room for those who abuse power or who treat the socially despised and disadvantaged uncharitably and unlovingly.

You remember the Naboth story. He has a vineyard that has been in the family for a long time. It is next door to the land of King Ahab who has been rebuffed in his efforts to buy the property. His wife Jezebel cooks up a plan to have Naboth killed. She hires two scoundrels who falsely accuse Naboth of cursing both God and king. Naboth is stoned to death. Ahab now has the land, but that is not the end of the tale. God speaking through Elijah strongly condemns the shenanigans and tells Ahab that he will die a gruesome death on the very land he has just so deviously acquired and that dogs will lick his blood. Ahab is now extremely sorry and asks God for forgiveness. This is granted and the gruesome death is postponed.

The message of the story is clear: God is a God of justice and therefore suspicious of those who abuse power and treat the powerless unjustly. God is on the side of the down-trodden rather than those who do the trampling. Humility is high on God's list of expectations for humans. The danger of overestimating oneself is much greater amongst the successful than the battlers. The balance between overestimation and underestimation is more likely found amongst those who have not arrived than those who think they have.

That is also the message of our New Testament reading in Luke 7:36-50. Here Jesus is the guest of Simon, who like his fellow Pharisees scrupulously observes the law and has great political power. He looks down on the woman who lives an immoral life in the town, kisses Jesus feet and wets them with her tears. Simon lets it be known that this is unacceptable behaviour upon which Jesus tells him the parable of the two men who owed money to a money-lender.

The money-lender is a very generous man as he remits both debts because the borrowers cannot pay. But one owes ten times more than the other and Jesus suggests that therefore the former will love the money-lender more than the latter, as so much more was at stake. Apparently Jesus compares the immoral woman with the one who needed much forgiveness and therefore had to repent more, whereas the Pharisee needed little pardon or absolution and therefore showed little if any repentance, love and faith.

The sting in the story is Jesus' implicit rebuke of his host. Jesus admits that the Pharisee was an exemplary citizen who went to great trouble of adherence to all rules and regulations of his society and his religion in contrast with the woman whose reputation was as low as one could get. And yet Jesus pointedly says that she had been forgiven and that her faith had saved her. By contrast, the Pharisee has obviously not committed many sins and is not saved by his faith.

Here too, as in the Naboth story, those with power, whether political or religious, invariably run the risk of being corrupted by that power. They become arrogant believers in their own intrinsic goodness and base their self-worth and integrity on personal qualities and accomplishments, untrammelled by the uncomfortable thought that in the process they have diminished God's authority by augmenting their own.

This theme is also picked up in our third reading for today: Galatians 2:15-21. Here St Paul says that strict adherence to the law does not necessarily lead to salvation, or personal wholeness. He goes even further by stating that Christ has died for nothing if personal integrity is nothing but scrupulous, outward, adherence to rules and regulations and not a matter of inward motivation, love, faith and understanding.

Both the parable in Luke 7 and Galatians 2 tell us that religious power runs the risk of corruption and distortion unless the different and yet compensating functions of systems of 'oughtness' (morality, law) versus systems of 'isness' (meaning, faith) are clearly distinguished.

I want to apologise in advance for introducing heavy sociology. For over thirty years my understanding of the essential difference between Judaism and Christianity, the Old Testament and the New Testament or morality and meaning, law and faith hinges on their separate function in an increasingly complex society. They serve different purposes, yet they also need one another. If a system of 'isness' (meaning) is to survive it has to be concretized through values and norms. If a system of 'oughtness' (morality) is to survive it has to be integrated by a transcendental source of order. They have to be linked, as meaning on its own can lead to rigidification and morality on its own can lead to distortion. Here again we have what I mentioned at the beginning: an incidence of social scientific knowledge about religion sunk in the swamp of information overload.

We feel it in our bones, don't we, that Ahab should get his just dessert for abusing power and that Simon should be rebuked for allowing rules and regulations to usurp the place of a loving and forgiving God. Yet these values and norms have to be reinforced, if a society is to be viable. A culture which condones corrupting power and arrogant self-glorification is likely to succumb, unless it can undo the social breakdown resulting from these vices through forgiveness, understanding and love.

Yet that same society also needs authority and constant strengthening of the moral order. The trick therefore is to both strengthen authority and moral order and yet to be constantly alert to the real possibility of power abuse and moral rigidity. Any society, whether ancient or modern, will need ways to do both. Any surviving religion was and is in the forefront of accomplishing both. Not to understand this and to declare religion as too narrow for present day society, is to fatally ignore one of the few means left for countering insanity and containing the explosion I mentioned in the introduction of this sermon.

There is more to be said, however, about the religious corruption implied in the parable of the moneylender. Jesus in Luke 7:26–50 and Paul in Galatians 2:15-21 warn believers of the danger of narrowly confining religion to following a set of rules, the law in their words. They suggest that salvation does not come by good works (as prescribed by law) but by faith (in Jesus Christ). True religion escapes the confinement to law. False religion succumbs to it.

Calvin makes similar distinctions. He distinguishes between the invisible and the visible church. The godly, as he calls them, represent the invisible church. Yet they must maintain themselves in society: '… any one, who, from hatred of the ungodly, violates the bond of society, enters on a downward course, in which he incurs great danger of cutting himself off from the communion of saints (*Inst.* IV i 16).' In other words, good Christians cannot escape responsibility for society and its laws.

Calvin distinguishes the spiritual order from the civil one. Civil order (*Inst*. II ii 13), reflects man's nature as a 'social animal' which disposes him 'to cherish and preserve society' and obey its laws. By contrast the spiritual order 'has its seat within the soul (*Inst*. III xix 15)' and comprises the invisible church, or as Calvin has it elsewhere, 'the Church as it is really before God (*Inst*. IV I 7).' In other words it is the Kingdom of God, as Jesus describes it in the parables of the mustard seed and the leaven (Matthew 13:31-33).

Calvin does not have a high opinion of the visible church. 'In this church there is a very large mixture of hypocrites, who have nothing of Christ but the name and outward appearance: of ambitious, avaricious, envious, evil-speaking men … hence it is necessary to believe in the invisible Church, which is manifest to the eye of God only … (*Inst*. IV i 7).' In other words, the visible church may very well harbour corrupt elements. By contrast the invisible church is incorruptible. It is an abstraction of pure order in a world where order and disorder are invariably mixed whether one considers the spiritual or the civil realm.

The contribution which up-to-date social science can make to this dilemma of the visible church hinting at, rather than concretizing the invisible church is through its insights in the necessity for and yet also the deflecting nature of organization. Any idea or faith worth its salt will have to be what sociologists call 'institutionalized.' That is to say, it has to be surrounded by ritual and reiteration and retraced in the grooves of order.

The problem is that the institutional boundaries around this idea or faith tend to become as important, if not more so, than the idea or faith itself. And this means that the boundaries tend to replace the content as the centre of commitment, mainly because humans find it easier to be loyal to something concrete rather than something abstract.

The French sociologist Emile Durkheim called this the 'contagion of the sacred.' In other words, the vessel of the faith becomes the object of veneration rather than the faith itself. The organization of the religious idea takes over from what it is only supposed to guard and protect. Calvin correctly observes this phenomenon when he says that the church's function is to be a faithful guardian 'to prevent the truth from perishing in the world (*Inst*. IV i 10).'

This means that Simon, the Pharisee in Luke 7, made the mistake of confusing the accoutrements (boundaries) of religion with the real thing. The law, Jesus intimates (and Paul does the same in Galatians 2) is a concretization of the faith. Yet it is not the centre. It may be a necessity, but it is not the soul. And the Bible makes it clear that the only way out of the mistake and the dilemma, is to repent and to confess one's short-sightedness and sin. Similarly King Ahab's reconciliation with God after the heinous crime he committed could only take place after his confession and sincere repentance.

Loyalty to denominational boundaries rather than loyalty to the saviour seems to be the crux of the religious controversies and massacres in Northern Ireland, Indonesia, the Sudan and India. There is no religious organization, whether Judaism, Christianity, Islam, Hinduism or Buddhism that does not preach reconciliation and understanding of other human beings. One example, they all believe in the golden rule: do unto others what you expect them to do to you.

Yet it is easier to believe in the superiority of the visible differences and the historical diversities of other tribes and nations than the less visible, actually invisible, underlying similarities of their beliefs and ethics. The variety of denominations in such nations as Australia, Canada, New Zealand and the USA correspond closely with the different ethnic origins of their populations. The division of church and state in those countries accommodate the checkerboard of different denominational origins in the countries from which the newcomers came. Still the underlying similarities of these ethnic religions could quite admirably reinforce the common identity and unity of these new nations. But unfortunately the boundaries separating them make the division of church and state necessary, although religion as such is closely bound up with one's national identity.

In 1969 at the request of the publisher Thomas Nelson in Melbourne I wrote a book entitled *Christianity in Chains*. It was supposed to be an antipodal version of Bishop Robinson's *Honest to God* that had become a controversial bestseller in the northern hemisphere. We had originally called it *The Shackled Vision,* because the book wanted to point to the organisational deflections, the mundane loyalties, the psychological functions, the social needs, the rigid traditions that formed the shackles of the Christian vision, or in Calvin's terms, the invisible church.

I still adhere to almost all I wrote then. The invisible church is still embedded in, and maybe even corrupted by, organisational boundaries and compromises it needs to survive. And yet the vision is infinitely more important than the shackles needed for its survival.

This was driven home vividly to me in the Christmas service in the unheated assembly hall of Halle Prison with hard labour (Zuchthaus) in 1944. The service had been completely Nazified. It began and finished with the Hitler salute and the sermon was all about the titanic struggle of the German race to civilize the conquered nations and soldiers dying on the various fronts for the sacred cause. And yet the consolation of the Christmas message was there in the readings about the suffering servant from Isaiah and about the birth of Jesus from Luke. It seemed to whisper to me that the suffering Messiah born as a defenceless infant in a hostile society was at one with other marginal and political prisoners, such as us.

Conclusion: The Old Testament story about Naboth's vineyard, Jesus' parable of the generous moneylender and Paul's remarks about the relative importance of the law has wider implications. They are all pointers to God's blueprint for His heavenly order, His Kingdom, Calvin's invisible church. They all point to the comprehensive intent of God's cosmic program straddling the ages. They are as relevant today as they were in ancient times. Even more so, because at least in those days, humans were not confronted with the explosive changes on both the personal and social level, I mentioned at the beginning of this sermon.

The corrupting power which I used as our theme is not just a matter of ancient history. It is a burning human problem right now. We may have thrown up better barriers against the blatant abuse of power by those who were tempted that way, such as King David and King Ahab. Yet our short-sightedness and our tendency to confuse the necessary accoutrements of religion with its core meaning are just as much a matter of deep concern and makes confession of our sin and our repentance just as crucial.

CALVIN 17

MISPLACED MILITANCY

(Or the slippery slope of total obedience)

We are servants and deserve no credit; we have only done our duty. Luke 17:10

Today's New Testament reading is one of those horrendously and agonisingly embarrassing Biblical puzzles. It compels us to sit up, rubbing our eyes to see whether we are not dreaming. Is this actually what Jesus is saying and Holy Scripture is actually recording? Isn't this parable subversive of everything we have learnt about God?

What does it say? God is compared with a harsh master who after a hard day's work in the fields expects his servants to prepare his supper, fasten their belts and wait on him until he has his meal and then have theirs afterwards (Luke 17:8). To cap it all, Jesus, who tells this parable, adds that the disciples like the servants must say: 'We are servants and deserve no credit; we have only done our duty (Luke 17:10).'

God here is the opposite of what we like Him to be and the way he is portrayed in other parts of the Bible: loving, compassionate, understanding, forgiving sinners. In those other parts He is concerned for the downtrodden and losers, those who mourn and those who are persecuted, those who suffer insults and injustice, the protector of the vulnerable and the weak.

Yet in this parable He is the autocrat with no feeling or respect for his workers, squeezing the last drop of blood out of them. Here he does not balance rewards and punishment, as we have learnt from the Harvard psychologist B.F. Skinner to be elementary for all human behaviour. Here God is depicted as a poor employer who still has to learn how to handle his labourers and farmhands.

The God of this parable does not fit with modern notions of workplace management. He takes rather than gives. He distances himself from his workers rather than reaches out to them. Mateship is not in His vocabulary. He fosters inequality rather than a sense of community. He demands total, unconditional obedience.

Total submission, is this what God demands? And if so, is Islam (which actually means 'submission') not very true to this Biblical picture of Him? After all Mohammad and the Qur'an (meaning 'recitation' in Arabic) recording his revelations, borrow heavily from both the Old and the New Testament. Unconditional obedience to Allah (Arabic for God) is central to what Muslims (the Arabic word for 'those who submit themselves') believe. And does not this belief fit like a hand in a glove with today's New Testament reading?

It also fits like a hand in a glove with the horrendous acts of destruction last month in New York and Washington. Total obedience to the point of giving one's life for a sacred cause is essentially what motivated the terrorists destroying the World Trade Centre and part of the Pentagon. The basic origin of this motivation seems to have escaped most of the journalists and commentators, although a cursory reading of the early Islamic tradition could have taught them that even more than Judaism and Christianity, Islam stresses total submission and blind militancy.

What does this early tradition say? Islam dates its calendar from the Hegira, the year in which Mohammad at the age of 53 had to flee from Mecca. The year was 622 AD and Hegira means emigration or departure. It was in this year that Muhammad became the founder of a new religion.

Why was his life in jeopardy? Mohammad had started out rather humbly as a shepherd and a camel driver. On his many journeys to the marketplaces of the Middle East he learnt much from the Jews and Christians he met. Later he became a wealthy merchant in his birthplace Mecca.

In those days Mecca was an important, but decaying religious centre. Its wealth was partly derived from the sale of water from the well of Zamzam, but pervasive vices of gambling, drinking and usury had begun to affect family and clan obligations. When Mohammad began to thunder against all these vices, his life became endangered and he had to flee to Medina, two hundred miles to the north.

It was here that he wrote the Qur'an stressing the single-hearted faith in God and the virtues of kindness to slaves, respect for parents and wives, charity for the poor, protection of orphans and widows. It condemned cruelty, impatience and mistrust. The faithful are urged to be honest, helpful, patient, industrious, courageous, generous and honourable. It was the common faith that galvanized Mohammad's followers into a united military force.

This disciplined force of 10,000 men marched to Mecca in 630 AD, took the town, worshipped at the Ka'bah (the temple with the Black Stone, probably a meteorite, which was believed to have come straight from the Garden of Eden). The soldiers took no booty. Instead they made sure that the neediest were looked after. They all believed that the eradication of corruption was their God-given duty and that giving their life for the good cause would assure them a place in paradise.

Later the conquest by Muslim armies of large areas of the Mediterranean basin was anchored in this fervent faith. The soldiers strongly believed that they carried out Allah's will and that sobriety, responsibility and reliability went together with order as much as intoxication, irresponsibility and deviousness went together with disorder.

Faith made the Muslims into a formidable fighting force. Yet cruelty, injustice and abuse of power, the very elements which Mohammad so strongly denounced, often followed in the wake of military conquests. And that was not just true for the Islamic armies. It was just as true for the Christian Crusades that took a heavy toll amongst the innocent, women and children.

Let us take stock for a moment. I started out by pointing to the embarrassing, yet indisputable image of God in our parable as a despot and tyrant demanding absolute obedience. Then I traced this theme of total obedience to the history of Islam, an offspring of Judaism and Christianity, all the way to the very recent atrocities perpetrated by the nineteen terrorists who in the name of Allah destroyed themselves and thousands of innocent victims in New York and Washington. All this has made the puzzle of the parable all the more real and pertinent. The time has come to try and solve the puzzle. I would like to do this under the following three points.

(1) *Pure Order*. Let us start with having a look at what other Bible scholars and preachers have said about the parable. George Buttrick was the famous, Scottish born minister of the Madison Avenue Presbyterian Church in New York who wrote a book about the parables. All he has to say about this one is that God is not a slave driver, that the parable is a challenge to endurance and that for strong souls, duty is a sufficient recompense. This to my way of thinking avoids the real purpose of the parable and is not true to the story. God is depicted as the aloof master.

Other scholars ignore the parable altogether. Not Calvin. The parable is right along his alley. 'We are God's property and therefore he owes us nothing.' To Calvin it is 'wicked arrogance' and 'diabolical pride' to think that God is in any way beholden to us. We are God's slaves. It would be 'foolish confidence' to claim that we deserve God's kindness and liberality, even when our behaviour is exemplary.

Elsewhere (*Inst*. III xv 3) Calvin uses our text to explain why humans cannot earn extra points for the good works they perform. Heaven and salvation are free gifts from God rather than founded on human accomplishments in Calvin's mind. Why? Because anything that humans touch is impure and imperfect. God alone is pure and perfect.

Could we translate this Calvinist kind of thinking by suggesting that existence is flawed because order is always mixed with a respectable amount of disorder? Or to put the same in Calvin's and Biblical terms: existence is flawed because pure perfection can only exist not in man's world but only in God's. Salvation contrasts with sin. Yet a vision of that pure perfection, salvation or order is a prerequisite for man's survival as chaos means extinction. If so, the image of God in this parable as a despot and tyrant may ultimately be an expression of the unassailability, impregnability or distancing of the pure order He represents.

This interpretation may even appeal to the many atheists and critics of religion I encounter in the social scientific study of religion. It may even appeal to some journalists, such as Robert Macklin and Simon Grose of *The Canberra Times* or Phillip Adams of *The Australian Newspaper*, whose naïve and unsophisticated treatment of religion never fails to irritate me. After all this interpretation fits with their view of evolution and the human condition.

This then is my first point: Jesus being part of a long line of prophets wants to restore God to His rightful place as beyond the mixture of good and evil, perfection and imperfection, order and disorder, integrity and corruption, salvation and sin. But that inevitably means separating God from the here and now in order that he can come into his own as a pivot of re-orientation, bolstering the first (evolutionary necessity, or, for instance highlighting order/salvation) at the expense of the second (evolutionary extinction, downgrading disorder/sin).

(2) *Authority*. My second point is closely related to the first. God's aloofness and apparent disregard for his workers' self-esteem may be Jesus' way of telling his disciples that God's authority is distinct and should not be obscured or rendered ineffectual through superficial chumminess. God is described as the source of constancy in our Old Testament reading for today (Lamentations 3:22). Calvin too uses the certainty of God's authority time and again.

In other parts of the Bible (e.g. Revelation 1:8) God is described as the Alpha and the Omega, the beginning and the end. In other words our entire existence is surrounded by His ordering authority. He is never the manipulable means to human ends. He represents the contour of all that exists, the source of meaning. Therefore he is not to be confused with those who depend on Him. He is unconditioned. By contrast all of us are conditioned.

The attraction of fundamentalism in all its forms, Jewish, Christian, Islamic, Hindu is particularly great in the areas of the world where ordinary people, rather than the well-to-do, feel rudderless, where change has either been too rapid or has left major sections of the population on the margin and sidelines of existence. That was certainly true for the exiles in Babylon ('The Lord is all that I have, Lamentations 3:24') who lamented their captivity in a foreign land (Psalms 137:1 'By the rivers of Babylon we sat down and wept').

Rallying around the traditional source of stability has always been salve for the wounds of the present. God has been the mainstay in times of trouble for countless generations before us. The Psalms are full of references to God consoling those in trouble. Even in our secular society people kept flocking to the ecumenical services all over the world after the 11 September calamities as if to say: 'we, Jews, Christians, Muslims are united in our grief.' Yet God was both implicitly and explicitly regarded and worshipped as the authority and source of order and stability in a world that had suddenly and dangerously become unhinged.

Fundamentalists of any stripe cling even more strongly than the rest of us to the structures, delineations and fundamental authority of the past, as if to say that security has not been altogether swallowed up in a society which bears cunning resemblance to the imploding World Trade Towers of New York.

So my second point of making sense of this disturbing parable is that Jesus may have wanted to draw the attention of the disciples to God being altogether different and possessing superhuman authority. He is to be worshiped rather than made into a chum.

(3) *Faith*. My third and last point is by far the most important of my attempts to understand this parable. It means going back to Scripture and discovering from the context what Jesus was actually attempting to say to his disciples in answer to their question, how they could increase their faith. Listening to God and obeying him had been central to their recent discussion. And they obviously felt that more faith would advance both better listening and would improve obedience.

Jesus accepts their worry about the quality of their faith and commitment. That's why he confirms (Luke 17:6) that even faith as small as a mustard seed can do miracles. Nowadays we would say: 'Faith is like a stem-cell.' Both have an amazing inner dynamic, a capacity to grow into something altogether different. Both provide the core, essence and roots of diversity. Faith or commitment makes us what we are essentially. If money, fame or power are our basic commitments in life, they will structure our beliefs as to what life is all about.

Yet I understand Jesus to say in the parable that that is not the way to live life to the full. Those commitments do not aim high enough. They are too narrow, concrete and actually make gods out of golden calves rather than revere the God who met Moses on top of Mount Sinai. Faith is God not just being the aloof, distant master, but also the one who stretches his arm to save.

Faith is being linked to God's order and trusting that this order will save you and make you whole. If the parable is nothing more than a summary of God representing pure order and authority it virtually abandons the commitment, feeling or loyalty element of the God-man relationship. By emphasizing exclusively the distance between the perfect and imperfect, order and disorder, wholeness and breakdown of that wholeness, identity and difference, salvation and sin, we are left with a sense of analytic coldness.

It is at this juncture that the faith relationship fills the gap and becomes pivotal. For it allows for a personal relationship to sustain the link and to suspend the coldness of the difference. If this is so the parable can be regarded, not as contrasting with, but as complementing God's compassion and love; as for instance in the parable of the prodigal son.

How relevant is all this for our present situation?

On 12 September this year we were booked to return to Australia via Texas. Yet no planes were flying and we had to stay a while longer with our youngest daughter and her family in Niagara Falls, Canada. We were glued to our television set all day. I vividly remember that soon after the destruction of the World Trade Centre an article appeared in the major American and Canadian papers by Jerry Falwell a well-known and powerful American fundamental minister suggesting that the events might have been God's warning and actual punishment of a wayward corrupt nation, upsetting God by immoral behaviour and sinfulness. Our daughter was fuming: 'How dare he say that, justifying an obviously criminal terrorist act by bringing God into it and actually hinting that the terrorists were God's messengers!' We agreed with her and her many friends. How could God possibly condone the death of all these thousands of innocent people?

We have to be careful not to fall in the terrorist trap of accepting their argument that they unselfishly gave their life to do Allah's will. Claiming to know God's mind is claiming too much. We too may be claiming too much when we counter that obviously false claim by suggesting that we do God's work by eradicating all the accomplices of the terrorists.

The will of God, as I see it, is to follow Jesus and all he stood for and to repent for our part in creating a world in which individuals feel alienated enough to perpetrate these heinous acts. If that is all Jerry Falwell is trying to say, good for him. Yet by claiming divine sanction for a crusade of punishment and revenge, we may also be claiming too much.

Christians believe that Jesus is the bridge between God's purity, perfection, order and authority on the one hand and our impurity, imperfection, disorder and sin on the other. The former are the very items that separate us from God, because none of them are fully represented in humans. Yet they are also the very items that allow the race to ultimately win the battle for survival of the fittest. In Jesus God showed us concretely how the gap between God's attributes and man's imperfection, sin and disorder could be bridged. Faith and obedience are a crucial link. So is humility and confession of sin.

The parable is Jesus' answer to the disciples' quest for increasing faith. It says unequivocally that one's faith increases if one accepts God as one's master rather than one's equal. God represents unconditioned order, not one that humans can concoct through insisting on their independence from Him. Jesus seems to suggest that the greater the distance between master and servant the stronger is the bond of faith. It has more to bridge and therefore has to be stronger to carry the load. Jesus did not advocate revenge. Jesus practised total obedience to the Father, yet followed a different path that led directly to the cross rather than to mass destruction.

It is possible to both understand and yet condemn identifying God's will with terrorist action. Yet we should not make the same mistake of justifying our counter attack, as similarly totally God's will. We should be ready to acknowledge that fundamentalism may be an understandable reaction to what we have been making of God's creation and civilization. Total obedience to God's word is a humble acceptance of his authority rather than convincing ourselves that we act on his behalf when we embark on a counter crusade.

Hymn 508 'O Jesus I have promised to serve You to the end', expresses this sentiment well.

CALVIN 18

GRATITUDE from a FOREIGNER

Could none be found to come back and give praise to God except this foreigner? Luke 17:18

Scripture to me is a never-ending source of interpretation of present events in the light of God's dealing with humans in the past. If we ignore this source of understanding we are inevitably thrown back on letting the facts explain themselves without the benefit of the larger context, thereby narrowing and even jeopardizing the truth of the matter. We will certainly overestimate the unstable character of the present day welter of events overwhelming us, unless we insist on the larger context.

And so last Sunday's lesson of the parable of the tough employer led me to interpret the recent events in New York and the underlying motivation of the terrorists blowing up these skyscrapers. My argument was, as you may remember, that God's order and authority separate us from man's fickleness and disorder. I also argued that our link of faith with God should not lead us to mistake misplaced militancy for total obedience and that neither Christians nor Muslims should fall in the trap of assuming that we know God's mind and can fully fathom God's blueprint for existence. My conclusion was that in following Christ we might avoid that mistake.

The question then arises as to whether the enormous progress made in our technical and scientific knowledge and the sophistication of the weapons of mass-destruction in just one century does not nullify the reliance on God's word as the deepest and most sophisticated source of interpretation. After all when the Bible was written it was quite impossible and even unimaginable for humans to visualize the events of the beginning of the third millennium.

My answer is that God's word can only be inadequately understood because of our being enveloped in a particular historical situation, but that yet there is a constancy and eternity in each situation that transcends that situation and therefore allows us to have a more comprehensive, though relatively inadequate interpretation of those events.

In the car on the way home last week my wife and I were discussing the structure of the sermon as it expressed those convictions and she wondered whether I was not paying too much attention to Calvin in my recent sermons. Didn't he live in an era entirely different from our own? My reply was that all of us, St Paul and Calvin included, could not avoid being the children of our time, but that they also invariably revealed a glimpse (and usually more than a glimpse) of the will of God.

This time the sermon theme is based on gratitude in the verses of Luke 17:11-19. What does it say? Jesus is travelling 'through the borderland of Samaria and Galilee (Luke 17:11)', where he is met by ten men with leprosy. He heals all of them, but only one of them (who also happen to be from Samaria and therefore a foreigner) returns to thank Jesus and praise God for being cured.

In Christ's mind faith and gratitude belong together. They both rely on the existence of God as the author and creator of order out of chaos as we discovered last week. To the believer order in pure form is not to be found in himself or in his society or culture. Here it is always mixed with forms of disorder, or 'sin' in a narrower sense. Under 'disorder' we can categorize such events as natural disasters or disease, whereas sin is a narrower kind of disorder. It is confined to our social relations where it means 'whatever leads to disrupting those relations.'

Yet in God order in pure form does exist. He is above the vale of tears. He dwells, as the Bible tells us (Matthew 6:20) in heaven, where neither moth nor rust can corrupt. It is from this vantage point that chaos can be overcome, that re-orientation can take place and a blueprint for order (in Calvin's vocabulary 'predestination') for survival of the human race can be established. The link of faith or commitment to God's design is a *sine qua non*, a prerequisite. Obedience and gratitude are major elements in this faith relationship and therefore Jesus links them together in his praise of the Samaritan who came back to thank him for his cure.

Being ungrateful or not meeting obligations and expectations is one way of disrupting social relations. Good social relations in turn are necessary for the proper running of a society. The Bible often calls bad social relations 'sin' and good social relations 'salvation.' Under the category of bad social relations the Bible has for instance the proscriptions of the Ten Commandments and the deadly sins of pride, covetousness, lust, anger, envy, gluttony and sloth. By good social relations we often understand altruism rather than selfishness, humility rather than arrogance, understanding rather than self-conceit, love rather than hatred, giving rather than receiving, self-restraint rather than self-indulgence.

We can also put this differently: good social relations can contribute to the common good, or the solidarity of one's community. Bad social relations usually disrupt a sense of belonging. When the Bible speaks about 'salvation', or wholeness, it often associates that with whatever builds up social cohesion and 'sin' when disorder or disruption is evident.

When the Bible says that God has created, and will continue to create, order out of chaos, there is a close correspondence with God encouraging whatever contributes to a healthy, well-oiled community. And conversely God discourages whatever takes away from the common good. Through faith in God we in turn contribute to the store of values and norms that consolidate a sense of belonging. In God all these expectations are summed up and personalized and through faith, if everything goes well, they are in turn internalized in our behaviour.

One of the problems of modern society is that patterns have been changing from one generation to the next. And this change is not just local but global. The children of my nieces and nephews in the Netherlands as well as our grandchildren in Canada, the USA and Australia are all carefully raised as little individuals with whom one reasons about all these norms and values mentioned above. Much time is taken by their parents to consciously instil in their offspring the set of attitudes leading to doing well at school, in sport and in their peer group. They usually say that certain kinds of behaviour are 'not acceptable' rather than wrong.

In our generation, however, discipline, rote learning and straight superimposition of these norms and values were more prominent, although love, affection and understanding were not less important. There is a subtle shift from the social to the self, from society orientation to individualism. Yet this point should not be misunderstood. 'Unacceptable behaviour' is nearly always behaviour that disrupts social or family relations.

All this is an introduction to understanding our text for today. Jesus expects gratitude, and rightfully so. After all, being rid of this crippling disease and the awful separation it caused from other citizens meant enormous change for all ten lepers. Yet nine of the ten took all this as a stroke of good luck that had come their way and for which they did not owe anybody any thanks. In other words the self was more central to them than Jesus or God.

By contrast Jesus felt that their healing should have been properly recognized as a gift from God whom they therefore should have praised. Physical integrity had won out over social obligation. The norm of gratitude was ignored to the detriment of the common good. The basic animal instinct of physical survival and health improvement had overcome their weaker sense of communal expectations and humbleness before God.

It is this contrast between the physical integrity innate in the self versus the loyalty to that which is beyond the self that is so prominent in the New Testament. St Paul again and again contrasts the 'flesh' as he calls it, (it is actually another word for the strong innate instinct for 'physical integrity') with the spiritual or loyalty to God and His Kingdom. Praising God in the Bible has precedence over concern for the body.

This is, of course, also Calvin's view. In the *Institutes of the Christian Religion* (III xx 28) he has a long section about thankfulness. To him thankfulness is a prerequisite in all prayers. It should be incorporated together with the prayers of adoration, supplication and intercession in all our communications with God.

What is his argument? It is the duty of believers to glorify and praise God, he says. 'God never ceases loading us with favour upon favour, so as to force us to gratitude, however slow and sluggish we may be.' This recognition should also give us a sense of guilt as He provides us with far more than we either deserve or can hope to get. (In parenthesis, it is again remarkable how closely this meshes with the enormous advantage in human history it has been for humans to learn to deny their physical integrity for the sake of a more robust social solidarity).

And if we don't like the cards existence has dealt us (and there is much pain, disorder, grief, disappointment and adversity) we still must remember God's love for us that will sustain and strengthen us. And this in itself is much cause for celebration and thankfulness.

To Calvin: 'God is the author of all good.' He curses those who confide only in themselves and disregard His will. 'We have no right to use the benefits proceeding from his liberality, unless we assiduously praise and thank Him.' God's kindness must also lead us to love Him although 'under the influence of moroseness, weariness, impatience, bitter grief, and fear we may murmur in our prayers.'

The mention of 'moroseness' in Calvin's observation made me think of his own poor personal health. He suffered from many ailments and just before he died in Geneva in 1565 at the relatively young age of 55 people described him as a walking corpse. Yet his indomitable spirit, enormous intelligence, his clear logical way of expressing himself, his unsurpassed learnedness stayed with him right until the very end.

Yet our text has more to say. It also mentions the foreigner, a Samaritan, who proved to be more thankful than the natives who took Jesus for granted. There is a lesson for us here too. Like them we take so much for granted that we forget to be grateful. We behave as though 'the favours', as Calvin called them, are not only our well-deserved patrimony, but inalienable rights.

We forget that almost anything that we are proud of is owed to previous generations. If we are proud of such diverse things as our freedom as well as our standard of living or our improved health record, we generally forget that we owe it entirely not to our personal contribution but to ancestors who fought for that freedom or to individuals who in the past built up the wealth of the nations, or denied themselves the consumption of their savings, but turned it into capital, or to inventors whose formidable minds discovered how to strengthen our immunity to disease.

Once you start making a list of what we owe to our culture, our society, our religious upbringing, the values of responsibility, reliability, kindness to others, instilled in us by our parents, our schools, our churches, the colossal list almost obliterates the incredible smallness of our individual contribution. Hopefully we feel obliged to pass these advantages to the next generations, but even here there is much room for more gratitude.

Just look around you in this church. Its impressive architecture, its stainedglass windows, the solemnity of its interior, the quality of its furniture, the inspiring music our organ produces, they are all the gifts of previous generations who could have selfishly used their hard-earned money for trips abroad or to extend their real estate or share-holdings rather than build this church.

And once we are embarked on listing our incredible dependence on others in the past or in the present, we should not forget the opportunities which have come our way, none of which are the result of our own doing or achievement. All of them are the result of the kind of society built for us in the past.

Where would you or I be if the free market economy, our democratic political institutions, our long established academic insistence on objectivity had not been sustained by past generations?

Let us just take one issue, as it is rather opportune in this season of both local and federal elections: our democratic institutions. There are still nations ruled by dictatorships or one-party monopolies outlawing opposition. In those countries religion is nearly always pressed into serving those in power. We may be alarmed at some of the unseemly smear tactics in yesterday's paper. Yet we are so much better off than fellow human beings in other countries where human rights are trampled and freedom of expression and religion don't exist.

Absolute power corrupts absolutely, whether it is in our political, economic, scientific, or any other system. Corruption anywhere is of course one of the destructive elements of human existence so well dramatized in the age-old story of the fall in Genesis 3. It has not only survived the rise and fall of civilizations, but is as relevant today as it has ever been. Our immense technical progress has in no way eclipsed the truth of Genesis 3, another item to be profoundly grateful for.

Our God is a just God (Deuteronomy 32:4) and therefore He utterly condemns abuse and corruption. That is one of the many ways that He creates order out of potential chaos. It also means that He is the God of all nations (Psalm 66:7, the Old Testament reading for today we did not use), whether he is called Jehovah by Jews, or God by Christians or Allah by Muslims.

Global justice cannot prevail if there is no universal penalty that can be implemented for injustices perpetrated by rogue nations. God and the Biblical traditions have time and again been used for reinforcing segmental identities, whether national, ethnic, or personal. This could remain unchallenged because often there are no arbiters or arbitrating institutions for these identities.

Fortunately this is changing now. The International Court of Justice in The Hague seems to have much more power than it had in the first half of the twentieth century. And the United Nations has also more clout than The League of Nations ever possessed.

All these developments, institutions and organizations transcending the local, ethnic and national identities make the monopolization of religion for their exclusive legitimation less likely. This is certainly to me an important item to be profoundly grateful for. The granting of the Nobel Peace Price yesterday to both the United Nations and its secretary Kofi Annan is a significant step in the right direction.

Yet there are other items on my long list of things transcending the narrow interest of my physical integrity often summed up in God. Can you imagine how bare and futile our lives would have been, and still are, without love, understanding, empathy, friendship, respect and fellowship of others? These too are summed up in God's being and as such remembered as 'eternal', 'sacred' and 'ever present.' All these have enriched our lives and made living an undeservedly pleasant experience.

I say 'undeserved' because the opposing elements, such as anger, suspicion, envy, arrogance, hatred, selfishness etc. have just as often marred those relations. Satan never seems to be far away when God lifts us above self-sufficiency and self-love.

There is one part of our text we have ignored so far. Jesus asks 'Could none be found to come back and give praise to God except this foreigner?' The implication is that the native Israelites took Jesus and his cure for granted and that only the foreigner from Samaria came back to praise God and thereby raised himself beyond self-satisfaction with his good luck. Jesus therefore praises him for his faith (Luke 17:19).

Jesus draws attention to the whole-making, or salvation by faith, not being confined to the nation of Israel. To him God's blueprint included other nations as well. He actually challenged his own nation to broaden their outlook by using the Samaritans as examples of charity (the famous parable of the Good Samaritan) and superior spirituality as in today's reading of Luke 17:11-19.

Israel was no exception to the general rule that foreigners can both disrupt a culture and contribute to its welfare through innovative and rational procedures. In Latin 'hostis' could mean both stranger and enemy. Yet in both China and Italy in earlier times only outsiders could be employed as officials and judges because of their greater objectivity.

All this is relevant as well for Australia with its large foreign-born population. On the one hand our faith requires us to be hospitable to strangers (Leviticus 19:33, 34 or 1 Peter 4:9), yet on the other hand it also insists on the unity of the nation under God. This means that indeed multiculturalism, an understanding and welcoming of foreigners is part of the Judaic, Christian and Islamic tradition. Yet it also means that once they are settled, immigrants are under obligation to fit with the ways of acting and reacting in their adopted country. It also means that unrestricted entrance of newcomers, refugees and asylum seekers runs the risk of jeopardizing the unity of the nation once the capacity of absorption has been exceeded.

We can learn from this passage of Luke that our gratitude for the large numbers of favours provided by God should be expressed continually, if only to keep a perspective on the large contribution previous generations have made and on the smallness of ours. It has also taught us that foreigners may help us to take our identity less for granted and therefore deepen our sense of gratitude for God's free gifts.

CALVIN 19

PEACE and POWER

May hills and mountains afford thy people peace. Psalm 72:3

Today is Epiphany Sunday. Epiphany means appearance and on this day the Bible readings deal with the three wise men from the East paying homage to the baby Jesus. They follow the star that they believe marks the birth of a new king of the Jews.

They arrive in Jerusalem, where they hope to get more information. Here they meet King Herod the Great (not to be confused with his son, also Herod, who had John the Baptist decapitated). Herod the Great was a rather paranoid and power hungry individual. He had ten wives and had at least one of them, together with her brother, grandfather and some of the children, murdered.

He was not Israelite by birth and had acquired the throne through his ability to raise taxes. He was not liked by his subjects and obviously did not feel very sure about his position. Naturally he feared potential rivals and pricked up his ears when he heard about the birth of a future king. And so he called a meeting of the chief priests and lawyers. They informed him that the Messiah, deliverer of the Hebrews, would be born in Bethlehem in the land of Judah, not far away.

Herod then sent the wise men to Bethlehem, asking them to report back to him, once they had found the child, 'so that I may go myself and pay him homage (Matthew 2:8).' They continue on their way, again guided by the star which 'stopped above the place where the child lay (verse 9).' They entered the house, found the child with his mother Mary, bowed to the ground and then offered him gifts of gold, frankincense (a white, aromatic, gum resin exuded from a tree, sometimes burned as incense) and myrrh (also a gum exuding from a bush-like tree and used as perfume).

After this they were warned in a dream not to go back to Herod and returned home another way (verse 12). This proved to be a very wise decision as it gave Mary and Joseph a chance to escape to Egypt before Herod could massacre 'all children in Bethlehem and its neighbourhood, of the age of two years or less, corresponding with the time he had ascertained from the astrologers (verse 16).'

The other reading for the day comes from Psalm 72:1-14. It pictures an idealized ruler, King David praying that his son (Solomon) may turn out to be such a king. He is not paranoid and cruel, as Herod, but fair and just. In verse one he is also described as righteous, which nowadays we would describe as 'having integrity.' And that integrity is often linked with piety and perfection.

Such a king is also deeply concerned with the poor, the needy and the oppressed (verse 2). He makes sure that peace prevails rather than war, prosperity rather than destitution. The psalmist compares such a king with 'rain falling on early crops, showers watering the earth (verse 6).'

What does Calvin have to say about today's readings?

The prayer of Psalm 72 asks God to give the king (Solomon) judgment and righteousness both of which, to Calvin, lead to well-regulated government in contrast 'to the tyrannical and unbridled license of heathen kings, who despising God, rule according to the dictates of their own will.' But, 'no government in the world can be rightly managed but under the conduct of God and by the guidance of the Holy Spirit.'

In his commentary on verse two Calvin elaborates why he thinks God is necessary for good government. One cannot just take the latter for granted. Also needed is 'the spiritual government of Christ by which all things are restored to perfect order.' Guided by that perfect order the poor and those who are oppressed unjustly are cared for. Only then peace will reign.

Peace, Calvin explains, does not only imply 'rest and tranquillity, but also prosperity.' For 'a happy life nothing is more desirable than peace; for amidst the turmoils and contentions of war, men derive almost no good from having an abundance of all things, as it is then wasted and destroyed.'

Peace is the native fruit of 'righteousness', all-pervasive justice that 'should be diffused through every part of the world.' Unless this 'spirit of righteousness' is perceived to come from heaven, government becomes 'a system of tyranny and robbery.' Without the God-given spirit of righteousness an increase in the power of an individual will be matched by oppression of the poor.

Yet a ruler can also be 'too gentle and forbearing. There is much truth in the old saying that it is worse to live under a prince through whose leniency everything is lawful, than under a tyrant where there is no liberty at all.' 'A holy and righteous government', Calvin concludes, 'will draw in its train true religion and the fear of God.' Perfect order is closely tied to the spiritual kingdom of Christ.

Psalm 72 has been used wrongly, according to Calvin, as a messianic pointer to the story of the three wise men in Matthew 2:1-12. The lectionary for today obviously has been composed with that idea in mind. Those who use this pointer, Calvin says, don't know their geography. The three kings bearing gifts (Psalm 72:10) came from the West and the South, not the East, from which the three wise men supposedly came (Matthew 2:1).

Yet that does not mean that Psalm 72:1-14 is not relevant for Matthew 2:1-12. In the latter also the Bible mentions a king (Herod the Great) who is too concerned with maintaining his personal power to be overly concerned with the wellbeing of his subjects.

Calvin suggests that there is a lesson to be learnt from the wise men 'adoring Christ in the stable where he lay amidst the tokens, not of honour, but of contempt.' Stripping the son 'of all earthly splendour' informs 'us that the kingdom is spiritual.' In other words, the Kingdom of God is qualitatively different from an earthly kingdom. It is as different as God's perfect order differs from the human mixture of order and disorder, or salvation differs from sin.

Herod trusted in his own power rather than God's. He was intoxicated with prosperity and man-made security and therefore pride had taken over from humility. The same with the people of Jerusalem who were also troubled (verse 3). 'For they were so completely worn down and almost wasted, by continued wars, that their wretched and cruel bondage appeared to them not only tolerable, but desirable, provided it were accompanied by peace.' Calvin characterizes the people of Jerusalem as 'unwilling to undergo any risk, and cared less about the grace of God than about the frown of a tyrant. The whole nation ... was so degenerate that they chose rather to be oppressed with the yoke of tyranny than to submit to any inconvenience arising from change.'

There are a number of things I always admire about Calvin.

(1) His admirable knowledge of the world around him and his broad vision. Yet that world was quite different from the one in which the many authors of the Bible lived. Their world in turn differed much from one another. Yet they had all the essentials of faith in God in common.

(2) Calvin's broad vision never restricted his Christian faith. If anything, his loyalty to the Bible strengthened it.

(3) His enormous intellect, his rational legal mind and his capacity to come up with apt quotes not only from other parts of the Bible, but also from the church fathers and the ancient philosophers.

With all this in mind, how can we make Psalm 72 and Matthew 2 relevant for our day and age?

If we are too swamped by, and impressed with, the differences between our various worlds, we might never get around to what holds us all together. And if that happens, not only will the essence of our Bible readings escape us, but we will also invariably make little gods, or little centres of commitment to the things of this world which are important for our daily living, but yet too tangible to have eternal significance.

Let us first agree about the ways our present world differs from Calvin's and the biblical authors. Then we can freely target the essentials that remain true for all ages, all situations and all cultures.

The massive explosion of technical knowledge and the even more intrusive global communication networks are certainly what would strike a visitor who lived 450 years ago as Calvin did, or 3000 years ago as the author of Psalm 72 may have or at least 1900 years ago as the author of Matthew did. All the things we take for granted, our cars, our planes, our trains, our radios, our refrigerators, our television sets, our electricity, our telephones all these could not even be imagined by any of the people mentioned. The knowledge of our universe, our planet, medicine, DNA, genetics, mind, body, nature, society, and culture would similarly have astounded them.

Not least is the increase in knowledge we now have of other religions, other denominations and how they have affected other countries and civilizations. Anything we want to know is at our finger tips on the internet. There is now infinitely more time and opportunity for at least ninety per cent of the developed world to spend time and energy on matters other than feeding oneself. And this allows for the massive explosion of knowledge and communication facilities.

Yet this explosion also evokes its opposite – a need for synthesis, for something that holds it all together. And this has not changed in the hundreds of years that separate us from Calvin, from Matthew and the psalmist. Human nature is still the same. There is still crime, oppression, poverty, anxiety, conflict, mental disease, hatred, and jealousy – some of the problems the good king of Psalm 72 was supposed to address and deal with.

Essentially what we do in this service and in all services, is to pay homage, to worship God who addresses the problems of an unchanging human nature. We also listen to scripture, the story of the fall and original sin. We listen to the word of God who represents the stabilizing antidote, or as Calvin called it in his commentary on Psalm 72, 'perfect order. '

This is also what we have in common with all those individuals just mentioned, Bible authors and theologians. We may differ enormously from them in our manner of living, but we have God and his consistent and insistent creation of order out of chaos, light out of darkness, salvation out of sin, in common. And, if anything we may need God's power here even more than they did.

The illusion that human power can now decide its own destiny is now stronger than ever, has made our hubris and pride all the more threatening and potentially disastrous. Man's overestimation of his power is equalled by his persistent underestimation of the unacknowledged need for a vision of God's 'perfect order.'

Yet this need is not just academic and abstract. It can also be expressed in concrete form. How relevant is all that we have learnt today from scripture for our daily living, our national and international existence? I will attempt to answer this question under the following three headings: (1) our increasingly more global order; (2) our relations with other denominations and other Christians; (3) the knowledge explosion.

(1) The global economic, scientific and political order is all around us. This order is just as much in need of God's blessing and stabilizing spirit, if not more so, than our personal, communal, civic, national order. Granted, it tends to proceed under its steam and impetus. Yet it fits just as much in God's larger, 'perfect order' design. It may be just as proximate (or 'imperfect') as the others, but Psalm 72 and Matthew 20 explicitly speak about other nations, or representatives of those nations paying homage to God and Jesus as the originators, curtain raisers, of a new dispensation for the entire world.

This global order and its economic, scientific and political institutions may have some sort of soul, or unifying centre of commitment, but it seems rather weak. If those unifying centres or souls are under-developed, they must be strengthened if they are to survive. Actually this is what Christianity and other religions have done traditionally with the other kinds of order, our personal, family, ethnic, national souls. Our Christian prayers have always supported them. The emerging global order should be just as much the subjects of Christian prayer and scrutiny. It is just as much in need of the gift of God's justice and righteousness as the king in Psalm 72. And this is particularly true, if it is a way station to God's heavenly kingdom, heavenly peace and perfect order.

(2) The universality of God's love, understanding and promise of salvation must also extend to our acceptance of the intense knowledge explosion of other denominations and religious organizations. Behind their organizational wizardry shelters much similarity which should not be dismissed out of hand. Nor should it lead us to a search for a shallow common denominator which often sacralizes secular structures localizing and inhibiting rather than universalizing God's perfect order.

Here Calvin's injunction to open the eyes of our mind (when commenting on Matthew 20:21) is very pertinent. Certainly the entire New Testament is testimony to both Jesus and Paul insisting on lifting religion beyond narrow ethnic boundaries to the wide universal vistas of God's blueprint.

If memory serves me well, the many ecumenical efforts at the beginning of last century in Australia were thwarted by the desire of the various denominations (usually of ethnic origin) to maintain the boundaries around their own organizations. The Baptists who were originally included in those efforts bowed out because they were not interested in the unity of organizations, only in the organic unity of Christian believers. For the latter, organizations were only means to the end of being organs for God's spirit.

Organization versus organism. Proximate order versus perfect order. God is interested in both and gives both his blessing. Yet the former has an auxiliary rather than essential character. The former is part of the mundane necessity to survive the here and now. It is intermediate. By contrast the latter is transcendental and intangible. It deals with an ultimate blueprint for existence or the heavenly kingdom, as Jesus called it.

The peace that he both promised and represented is a by-product of that spiritual order. On the other hand the inequality of power is a much more ad hoc, transitory, spasmodic way of infusing order in a viable society. Yet, as we have seen in Psalm 72, the spiritual kingdom infuses the earthly kingdom with a break on power abuse through its expectation of justice, righteousness and integrity.

Cutting ourselves off from other Christians tends to reinforce and even idolize mundane, organizational boundaries at the expense of the potential impact of the universal message of Christian salvation. Both Jesus and Paul penetrated the exclusive bonds of the Hebrew understanding of God's kingdom and replaced it with an inclusive appeal to the gentiles.

One can also put this in another way. Organization of any kind is always a means towards an end that needs protection, expansion or consideration. It should not be underestimated. It is an important way to guarantee the survival of that particular end. Yet it should not be confused with that end. It assists, but cannot take the place of whatever it assists. So it is with our churches and ecclesiastical organizations. They are necessary, but cannot take the place of the message of salvation.

Our Australian denominational structures reflect the ecclesiastical organizations of those countries from which our original colonists and immigrants came, England, Scotland, Ireland, Poland, Italy, Greece, the Netherlands, etc. They are part of our heritage. Yet they should not be treated as exclusive islands of veneration. That veneration should be reserved for religious content which happens to be very inclusive indeed. After all it deals with the 'perfect order', or the kingdom of God that Calvin spoke about.

There is this somewhat irreverent, yet delightfully humorous story about St Peter guiding a group of visitors who were curious about the precincts of heaven. The group came to a big wall and St Peter asked them politely not to speak and tiptoe around the structure. When they had passed it, they asked him what was behind the wall. 'Oh', said St Peter, 'they are the Fundamentalist Presbyterians and we don't want to destroy their illusion that they are the only ones in heaven.'

Of course, the story can be adjusted to other kinds of fundamentalism, or indeed to any other kind of exclusive belief, such as atheism or liberalism. When I tell the story I usually insert one or other of the Dutch denominations to which I have either belonged or for whom I have a deep respect. The story helps at least me, and I hope some of you, to appreciate the inclusive rather than the exclusive inclinations of the Christian churches. Exclusivity moves too much in the direction of divisive earthly power at the expense of the heavenly kingdom and 'the way of peace' into which Jesus 'guides our feet (Luke 1:79).'

(3) The three wise men from the East represented the knowledge, learning and philosophy of their age. They came to worship, as Calvin said, 'Christ in the stable where he lay amidst the tokens, not of honour, but of contempt.' They humbly worshipped not their own knowledge, but the wider context in which this knowledge was placed. And this wider context had a dimension which the rational mind could not fathom because it was restricted to the self-justifying canons of reason and objectivity. It has to do with simple acceptance and humble reverence rather than self-sufficiency and arrogant bigotry.

This spirit is well represented in the motto of my own university (McMaster in Canada) which runs as follows: *Ta Panta En Christoi Sunesteken* which is Greek for 'In Christ everything hangs together.' It is based on a statement in St Paul's Letter to the Ephesians (1:10). Like all other universities it gathers all knowledge in numerous departments and even more numerous research projects, adding to the knowledge explosion I have mentioned before.

Although McMaster, like most universities in Canada, started out as a religious institution, there is nothing less true than that all knowledge is held together in Christ. Like any other university in the world it assembles knowledge on a large scale without even attempting to unite it all. As I have said before, modern universities represent an exploding fire ball familiar with New Year's Eve fireworks. But most of that knowledge seems to have been lost in space.

What the three wise men from the East represent is an acknowledgment that the cohesion necessary for survival of the inorganic, the organic and the social must be found somewhere else. Reason and objectivity on their own, don't seem to fill the bill of comprehension. Other dimensions of living, such as love, loyalty, faith, commitment are some of the elements equally necessary to make existence whole.

The three wise men found this other dimension in a manger in an inconspicuous inn in Bethlehem. It is here that earthly power and knowledge is depicted as maybe a necessity for proximate order, but not for something as ultimate as 'perfect order.' Here they found the Prince of Peace, as he is called in Isaiah 9:6. Maybe that is where we should look as well, if we are interested in living life to the full. And as we shall sing later in Hymn 448:

> Christ does call
> One and all:
> Ye who follow shall not fall

CALVIN 20

ABUSE of RELIGION

Scripture says: 'My house shall be called a house of prayer, but you are making it a cave of robbers.' Matthew 21:13

Jeremiah lived from approximately 650 BC to 570 BC, when according to tradition he was stoned to death in Egypt for upsetting his exasperated fellow exiles. Now upsetting people was a bit of a hallmark for Jeremiah. He was born in Anatoth, a village two miles north-east of Jerusalem. His father, Hilkiah, was the local priest.

The Lord called him to prophesy in the thirteenth year of King Josiah's reign which must have been in the year 626 BC, when Jeremiah would have been in his early twenties. The event of his calling is described in the first chapter of the book named after him. Jeremiah does not like the call and says: 'Ah, Lord, God! Behold I do not know how to speak, for I am only a youth (verse 6).' But 'the Lord put forth his hand and touched my mouth; and the Lord said to me, 'Behold I have put my words in your mouth (verse 9). I have set you this day over nations and over kingdoms, to pluck up and to break down, to destroy and to overthrow, to build and to plant (verse 10).'

Unfortunately, the Lord was not always pleased with his people and so Jeremiah often caught the brunt of God's displeasure and had to faithfully transmit to the Hebrews why He was upset and what had to be changed in order to get back into His favour. Plucking up and breaking down, destroying and overthrowing, building and planting were not always pleasant business. No wonder Jeremiah's utterances received a rather mixed reception. And today's prophesies about the abuse of God's house (it being made into 'a cave of robbers') is certainly not an exception.

As long as King Josiah was on the throne of Judah, the Lord and Jeremiah as his spokesman had little to complain about, but when Jehoiakim succeeded his father in 609 BC the rot set in. Our Old Testament reading for today, Jeremiah 7:1-20, shows God's displeasure. Apparently the king and the people felt that attending the temple in Jerusalem was all that was necessary to be saved and forgiven. After superficial worship they apparently had no qualms 'doing all these abominations (verse 10)' all over again.

Jeremiah lists these abominations: stealing, murdering, adultery, swearing falsely, burning incense to Baal, and going after other gods (verse 9). Then he uses the text for today: 'My house shall be called a house of prayer, but you are making it a cave of robbers (verse 11).' For good measure he adds the warning: 'Go to my shrine at Shiloh, which once I made a dwelling for my name, and see what I did to it because of the wickedness of my people Israel (verse 12).'

In the early nomadic period of existence Shiloh had been the place where the ark (the centre of worship travelling with the Israelites) had been stationed. It had been captured by the Philistines while in the safekeeping of the wicked sons of Eli. The point of the comparison is that both the temple and the ark were pointers to, and symbols of, a source of prayer and inner motivation rather than pieces of wood and stone with intrinsic sacred value.

And that seems to be the crux of today's Old Testament reading: the tragedy of human existence and a major source of men's temptation is the inevitable propensity of humans to invest emotions and commitments in what is concrete and discernible. The Bible struggles again and again (the golden calf in Exodus 32:4 is another good example) with the problem as to how humans can learn to lift their sights beyond the immediate and the tangible to the intangible and the cosmic.

This is also the central issue in today's New Testament reading, Matthew 21:10-17. In his little speech at the temple Jesus actually borrows Jeremiah's metaphor of the robber's cave. The purpose of the temple to direct humans to God is sidetracked to make room for the very mundane efforts of the money-changers and the pigeon salesmen to make money. Jesus is indignant, upsets their tables and other gear and chases them out of the temple precincts and says: 'Scripture says; My house shall be called a house of prayer, but you are making it a robber's cave (Matthew 21:13).'

Again the transcendent is sacrificed for the immanent, the cosmic for the immediate, the heavenly for the earthly, and the austere for the indulgent. To Jesus the temple, like the ark before and the church in our day and age, is the house of God. It is to be revered not because of what it is made of, but of what it points to. Jesus appears to think that the human need for boundary is to be countered by openness to God's presence and influence.

What does Calvin say about today's readings and particularly our text? Times have not changed much, he says. What were called the ark and the temple in those days are the churches of today. Satan's intention to corrupt has in no way diminished. There were just as many 'hypocrites' within their walls then as there are now. And the problem is that by worshipping the wood of a chest (the ark) or the brick and mortar of a temple or a church, worshippers allow 'themselves greater liberty in sinning.'

And what is the sin these hypocrites commit? They ignore 'the design of God to employ outward symbols for instructing the Jews in true religion' and by doing so they satisfy 'themselves with empty pretence.' And he adds that it is not enough 'to give attention to outward ceremonies' backing his opinion with a quote from Paul's letter to the Romans (1:25) that these hypocrites and godless have changed 'the truth of God into a lie.'

To Calvin 'a cave of robbers' is a 'metaphor of all corruptions.' And Christ's chasing the sellers of pigeons and the money-lenders from the temple precincts were his attempt to restore 'the reverence and majesty of the temple.' Purifying the temple to prevent its profanation is the way St John (2:16) describes the act of Jesus. To Calvin the purpose of the temple is 'to be a shadow of those things the lively image of which is to be found in Christ. That it might continue to be devoted to God, it was necessary that it should be applied exclusively to spiritual purposes.'

These purposes are also cosmic, intent for the entire human race, not just for the Jewish nation, according to Calvin. God's order is universal. According to St Mark's record of the event, Jesus quotes Isaiah 56:7 that the temple is a house of prayer for all nations and Calvin remarks that hypocrites may be excluded; but foreigners and strangers who were formerly excluded are now included 'so that henceforth the distinction between circumcision and uncircumcision shall be abolished.' Gentiles are now 'united to the Jews so as to form one body … the assembly of believers.' They are reconciled to one another and enjoy 'the peace of conscience which Paul ascribes to the Kingdom of God (Romans 14:17) and which we enjoy when we are reconciled to God by Christ (Romans 5:1).'

Still on abuse and corruption of religion and the church, Calvin has some interesting observations in his commentary on 1 Corinthians 1:10-13, where Paul addresses himself to conflicts and divisions in the Church of Corinth. Paul accuses the congregation of splitting itself into parties crystallized around leading personalities, such as Apollos and Cephas and exhorts the Christians to unite around Christ rather than flesh and blood followers.

Calvin comments that these divisions are 'the fountain of all evils', 'the most hurtful of all plagues', 'the deadly poison of all churches.' They violate the most sacred of bonds. They 'tear Christ asunder.' They are 'the most destructive enemies of our faith.' If these leaders 'do not adhere to Christ alone – that very thing would make them covenant breakers.'

By contrast, 'harmony of affections' should prevail. Christian unity consists of 'fitting and suitably joined together … just as the members of the human body are connected together by a most admirable symmetry.' Religion is a most powerful force 'to unite us.' Yet 'on the other hand, if any disagreement has arisen as to matters of this nature … in no other department are there fiercer battles.'

Calvin's realism about human behaviour also leads him to think that humans cannot achieve perfection in even the most sacred of duties, such as witnessing to salvation through faith in Christ. Yet organization is necessary and so Calvin feels that Christians can at least strive for minimal conflict. Therefore he suggests a system of checks and balances, whereby the power of leadership is checked by 'common consent (*Inst.* IV iv 2).' Yet one has to be careful, 'lest as usually happens, from equality dissension can arise' and therefore elders and presbyters should be appointed. Yet they should always be individuals whose genuine humility must surpass any ambitions they may have.

The real issue that both the readings from Jeremiah and Matthew are grappling with is the enshrining of religion, the embedding of basic religious/spiritual ideas in concrete structures. The perpetual temptation is not just to assign equal value and commitment to these structures, but to actually assign more value and faith to their embodiment than to the core of those religious/spiritual ideas.

And when I mention 'enshrinement' and 'embeddedness' I do not just mean the wooden box or ark carried around by the ancient Hebrews to the promised land or the stone temple they built once they settled in Canaan. I also mean the necessary boundaries erected around the specifics of their faith. I say 'necessary' because our Christian faith needs bolstering through a context of transcendent order. It needs commitment and loyalty of fellow believers. It needs the protection of ritual retracing the grooves of order. It needs the acting out of the conflict between tradition and change.

Yet these necessary boundaries can readily become what our text for today calls 'a cave of robbers' by which first Jeremiah, then Jesus, quoting him, and Calvin interpreting both, meant a replacement of core elements by human needs for concretization and enshrining, as though these needs can comprehensively and conclusively explain what man's religion is all about.

They are all necessary and yet only a help, an adjunct, to the pivot of faith around which our most basic commitment and motivation turns. These needs put men's thoughts and constructions at the centre of creation and thereby prematurely and erroneously enclose God in a man-made box and isolate ourselves from the openness of the heaven where God actually dwells.

Reduction to human needs is a very contemporary corruption of our faith in Jesus Christ as Lord and saviour. And not just individual needs but also social as distinct from individual needs tend just as much, if not more, to succumb to the temptation to abuse religion, to direct rather than serve. The flesh, as St Paul and Calvin insist on pointing out, may be an anti-social kind of corruption or a 'robber's cave', but then society as such has its own temptations of tearing down the heavenly for the earthly by sacralizing the idols of human achievements and self-sufficiency.

There are many examples. The burning of a mosque by Hindus in India; the massacres of Christians by Muslims in Indonesia and the Sudan; the conflicts between Catholics and Protestants in Northern Ireland; the destruction of Buddha statues in Afghanistan; the killings during the Crusades in Europe. Essentially these are travesties resulting from faith in the concrete representations of a religion rather than from commitment to the explicit teachings and the implicit symbols of those religions. The latter (the symbols) are invariably non-violent. They invariably stress self-denial rather than commitment to the organizational boundaries of those religions. The former (the enshrinements and conflicts) sometimes become the corruptions which our text today calls a robber's cave. They all rob the religious message of its real intent.

This is also true for the supreme sacrifices of young Muslims destroying themselves in New York and Jerusalem. The causes for which they self-destruct are invariably the hatred of an economic system such as capitalism or the hatred of another race, such as Jews. In other words it is the hatred for mundane structures rather than the contribution their death makes to the pure order at the heart of their respective religious organizations. It confuses enshrinement with the content of what it enshrines. It confuses the embeddedness of faith with faith itself.

Actually to think about individual, organizational and social needs as 'abuse' is maybe too strong a term. All three are both inevitable, unavoidable, closely linked to human survival and therefore necessary. Yet in Christianity they may also narrow the Biblical vision. They can lead to replacing the centrality of God with the centrality of human needs and endeavour. Or to put it differently, they may prematurely lock out God's pure order, immortality and omniscience from an instinctive, human, inward-looking faith in the concrete, tangible and mundane. They may very well make the ark, the temple and the church into a 'cave of robbers.'

The fall and original sin is the concept that the Bible uses to sum up the corruptions symbolized by 'the cave of robbers.' Original sin is deeply embedded in human existence. So deeply, in fact, that only an extraordinary measure proved necessary to rescue humans from its grip. This extraordinary measure, the Bible says, is the incarnation, God coming to man in Jesus Christ, to show that even in this mortal vale of tears sinlessness can exist.

The story of the purification of the temple as recorded in Matthew 21 took place after Jesus had triumphantly entered Jerusalem and just before his crucifixion. The crowds had hailed him as 'the prophet from Nazareth in Galilee (Matthew 21:11)', but the chief priests and the elders of the nation 'wanted to arrest him, but they were afraid of the people, who looked on Jesus as a prophet (Matthew 21:46).'

Jesus, like the prophets before him, stood for liberation, the opening of the heart to God's message of salvation. By contrast the priests stood for the status quo and the implicit petrifaction and routinization of religion. Jeremiah was stoned to death, John the Baptist decapitated and Jesus crucified for denouncing the religious and mundane status quo.

Religion had become denigrated to what fitted society and influential individuals within it. It had become nothing but a reflection of the human need for man's control of his existence. For Jesus that control was in God's hand rather than in men's. Yet that also meant, as the apostles, the church fathers and in our case Calvin, understood so well, that faith and commitment were more than man-made projections.

Where does all this realism, all this confrontation with our imperfections, all this awareness of sin even penetrating into the heart of our sacred religious institutions leave us? To me a sermon presents only half the picture if it confines itself to the realism of human nature. After all, the gospel is good news. It is the 'euangelion', the story of the evangelists. And to come to the good part counterbalancing the perplexing, negative one, we have to go back to our Bible readings.

And the good news is explicit in both the books of Jeremiah and the Gospel of St Matthew chapter 21. They speak not only about the robber's cave and the corruptions for which the cave is a metaphor. They also mention God's determination to rescue existence from these corruptions. They speak about God's guidance beyond the mundane and concrete. They give us a vision of God's pure order beyond the human disorder.

Jeremiah, after decrying false religion and warning the Hebrews of God's punishment, also says that God will not 'disregard his people (Jeremiah. 9:7)' and will continue to 'show unfailing love (Jeremiah 9:24).' Later God says through Jeremiah as his mouth piece: 'But if the nation which I have threatened turns back from its wicked ways, then I shall think better of the evil I had in mind to bring on it (Jeremiah 18:8).' Or further in Jeremiah 29:12, 13: 'If you invoke me and pray to me, I will listen to you. When you seek me, you shall find me.'

And in the New Testament in the same chapter 21 of St Matthew's gospel verse 42, God is not just represented as the one who rejects man's corruptions. Much more positively he also provides 'the main cornerstone' on which his kingdom is erected. There is a foundation stronger than man's squandering and disobedience. That cornerstone and foundation is Jesus Christ in whose name sins of corruption can be forgiven and expunged. Man's impurity has not undone God's purity. On the contrary, the latter is both stronger and more enduring.

CALVIN 21
MARTYRDOM and SELF-DENIAL

So they stoned Stephen, and as they did so, he called out, 'Lord Jesus, receive my spirit.' Then he fell on his knees and cried aloud, 'Lord, do not hold this sin against them' and with that he died. Acts 7:59-60

Stephen was a foreigner in Jerusalem. He belonged to a group of Greek-speaking Jews who were born outside Israel but had decided to resettle in their religious home, the centre of Judaism, Jerusalem. In their host country Jews often had to live on the margin of society, neither belonging nor totally accepted. They were often discriminated against because of their religion. What was more natural than to return to the mother country, its temple and the core of what was most precious to them, their belief in, and worship of, Jehovah? Yet when they arrived in Jerusalem, they soon discovered that they were now regarded as foreigners in Israel. Their native language was Greek, not Hebrew or Aramaic.

And then they discovered John the Baptist and Jesus, men who did not discriminate, but were full of the Holy Spirit. The enthusiasm of Pentecost infected them and warmed their hearts. The alienation they had felt evaporated as by magic. They felt as one with both the authentic Jews, such as Peter and the other disciples, but also with other foreigners present at the occasion. The Holy Spirit transcended the barriers of language and united all those present.

Yet even amongst that first band of Christians the sense of belonging and unity had begun to weaken. Just preaching the good news of salvation had not been enough. People also had to eat and particularly the widows of the Greek speaking Jews (they were usually called 'Hellenists') had been starving and had not been given their fair share of the handouts. Therefore a meeting of all followers of Christ was called and a committee of seven Hellenists was appointed to rectify the situation.

They were called 'deacons', Greek for servers, almoners. Nowadays we would call them welfare workers. They were put in charge of the fair distribution of gifts for the needy. This would free the disciples to concentrate on evangelism.

Stephen was to be the first and most prominent of the deacons. He stood out in the crowd of Christians partly because of his eloquence and strong Christian conviction, but mainly because he represented what nowadays would be called 'charismatic leadership', those who inspire. He felt at home with the Hellenists, but he was also thoroughly acquainted with the Hebrew heritage. This was clearly shown in the speech he made before the Sanhedrin, the powerful Supreme Court of Jerusalem.

Charismatic leadership often forms a bridge between contrasting cultures. Stephen was such a leader and could interpret each group to the other while simultaneously rescuing the most vulnerable group from oblivion. Charismatic leaders usually inject new vitality in downhearted groups such as the Hellenistic Jews. They inspire new religions, such as early Christianity, emotionally stripping old patterns and welding their followers to new ones.

There was a tradition of charismatic leadership in Israel. The prophets had usually been inspiring individuals. The Biblical vocabulary of the authors was not large enough to call it charismatic leadership and so it was described differently in Exodus 34:29. Moses' skin is described as shining 'because he had been speaking with the Lord.' In the New Testament (Luke 9:29) the face of Jesus is described as having changed while he was praying to the Lord. Moses, Jesus and Stephen had become magnets to their followers, all inspired by the contagious faith in the Lord.

The speech of Stephen elaborately recorded in Chapter Seven of the Book of Acts was his defence against the accusation that he had slandered God's temple and the Law of Moses. He had been hauled before the Sanhedrin, where he showed his intricate knowledge of Jewish history and its fit with his Christian conviction. The disciples had more or less said the same thing, but being authentic and born locally they were protected by public opinion. By contrast Stephen was more vulnerable. The Greek speaking Jews were regarded as strangers and therefore the Sanhedrin, hostile to the new sect, hoped that by bringing Stephen into disrepute it would undermine the entire Christian movement.

Stephen established his credentials by beginning his defence with the importance of Abraham, Joseph and Moses. He followed this up with the story of David and Solomon. All very correct and acceptable, but then finished very controversially (Acts 7:51-53): 'You always fight against the Holy Spirit. Like fathers, like sons. Was there ever a prophet whom your father did not persecute? They killed those who foretold the coming of the Righteous One; and now you have betrayed him and murdered him, you have received the Law as God's angels gave it to you and yet have not kept it.'

This touched the priests and other members of the Sanhedrin 'on the raw and they ground their teeth with fury (Acts 7:54).' But Stephen was unperturbed. He was filled with the Holy Spirit and said: 'I can see the Son of Man standing at God's right hand (verse 56).' This was obviously too much for his accusers. They stopped their ears, 'flung him out of the city and set about stoning him (verse 58).'

Then follows our text for today: 'So they stoned Stephen, and as they did so, he called out 'Lord Jesus receive my spirit.' Then he fell on his knees and cried aloud, 'Lord, do not hold this sin against them', and with that he died.'

What does Calvin have to say about this episode?

He sees it as a conflict between God, represented by Stephen, and Satan, represented by the Sanhedrin. Stephen has the eye of his mind so strongly on Jesus that not even the cruel and extremely painful death through stoning could affect his faith. The Sanhedrin consists of 'the adversaries of the word' whom Satan has stricken 'with madness.' They are 'raging enemies, oppressing the goodness of his cause, partly with false accusations and malice, partly with violence and outcries.' By contrast Stephen surrounded by hostility and cruelty on 'every side, destitute of man's help, turns to God.'

Calvin interprets Stephen's prayers as the acme, the pinnacle and culmination of godliness. In the first one (commending his spirit to Christ, verse 59) he 'does not lean on the judgment of the flesh, but rather assures himself, even in very destruction, that he shall be saved and suffers death with a quiet mind.' In the second one (praying to the Lord not to hold this sin against his enemies (verse 60) he admires Stephen for not indulging in revenge, but showing what 'affection he bears toward all other men.'

Stephen does not waver, but clings to the very understanding so typical of Jesus on the cross who also prayed: 'Father forgive them, for they do not know what they are doing (Luke 23:34).' Understanding one's enemies and murderers and not seeking revenge for their palpable injustice shows a wideness of spirit which is from God rather than man.

Calvin quotes Augustine writing 'that unless Stephen had prayed the Church should not have had Paul.' It was Paul who (verse 58) looked after the clothes of the witnesses who participated in the stoning but was later converted on the road to Damascus. Calvin feels that Augustine's statement is a bit strong, but admits 'that Stephen's prayer was not in vain.' Or to put it differently in our own terms, Stephen's charisma had its effect on Paul who not only had a similar background (he too was a Greek speaking Jew born outside in Tarsus, Cilicia) but similarly enthused by the Holy Spirit unstintingly built the various communities of believers all over the Mediterranean basin until he himself was executed.

Calvin, intellectually as fair-minded as ever, then brings up the awkward question of the Sanhedrin justifying the stoning in scripture. Chapter 13 of Deuteronomy deals with stoning as punishment of false prophets. Were those who stoned him sincerely convinced that Stephen and the early Christians were a collection of 'false prophets?' Calvin's answer: 'The stoning of Stephen was both unjust and also wicked, because he was unjustly condemned … it is the cause alone which makes the difference; but this difference is so highly esteemed before God and his angels, that the reproaches of the martyrs do far excel all glory of the world.'

Calvin's stress on the cause as a critical factor in martyrdom helps us to answer the topical question as to the difference between the Christian martyrs and the young Muslim ones who recently destroyed themselves for what they believed was a holy cause. To them the WTO Towers in New York were a monument of evil capitalism and the Israeli enemies who occupied the land that had belonged to their forefathers. And they believed that Allah would reward them for their self-sacrifice.

The difference is that the Christians martyrs died for their faith in a saviour whereas the Muslims died for a partisan principle of political self-determination. Identification with Jesus versus identification with a local cause. Jesus stood and stands for a transcendental system of meaning. The young suicide bombers stood and stand for the concrete mundane goal of winning a power game between nations.

God is a God of universal justice rather than a local warlord applying different standards of justice according to the local boundaries of one's bailiwick or one's base of power. God encourages global rather than local order if that is the difficult choice. One of the fundamental differences between the Old and the New Testament is that the former tends to sacralize an ethnic identity but the latter a universal one. Jesus and Paul burst the narrower boundaries of national justice, thereby promoting a global one. Jesus is the prince of peace rather than a partisan in a local squabble.

Therefore the questions become: does martyrdom caused by witnessing to Jesus or witnessing to Allah have practical consequences for more mundane goals? Does the faith in question lead to a better society or culture? Does 'walking with Jesus' or alternately defence of one's territorial aspirations and clashes or economic ideology get us closer to the pure order both God and Allah ultimately represent? Does martyrdom fits God's creation of pure order out of human disorder? Does the martyrdom in question aggravate or advance global peace and justice and relations between nations? Is giving one's life for a noble cause different for Stephen and the many Christian martyrs after him as compared with the Muslim suicide bombers?

There is quite a difference. The former advances global order whereas the other puts that order in greater jeopardy. The early Christian martyrs made a difference to culture. They reinforced universal standards of justice for everyone. Their extreme self-denial to the point of self-sacrifice carried in its wake a host of implicit examples for improving the quality and cohesion of their society and culture. Their Lord and saviour represented gentle understanding, integrity and above all reinforcements of those values and norms making for a saner and safer society. Global order is not advanced by hatred for other nations or hatred for their economic systems, but by understanding, empathy and love for one another.

This is the big difference between the Christian martyrs, of which Stephen was the first and foremost and the present day Islamic suicide bombers: the former, following Jesus, rather turned the cheek spreading peace and mutual understanding. By contrast the latter did the opposite. They stand for revenge. Their salvation is in aggressive defence and aggravating division and conflict. Stephen's martyrdom, by contrast stands for embodiment and identification with Jesus and what he stood for. The Christian martyrs represented a noble cause. The Islamic suicide bombers characterize a narrower and therefore ignoble cause, national/ethnic advantage at the expense of peace and justice for all.

The early Christian martyrs were the seed of the church. They also perpetuated the old tradition of preventing the priestly heritage from ossifying culture and society and keeping the change-oriented prophetic tradition not only legitimate, but also alive. It was centred on a person, the Messiah, who represented in his acting, living and dying, self-denial and self-sacrifice, the pure order, his Father had in mind for all mankind.

Our other reading for today (1 Peter 2:1-10) elaborates that theme. It gives details of the cause, which to Stephen was so precious that he was prepared to lay down his life for it. It is Peter's letter to the small communities of Christians in Asia Minor, now Turkey. They were often people like Stephen: Greek-speaking Jews who had maintained their Jewish beliefs in a foreign land far away from Jerusalem.

Being marginal in their host country the message of the suffering Christ appealed to them. They suffered too. They did not altogether belong in their pagan communities and yet they had invariably adopted some of the culture of their surrounding, such as the Greek language. Jesus, the crucified prophet, was a figure with whom they could identify. More importantly they could accept him as the central divine figure around which their unifying faith could take shape and be the core of their motivation and values.

That's why Peter's imagery of living stones (verse 5) building the spiritual temple around Jesus as the cornerstone appealed to them. They were the 'living stones' constructing through their faith a stable frame of reference in a less than stable and comfortable environment. Through bearing witness to the saviour they made a dignified place for themselves in a less than accepting and yet also dissipated dissolute pagan community. Their inspired dynamism, typical for the Old Testament prophets, fitted the suspicion of a religious, priestly, establishment, smugly convinced of their superiority.

With any luck the witnessing of these early Christians in Galatia, Pontus, Bothynia, Cappadocia, and Asia might attract their neighbours, curious as to the source of their exemplary acting and living. But Peter warns them, this potential for Christian growth will not come about when they think about themselves as 'establishment', people resting on their laurels of respectability, but as individuals still growing in faith and 'like newborn infants craving for pure milk (spiritual milk, I mean), so that you may thrive upon it to your souls' health (verse 2).'

This is also the theme that Calvin stresses in his commentary on these passages. He actually translates the verses one and two as saying: 'Malice and hypocrisy belong to those who are habituated to the corruptions of the world; they have imbibed these vices; what pertains to infancy is sincere simplicity, free from all guile. Men, when grown up, become imbued with envy, they learn to slander one another, they are taught the arts of mischief; in short, they become hardened in every kind of evil: infants, owing to their age, do not yet know what it is to envy, to do mischief, or the like of things.'

There is more. Peter in this section of his letter (verse 6) mentions that these 'living stones' or dedicated Christians also 'offer spiritual sacrifices to God through Jesus Christ' What does he mean by 'spiritual sacrifices?' Peter believes that 'visual sacrifices' such as those of animals are less important than heartfelt dedication of the worshipper in God's kingdom. And that meant self-denial or close identification with Jesus the crucified saviour, 'the image of the invisible God (Colossians. 1:15).'

Self-denial is the first concept that comes to mind when we think about Stephen. Yet it is also a prerequisite for whatever creates the healthy solidarity of a community to which it is a privilege to belong.

Calvin devotes a whole chapter (*Inst*. III vii) to what he calls 'a summary of the Christian life, self-denial.' The Christian life he says can be summed up in being owned by Christ 'so that man himself no longer lives, but Christ lives and reigns in him (Galatians. 2:20).'

'For when scripture enjoins us to lay aside private regard for ourselves, it not only divests our minds of an excessive longing for wealth, or power, or human favour, but eradicates all ambition and thirst for worldly glory and other more secret pests.' And in section two of that chapter Calvin says: 'Deny yourself, renounce your own reason, and direct your whole mind to the pursuit of those things which the Lord requires of you, and which you are to seek only because they are pleasing to him.'

There are practical, social consequences of this self-denial. It leads to sobriety, puts us on the road of pilgrimage to perfection. It leads to humility and modesty, respect for others, all leading to the 'common good', 'the good of our neighbour.' 'In this way only we attain to what is not to say difficult, but against nature, to love those that hate us, render good for evil, and blessing for curse, remembering that we are not to reflect on the wickedness of men, but look to the image of God in them, an image which, covering and obliterating their faults, should by its beauty and dignity allure us to love and embrace them. (*Inst*. III vii 6).'

This capacity for self-denial 'makes a way through all obstacles, and brings everything to a joyful and favourable issue.' Resigning oneself entirely to the Lord leads to 'tranquillity and endurance' and extends 'to all the accidents to which this present life is liable (*Inst*. III vii 10).'

There is an intriguing, fascinating, similarity between our present society and the ones that are addressed in Peter's first letter. Our society too is scattered (1 Peter 1:1). It too is torn by 'dog eat dog' factions, obsessed by adversarial coldness and rampant individualism. The balance between too much individualism and too much conformity is presently broken. There is too much of the former and not enough of the latter. More self denial, as Peter suggests may advance the health of our soul (1 Peter 2:2).

The tendency towards political and religious conservatism in many countries is a cry for the stability of delineation, or as our readings for today call it 'the corner stone of Jesus Christ' particularly on the part of those who live on the margin of our society, rather similar to the Hellenists in Jerusalem or the early Christians in Bithynia and Cappadocia in Peter's letter. Ignoring their cry will be to the detriment of those who seek their salvation in the comforts of material and technical wellbeing.

Our society also cries out for the wholeness, salvation, warmth and strength of a community of believers united by faith in Jesus Christ, the cornerstone in God's kingdom. It also longs for the inspiring dynamism of a Stephen and the self-denying, self-sacrificing crucified Jesus who is alive and well in the hearts of his followers.

With Christ as our foundation, or as the corner stone of our commitment and faith we can become what Peter suggests is a genuine Christian community and what Stephen was prepared to give his life for. It is this that our final Hymn 207 sums up appropriately and beautifully:

> Christ is made the sure foundation,
> Christ the head and cornerstone,
> Chosen of the Lord and precious,
> Binding all the Church in one.

CALVIN 22

The GRACE of GOD

(Or God's footprints in history)

...our Lord Jesus Christ through whom we have been allowed to enter the sphere of God's grace, where we now stand. Romans 5:2

The *Sydney Morning Herald* (27/4/02 Spectrum p. 5) recently published an interview of Gregory Benford, Professor of Physics at the University of California in Irvine, with his famous colleague Stephen Hawking in Cambridge, England. The latter wrote two bestsellers *A Brief History of Time* and recently *The Universe in a Nutshell*. Hawking has Lou Gehrig's disease. He lives in a wheelchair and cannot speak any longer. All communication is done via a special voice-automated keyboard.

In this interview at the University of Cambridge, Hawking refuses to either 'say that the universe is pointless or that it is designed for some purpose' and then adds that to pursue the quest for meaning 'would require one to stand outside the universe, which is not possible.' Yet he is also overwhelmed by an impression of order adding: 'the more we discover about the universe, the more we find that it is governed by rational laws. If one liked, one could say that this order was the work of God. Einstein thought so.' Later in the interview he says that 'we could call order by the name of God, but it would be an impersonal God. There is not much personal about the laws of physics.'

If one accepts Hawking's assumptions that nothing can be known outside the capacity for reasoning of the human brain, he is probably right. Yet these assumptions are too narrow for what we know nowadays about the complexity of our mind and psyche. The assumptions ignore the whole-making capacity of our commitments, feelings and emotions. They also ignore the laws governing social behaviour which also transcend pure reason.

This brings us right to the readings for today. The assumptions underlying all readings are that there is a God who transcends human understanding and who is more than human reason can encompass. What is more, this God can be approached through faith rather than through reason which in final resort is assumed to be more than equal to Him and confine Him to our limited conceptions. We affirm every Sunday that we have a point of reference outside the universe. In other words there is a sharp and basic difference between the Hawking view of the world and the Biblical one.

The first one is too narrow. It is exclusively centred on man and his capacity for reason. It assumes that one cannot say that there is meaning or purpose in the universe, falsely assuming that the agnostic position does not have an implicit sense of meaning, however negative that view may be. The second, Biblical view, by contrast, is much wider and is centred on God who is beyond human understanding and reason and yet is in benign communication with humans, in spite of their arrogance, self-centredness, imperfection and disorderliness.

Let us take all these readings in turn. There is first of all the story of Abraham's wife Sarah conceiving her first child (Isaac) long after this seems humanly possible (Genesis 18:1-15). Strangers who prove to be heavenly messengers in disguise visit Abraham and predict that he will have a son within a year. The crux of the story is verse 14 where the Lord asks: 'Is anything impossible with God?'

Calvin in his commentary on the passage suggests that all of us are like Sarah who cannot suppress a laugh of unbelief. We too, Calvin says, 'measure the promises and the works of God by our own reason, and by the laws of nature.' Sarah 'having fixed her thoughts too much on the accustomed order of nature did not give glory to God' because she was unable 'to conceive a miracle in her mind.' 'She limited the power of God within the bounds of her own sense ... the power of God ought not to be estimated by human reason.'

And then Calvin sums it all up as follows: 'He who does not expect more from God than he is able to comprehend in the scanty measure of his own reason, does him grievous wrong.' It is as though Calvin all of a sudden leaps the distance of four and a half centuries and counters Hawking's agnostic position with a much more sophisticated, true to nature, vision that the search for meaning and order is, and always has been, a mark of humanity's greatness and source of scientific progress.

Psalm 116:1-2; 12-19, today's second hymn, also thinks about God's grace and gifts as way beyond what humans can repay (verse 12). God is the one who has 'undone the bonds that bound me (verse 16)' and therefore is entitled to 'thank-offerings' (verse 17). Calvin, commenting on verse one states that one cannot gain the experience of God's grace unless one places one self 'entirely under his guidance and guardianship' and 'extols the grace of God as highly as one can (verse 12).' In other words to experience God's grace requires standing firmly outside the observable world of the senses and adopt an openness that transcends a man-centred view of the world.

Similarly Romans 5:1-11 is about the grace of God. Paul says that humans can be made whole (saved) through faith and commitment to Jesus Christ. Therefore we can enter the realm of peace, serenity and confidence that otherwise would elude us (verses 1-2). He suggest that it will allow believers to endure suffering and even use that very suffering to become stronger in the faith and provide the proof that one has stood the test (verses 3-4). All this is possible through the

Holy Spirit which is the channel through which God floods the human heart with love (verse 5).

That love of God is based on a new relationship of grace. Jesus' sacrifice on the cross is at the core of this new relationship. Jesus gave his life to make up for, to atone for, man's sin. This was an act of reconciliation on God's part. He wiped off old scores, thereby, as J. B. Phillips puts it in his translation of the passage, allowing us to 'be perfectly certain of our salvation through His living in us (verses 6-11).'

In Romans 5:3 Paul says that 'tribulation works patience' or in Latin: 'tribulatio patientam efficiat.' Calvin therefore uses the word 'effect' in his commentary. He says: 'Christians, with all their glorying, are yet strangely harassed and distressed in this life, which condition is far from being a happy one' and then continues to argue that 'the godly are prevented by these calamities from being blessed, but also that their glorying is thereby promoted. To prove this (Paul) takes his argument from the effects, and … at last concludes, that all the sorrows we endure contribute to our salvation and final good.'

By correctly changing the verb 'working' into 'effecting' Calvin allows me to introduce the essence of this sermon, that in sharp contrast with Stephen Hawking's observation that standing outside the universe is impossible, Christians believe that the effects of God's footprints in history are there for all to see. The entire Bible and all the readings for today testify to God's grace. They show that the Holy Spirit concretely and actively 'effects' life on this infinitely small bit of earth in the immense and apparently infinite universe.

This is also true for the last of today's New Testament readings, Matthew 9:35–10:23. Here Jesus teaches the good news of the kingdom (Matthew 9:35) because he is moved to pity seeing the people scattered like sheep without a shepherd, harassed and helpless (Matthew 9:36). Leadership is missing and those who are not fortunate enough to possess the worldly security of position and power are rudderless and like sheep harassed by the wolves of greed, cruelty, savagery and oppression.

Jesus by contrast is filled with compassion. To maximize the potential he fills the void by transferring his authority to the disciples (Matthew10:1) proclaiming the message: 'The kingdom of Heaven is upon you (Matthew 10:8)', to cast out unclean spirits and to cure the sick. His instructions are quite specific: they are not to charge for their services (Matthew 10:8). They are not to take any gold, to pack for the road, to take a second coat or shoes and no stick (Matthew10:9). It looks as though Jesus is foreshadowing that organization has it own pitfalls that detract from carrying out his and his disciples' mission in the world.

They are sent as sheep among the wolves, wary as serpents, yet innocent as doves (Matthew 10:16). Therefore it is not enough to just shut oneself off from the dog-eat-dog world, a world of sin both within oneself and without because surrendering oneself to that world is to be defeated by it and even to become like it. It has to be countered with love and compassion, Jesus says. Wary like serpents means not only to understand that world, but also to counter it with wisdom, common sense, understanding and concern for others.

Yet it also means that understanding and countering that world implies strong opposition, as indeed Jesus himself experienced when he was crucified by the very people he was sent to heal and save. So with the disciples, they might be hauled into court. And if they are, they are not to worry about how to speak, but to let the Holy Spirit do the speaking for them (Matthew 10:19-20). To be effective in this world it is not enough just to trust in one's talents, or lack of them. No, one has to allow the Holy Spirit to do it for you.

If the Bible readings this morning are rather long it is because I included the optional part of the lectionary (Matthew 10:9-23). I read them carefully and began to wonder whether they are optional because they are a bit embarrassing. In contrast with the image of Christian ecclesiastical organization in Paul's letters and what subsequently the Christian churches anywhere in the world have become, these passages stress an absolute minimum or actually, absence, of organization.

If that is what Jesus wanted the church to be, it is an implicit indictment of both fundamentalism and worse, the establishment character of most, if not all churches. If fundamentalists insist on barring women from the eldership and ministry (according to 1 Corinthians 14:34-35) they must also logically and consistently insist on ministers and elders going around without shoes, no second coat, no home, staying with whomever would have them, no possessions, such as gold, silver or even copper in their purses, no pack for the road and certainly no charge for services.

Yet it is also an indictment of the establishment character of most, if not all churches. And by this I mean the beauty, solemnity, orderliness, loftiness of our buildings and ways of worship. They contribute to our edification and as such are not to be scorned and despised. They belong to a particular style of life which contrasts with the very simple description of what the church's beginning was all about.

What makes the comparison actually worse, are other observations of Jesus in the Gospel. There is first of all the story (Luke 16:22) of the rich man in hell being jealous of Lazarus enjoying the bosom of Abraham, where as Calvin thinks, 'the scattered children of God meet during their pilgrimage on this earth' and which he compares with 'a quiet harbour at which believers arrive after navigating present life.'

There is also Jesus saying (Matthew 19:24) that 'it is easier for a camel to pass through the eye of a needle than for a rich man to enter the kingdom of God.' Calvin solves both examples of the predicament of the powerful and the rich by pointing to Jesus also saying (Matthew 19:26) that what is impossible for man is possible for God and further insisting that 'the Spirit of God ... exceeds all our senses.' Augustine, says Calvin, informs us 'that riches do not shut against any man the gate of the kingdom of heaven, but that it is open alike to all who have either made a sober use of riches, or patiently endured the want of them.' Yet the clue to it all is 'God's grace which assists men to keep the way of salvation.'

It is also not to be forgotten that to Calvin (commenting on Peter's sermon at Pentecost in Acts 2:17) prophets were 'accurate observers of their times' and spoke figuratively 'to fit their time' and applied 'their style unto the capacity of their time.' I interpret this to mean that in this day and age (so much more complex than the days of Jesus) God's authority and grace remain a beacon of hope and stability and that our luxuries, our organizations should never occupy pride of place in our basic commitments and motivations.

Still on organization, I believe that the Calvinist or Presbyterian and Reformed ecclesiastical organization more than other forms minimizes potential corruption of power and maximizes orderliness. Yet it is also an organization, and as such not different from the Episcopal and congregational modes of organizing church affairs. All I am trying to say is that if we take Matthew 10:9-23 seriously we must be careful not to sacralize what is a necessity if we want God's word to survive in a hostile environment.

Calvin makes the distinction between the civil order and the kingdom of God. The first one is proximate, the latter absolute. That is the way it should be. Calvin interprets Matthew 8:33 and Luke 8:39 as having 'symbolic significance' by which is meant 'the last and most erudite of meanings.' He calls it 'anagoge' (Greek for 'lifting things to a higher level.') In the particular context of Jesus casting out demons, Calvin explains 'that the cures of bodily diseases, performed by our Lord, were intended to be symbolical of the removal of spiritual diseases by the power and grace of the Great Physician.' Applying this kind of interpretation to Matthew 10:9-23 we may conclude that Jesus meant to say that God's grace is actually the real and essential message behind the specific instance of the earliest beginnings of Christianity before it had to be organized as a viable movement and that the specifics may differ according to the embeddedness of the gospel in time and place.

Calvin's commentary, on Matthew 9:35, is that the kingdom of God has the purpose of making the 'sadly scattered' become whole (saved) so that they gain 'perfect happiness.' But there is a condition. They have to let themselves be guided and guarded by God. It will not do, as he says in his comment on Matthew

10:19 'to measure themselves by their own strength which is always small or nothing.' No, 'Christ forbids the disciples to look at their own strength, and enjoins them to rely, with undivided confidence, on heavenly grace.' And then he adds: 'Frequently does it happen that the Lord leaves believers destitute of the gift of eloquence, so long as he does not require that they give him a testimony, but when the necessity for it arrives, those who formerly appeared to be dumb are endued with more than ordinary eloquence.'

Let us think a bit more about the meaning of God's grace. It has already become obvious from today's readings that it is a gift experienced by countless generations before us and that it has been there from the earliest beginnings of Biblical history right up to the present day. Jewish, Christian and Islamic history insists that God's footprints are abundantly clear in all of history, for all who are not blind. Actually the story of the gift of God's grace sums up what all those Biblical authors spanning so many centuries are all about and want to say. Yet just as real are the efforts of Satan to undo God's grace and the immensity of sin.

The Greek word (Charis) that is used in the New Testament and translated for us by 'grace' actually means 'favour.' It means that someone (in the Bible always God) has done us a favour. It is the opposite of being wrapped up in oneself. It means being liberated, not being bound anymore (Psalm 116:16). It means the freedom of not being imprisoned any longer in one's own little world. It means the opposite of the echidna on our property who rolled himself in a ball of prickles when I almost stepped on him yesterday. Echidnas have developed a very effective way of surviving in a hostile world: rolling oneself up in a hard shell of spikes.

Humans are a bit like that, aren't they? Yet this anxious way of encountering the world can become a veritable neurosis, a misplaced trust in the immediate and tangible. God's grace is different; it liberates and encourages the openness of love, compassion and affection. It encounters the world as a lamb amongst wolves. It encourages Christ's followers and disciples to be as innocent as doves. This may lead to a cross, but it also and ultimately leads to the God-given peace which 'passeth all understanding (Philippians 4:7).'

God's grace is not necessarily to be identified only with a win in the lottery, a piece of good luck, evidence of material success or improved security, as obviously is the case with my echidna. It often means a hard won integrity in the face of hardship rather than surrender and compromise. It means to let God determine one's next step rather than over-anxiously defend oneself solely with the weapons at hand.

This also means that God's grace is closely bound up with obedience and trust. One cannot expect to receive the benefits of God's gift of salvation or wholeness without faith in the giver. If one denies or doubts his existence and one believes that the universe can only be explained in terms of the concrete windings and turnings of one's superior capacity for thinking, the world must exclude God. Then obedience and trust can only be found in the self and other thinking selves.

The grace of God is like the love of the father in the story of the prodigal son. The father's heart went out to him while he was still a long way off and ran to meet him. He ordered a feast to celebrate the day and said: 'This son of mine was dead and has come back to life; he was lost and is found (Luke 15:24).' The grace of God is like the reconciliation between father and son. The father's forgiveness is matched by the son's return and obedience.

Very similarly, Jesus' sacrifice on the cross stands for God's love reconciling God and man. It expresses God's grace and favour to redeem man whose rebellion has alienated him from the creator. But now the rebel has returned and has promised to fit with the father's running of the land. Faith is restored, the covenant is renewed and man's wellbeing guaranteed.

As is to be expected, Calvin strongly stresses God's authority when he touches on grace. And he is right. After all grace is primarily a favour and a gift, and as Calvin emphasizes, an unmerited, undeserved gift, like the prodigal who had nothing, no merit left to claim the right of acceptance by the father. To Calvin living in the turbulent, insecure age he experienced, the counterbalance of God's shepherd-like authority had to be equally, if not more, strong to hold it all together. To expect that humans could climb to a man-made salvation through their own efforts or good works just was not realistic and would not do. Something much more drastic had to be accomplished, such as Jesus dying for the sins of the world and God's grace being miraculously injected in existence in order to rescue man from perdition.

Therefore he says in the *Institutes* (III ii 11) that he 'holds it to be a most pestilential delusion for man to be a fellow-labourer with the grace of God.' He does not object, he says, for humans to 'voluntarily follow the movement of grace', but that is as far as he wants to go. Obedience, faith and goodwill are God's gift to man. 'Whence it follows, that nothing is left for the will (of men) to abrogate as its own.' And to add strength to his argument he approvingly quotes from Paul's letter to the Philippians (2:13): 'for it is God who works in you, inspiring both the will and the deed, for his own chosen purpose.' This accords with Jesus' commendation to the disciples to let the Holy Spirit do the inspiring and speaking if they are hauled before courts.

The time has come to be more specific about God's footprints in history. After all agnostics, such as Stephen Hawking and many of my colleagues in the social scientific study of religion are hardly persuaded by the arguments as I have built them so far on the basis of scripture and Calvin's interpretations. They will dismiss them as Sigmund Freud did, as ever so many fantasies and wish dreams, concocted to compensate for deplorable inadequacies of life, to provide us with what we want from it or as a crutch for those who cannot cope with their helplessness.

Fortunately it is possible to argue for God's footprints in history even from the factual, scientific set of assumptions of my agnostic colleagues. I am thinking about the effect of belief in God on a large range of moral issues. This effect can and has been expressed in figures and statistics. The Religion in Australia survey, which I conducted at The Australian National University in the 1960s and updated in the 1980s, allows me to compare those respondents who believed in God without doubt and those who did not.

Sex relations after marriage with someone other than husband and wife were generally disapproved, but more by believers than non-believers. Much larger, however was the difference (39%) between believers and non-believers on the issue of sex before marriage. The orthodox believers (56%) were also much more likely than the non-believers (21%) to disapprove of the person who had a small job on the side and did not declare it for income tax purposes or to disapprove of the person who takes too much change when the shop assistant has made a mistake (94% versus 71%).

The effect of evangelical religion on denominational statistics is also well-known. If in the provinces of New Brunswick and Nova Scotia the percentage of Baptists is four times larger than in the rest of Canada, the increase is largely the result of very successful revivals and Christian conversions in the last quarter of the eighteenth century. The Baptists managed to become the heirs of what actually had begun amongst the Congregationalists who had escaped north during the War of Independence of the American colonies (1776-1783).

Yet winning arguments with non-believers in terms of their own assumptions is not the main theme of this sermon. The unifying theme of all of today's Bible readings is God's loving care and offer of salvation to all those who are burdened by their sins or the disorderliness of their personal and social existence. Actually I cannot think of any book in the Bible written many centuries apart that does not focus on God as the immortal, invisible, eternal source providing a frame of reference in the beyond for all the mortals who yearn for peace and salvation.

This is the tangible effect of our Christian faith that we celebrate today. It is God's free gift. It is God's grace which underlies all of scripture and the very foundation of our church. And it is this sentiment that is so well expressed in the third verse of Faber's Hymn 395 which we will shortly sing together:

> There is a wideness in God's mercy,
> Like the wideness of the sea;
> There is a kindness in His justice,
> Which is more than liberty.

CALVIN 23
ORDER and DISORDER

(Or salvation and sin)

Authority and awe rest with him who has established peace in his realm on high. Job 25:2

Today's Old Testament reading comes from the book of Job, chapter 25:1-6. It is a speech by Bildad, one of Job's friends who have come from afar to console him in his misery and attempt to help him to make sense of the suffering that Job regards as undeserved. Is God capricious and is his order a sham?

The friends maintain that there must be something in the past that Job has overlooked. That must be the real cause why God has sent him all these calamities. But Job cannot think of any charge that God could bring against him (chapters 23 and 24). Is his suffering maybe part of a universal problem with justice? After all the poor suffer unnecessarily and the wicked go unpunished. The latter may eventually get their just dessert and come-uppance, but even that is not always the case.

In other words, Job says, he cannot see why God would treat him the way he did. He is mystified. Is God's sense of justice failing? Or is there more to God's order that he cannot fathom? Is punishment for bad behaviour and reward for being good part of a larger scheme in which this easy 'cause and effect' is sometimes suspended? Is God maybe more than a moral policeman orchestrating social relations? Is salvation more than obeying the law? Is there more to life than following the Ten Commandments (Exodus 20:1-17) and the golden rule of doing to others what you expect them to do to you (Matthew 22:39)? Both Jesus and Paul say that God's order deals with more than law and justice and Job too (chapter 42:5) comes to that conclusion when he meets God at the end of the book.

But all that comes much later. Today our concern is with Bildad's argument in chapter 25. He says that all authority and awe rests with God (verse 1). God has established heavenly peace (verse 2). Furthermore no mortals can be innocent and nobody can be justified in God's sight (verse 4). Not even the moon and the stars are pure (verse 5). How therefore could mere mortals who are nothing but maggots and worms, be justified (verse 6)? In other words he comes close to saying that it is not for humans to understand God's justice.

Major Biblical scholars, such as Samuel Terrien and Paul Scherer, associate editors of the prestigious 12 Volume *Interpreter's Bible*, regard Bildad's argument as false. They say that he equates man's finitude with his corruption or man's limitations with his sinfulness. They feel that Bildad is 'theologically inept' and 'morally insensitive.' To them it is not fair to reduce humans to nonentities 'from which the divine image has been completely eradicated.'

In sharp contrast Calvin likes Bildad's argument. Actually Calvin's interpretation could not be more different. What does he say? In his ninety-fourth sermon on Job which deals with Chapter 25, he begins by praising Bildad for taking the wind out of man's self-aggrandisement or the puff out of his blown-up self-justification. He calls Bildad's argument 'a good and very useful advertisement' for attributing glory, power, majesty, authority and justice to God rather than to man. The latter is always inclined to pride rather than humility. He actually feels that Bildad is guided here by the Holy Spirit.

He then strengthens that argument by pointing to God's 'heavenly order' on which humans should cast their eyes. That heavenly order is a blueprint for peace and extends its relevance to the earthly order that is also ultimately in God's hand. Humans would do well to take their cues from that heavenly order. It shows the road to not just peace, but also to ordered rules and regulations.

Unfortunately, Calvin says, man is a rebel who prefers to go his own way, or to contrast it with the Interpreter's Bible approach, has not come to terms with his finitude and gives divine status to purely human accomplishments. Therefore humans should be more serious when they say 'Thy will be done' in the Lord's Prayer. Only then can God's infinity and peace become the norm for the order that he has in mind for his earthly kingdom.

Amidst all the changes, the unrest, revolutions and muddle of human existence God does not lose sight of the order he seeks for mankind. God follows his own counsel. To Calvin God's providence, predestination and election are all part and parcel of this heavenly order (Commentary on Psalm 96:10). It is the blueprint for existence established once and for all. Yet it is beyond the reach of humans, unless we surrender our false sense of autonomy and trust his authority.

The difference between Calvin and twentieth-century interpreters of Bildad's little speech may well consist in Calvin's denial of the modern confident belief in individual wholeness alone and their acceptance of the same. Calvin follows Paul in his distrust of man's incapacity to surrender to what lies beyond his instincts for personal survival and pleasure. Submission and modesty are required if one is to overcome this flaw in human nature. Man's self-esteem is not his real salvation. The social system is precarious and cannot be taken for granted. Naked individualism must be contained. Individual wholeness is not a sacred good. Yet reconciliation and therefore personal wholeness can be achieved through acceptance of God's absolute authority.

Looking at Calvin from the social science point of view, the reformer's elimination of the supports of institutional mediation between God and man appears to directly put all the more stress on God's authority and sovereignty alone. Strong heavenly authority seems to make up for the more earthly authority of human structures, however necessary those structures are for mundane order.

It is as though Calvin fears the consequences of the very individualism that is his point of departure at the beginning of his monumental *Institutes of the Christian Religion*. Here he insists on the fundament of Greek and consequently Renaissance philosophy that man's greatest good is to know himself. Here he seems to anticipate the rational individualism of Descartes who severely qualified his own statement of 'cogito ergo sum' by adding if one lives 'in a society where moral customs are not corrupt.'

Maybe this is the clue to Calvin's insistence on man's sinfulness and God's authority. To him man's sin was closely associated with his rebellion against God's infinity and the moral constraint imposed by society on his instincts and his finitude in the total scheme of things. If this is the case, the interpretation of Scherer and Terrien may hinge on a narrow view of sin. It should be enlarged to include the human propensity for social sabotage.

If sin is rebellion against God (according to the generally accepted definition) it is more than moral, ethical aberration. It is also denying what God stands for. It is appropriating for oneself such ideas and concepts as integrity, justification and infinity. The purity contrasts with what Bildad (Job 25:5) calls the impurity of even the moon and the stars, let alone mortal humans, whom he calls maggots and worms (Job 25:6).

Implied in Bildad's conception of the world, is God's purity and perfection distilled (or in psychoanalytical terms, sublimated) from a not so pure, not so perfect, not so orderly, finite, mortal, existence. Yet God's order is not just an unreal fantasy of the mind. It is not just a figment of man's imagination or a retreat from reality. God's order and authority are linked with faith. But for this we have to go to the end of the book where Job meets God.

Christians go further. They maintain (and that's what the New Testament is all about) that in Jesus Christ God became real, became concretized. That's why this sermon would be incomplete unless we also paid attention to our New Testament reading, Romans 6:1-11.

Romans 6 begin with contrasting sin and grace. Is it true that the more we have of the one (sin), the more we appreciate the other (grace or salvation)? Or to go one step further, is it not true that the more we are mired in the numerous idols or sham securities of this world, the more we are likely to find the miracle of the opposite, salvation, as Jesus did (Philippians 2:7)? Or is it not true that the more we are dislocated and emptied of all earthly supports the more we are likely to be open to God's impact in our lives? Or to put it somewhat differently: is it not true that the more we are separated from God's order and wallow as worms and maggots (to stay with Job 25:6 a bit longer) in our mortal, finite existence of sin and disorder, the more preferable and delectable our adoption as God's child will be? In final resort isn't reconciliation with God's infinity and authority the clue to what true living is all about?

Yes, says Paul, but that final goal of existence, would be in total jeopardy, if not right from the beginning we set out on this path rather than go in the opposite direction for awhile in order to all the more appreciate the good ending, a safe homecoming. Therefore it is a ghastly thought (Romans 6:2) to avoid separation from God or worse, to increase the distance to all the more glory in the final arrival.

One can put all this in very secular terms: Christianity (actually all religions) bolsters the forces that lead to greater order and integrity. Therefore the Bible determinedly discourages sin and disorder, even if the most enduring and successful of these religions also realistically anticipates the strength of sin and disorder. As much as possible it gobbles up those forces of instability and corruption and reinstates a now enhanced form of wholeness or salvation.

Therefore Paul continues in verse three to point to Jesus Christ, restorer and reconciler of a new order replacing the old one corrupted by both secular and sacred authorities. This new order was built on the ruins and death of the old testimony yet saving numerous and essential elements of that interpretation, such as commitment to transcendental order, the saliency of integrity, recognition and worship of Jehovah, who embodied justice, eternity and salvation.

Baptism (verse 4) was the sign and seal of this new order unifying the believers through a new symbol. Like the crucified Jesus they bore witness to the death of the old interpretation and the birth (resurrection) of a new one. The head and cornerstone of this new path was the very person whose death and life was to all intents and purposes identical to what the new faith was all about. And it was this faith, or the Holy Spirit that cemented the unity of those who together walked the new path of life.

It is this identification with Jesus, his life, rejection, crucifixion, resurrection, integrity and eternity that saves the believer (verse 5). He is the new being representing wholeness and salvation replacing the old one, Adam, who represents fragmentation and sin. For the believer it is like destruction (crucifixion) of the old self and rebirth (resurrection) of the new self (verse 6). It is being stripped from an old identity and welded to a new one.

This new being, as Paul calls his Roman converts, is now immune to the destructiveness (sin) of his old existence. The old attachments and securities have been shed like old, threadbare clothes. He or she is now robed in new ones.

He or she is now cleansed. Sin has been washed away like water dissolves dirt. Baptism has proclaimed him or her to be immune to an old life of fickleness, formlessness and fragility and to be provided with a new bill of sanity, of fixedness, firmness and faith (verse 7).

Nothing can destroy that new life. Order and meaning are not subjected to decay and death anymore. Order has triumphed over disorder. That order is not just a passing fashion or a whim from the past, come today, gone tomorrow. No, it is eternal, firmly established by God who in his own being represents eternity, truth and stability (verse 9). It is concretized in Jesus, the first-born of every creature (Colossians 1:15).

Yet that eternity and stability can be mistaken for, confused and identified with, the very human inclination to draw it down to the level of human control and segmental power accessible to a privileged few. God's eternity and power then become distorted as a facade for security rather than its essence. Then it loses its purity and becomes a form of oppression for the underprivileged, the marginal and the dispossessed. Then it is corrupted to serve some rather than all humans.

Jesus, like John the Baptist and an impressive line of prophets all the way back to Moses and the beginnings of Hebrew history, became the leader of the latter category. He not only suffered, but was crucified. Yet his death was the beginning of a new reintegration and reconciliation. God put his seal on the reformation of a corrupted Israel and restored an ancient tradition of homage to his purified order as over against the human corrupted one. Sin's power was now destroyed and salvation, integrity and faith were now invested in Jesus Christ and his Roman followers and believers (verses 10-11).

Calvin's commentary on Romans 6:1-11 similarly stresses the pivotal importance of the crucifixion and the death of an old regime. He contrasts it with the resurrection and the birth of a new order more in tune with God's heavenly blueprint. 'Without God's gift of regeneration the faithful are never reconciled to God.' To keep in tune with God's heavenly blueprint (His kingdom) the faithful must 'mortify the flesh' and 'lead an incorruptible life.' To be regenerated one must identify through the Holy Spirit with 'Christ who lives a life subject to no mortality in the immortal and incorruptible kingdom of God.'

Karl Barth in his exegesis of Romans 6:1-11 stresses the strict symbiotic relation between the old and the new world, the world of sin and the world of righteousness/integrity/grace, the world of Adam and the world of Christ. He expands Calvin's view by interpreting it as follows: 'Fall and grace stand to one another in an eternal tension or polarity or antinomy.'

Barth understands the passage to contrast the disorderliness of human life 'as mirrored in this world' with the order of God's grace in the heavenly one. This heavenly world points significantly beyond the concreteness of the earthly one.

The point of observation outside the latter (the earthly world) allows one to recognize one's 'complete identity with the old man.' But 'the death of the old man and the dissolution of my identity with him also involve the doing away of my union with this body.' One has to surrender to this point of reference beyond the body. Surrender means faith and 'faith means seeing what God sees, knowing what God knows, reckoning as God reckons.'

How relevant are both Bildad's speech and Paul's little sermon to the Christians in Rome to our day and age? Hasn't our impressive technical advance made us puffed up? Hasn't our immense and total control of nature made us gods in our own right? Don't we now have the kind of freedom from nature that not even our recent forefathers could imagine? Don't we now have the most detailed information about the universe, our society, our culture, and our bodies at our fingertips? Hasn't our immense increase in knowledge made the biblical stories about God's creation and Jesus quaint and obsolete?

And yet when we look around us what do we see? Has the cruelty of man to man diminished? Aren't levels of tension and anxiety in our most affluent homes often as bad as in the poorest, drug and alcohol-addicted parts of our communities? How many civil servants do not heave a sigh of relief when an opportunity for early retirement from a dog-eat-dog world opens up? Aren't there a respectable number of our young people who cannot cope with bullies at school, who feel isolated or who succumb to peer-group pressure to experiment with drugs and sex? Isn't there much bitterness amongst the divorced or amongst those who have been denied progress on the career ladder? How many in business have not experienced shaky or dishonest dealings, cheques bouncing or uncollectible debts?

Today's readings are relevant to all of us. They speak of an order that is not just pie-in-the-sky, but has been established once and for all. They speak of a God whose blueprint for His world is rather different from the one we experience every day and yet is accessible to us as a point of reference for peace, hope, understanding, forgiveness and stability. They speak of a world in which death and Satan have been overthrown and replaced with eternal life and integrity. They speak of a saviour who practically leads all his followers out of a world of pain and sin on a path of serenity and salvation.

There is a source of incredible firmness, balance and equilibrium around which our motivation and will to act can shape it. It is this source that frees us from all that ties us to our anxieties, depressions, paralyses and impotence. It is this source that all through the ages has been refined, honed and inspired countless generations before us. These generations have handed this faith to us, fortified by its biblical foundation and its concretization in a living saviour, Jesus Christ. Both Bildad's speech and Paul's little sermon witnessed to this source. It is ours to adopt, provided that an obsession with our technical and scientific advances have not obscured its splendour and salience and hindered its adoption. Calvin's insistence on modesty and humility before God's purity and authority is an important way to be true to that eternal wellspring of salvation.

And therefore we can leave this house of God, re-assured that sin within or around us is not the final word, that we are in good hands and that we are invited to walk on the path that Jesus is showing us. Hallelujah.

CALVIN 24
WORK

These last individuals have only worked one hour, and you have made them like us, who have suffered the burden and the heat of the day. Matthew 20:12

Sometimes the Bible confronts us with some fascinating and intriguing puzzles. Today's readings provide one of those. What do the readings say? The one from Job 7:1-11 assumes that work deserves appropriate and corresponding rewards. By contrast the reading from Matthew 20:1-16 presents God as an employer who does the exact opposite, and does not reward according to labour provided. What is worse, he actually insists on getting away with it. How can we resolve the inconsistency and discrepancy?

Let us first look at what the readings actually say. Work in the Bible is portrayed as necessary in a healthy society, contributing to a sense of fulfilment and worthy of appropriate rewards. However, before we find this sentiment, expressed in Job 7:2, we must attend to the background of the story.

Chapter seven represents Job's response to an argument advanced by Eliphas. He is one of Job's friends, who have come from afar to comfort him in his misery and to genuinely help him make sense of his misfortune. In Job 5:17 Eliphas suggests that the man whom God corrects should be happy and that therefore Job should not despise 'the chastening of the Almighty.'

But Job does not buy that argument. He contrasts himself here with a worker who gives his employer a good day's work and at the end receives the appropriate reward for his labour (Job 7:2). This to Job is the normal rule in a just society. It is the kind of justice one should expect. It is also what naturally and reasonably a just God would approve.

But, says Job, that is not the way God has treated me. He has not treated me justly. I am at the end of my tether. I am not rewarded for my good works. If anything I am suffering for no reason at all. There is nothing that I have done that deserves the treatment I have received from God. It is all blatantly unfair. I am tossing and turning all night (Job 7:3-4). I am riddled with worms, covered with terrible sores (Job 7:5). I despair of life (Job 7:6). I am like the wind, relegated to a nothing (Job 7:7-8). Life to me is like a cloud that vanishes. Life to me is like death and being buried (Job 7:9). My spirit is nothing but anguish and my soul is bitter (Job 7:11). And all this, Job suggests, is in contrast with a worker who gets his just rewards. If he were unfairly treated, like I am, he would similarly feel hopeless, meaningless and bitter. It would similarly make him a rebel. In a just society, run by a just God, this kind of injustice should not exist. What does Calvin have to say about this passage?

He is adamant that without God's sovereignty and rule there would be no order in society or in the entire world (commentary on Psalm 96:10). If there were no society to serve basic needs, humans would be like 'cattle and preying beast (commentary on Isaiah 24:2).' Division of labour is a necessity in a viable community and 'makes humans dependent on one another (sermon 101 on Job).' Work therefore is an essential element in a just society.

Work is necessary not just because God demands it, but also because it binds master and servant (commentary on Ephesians 5:22) It also binds humans to their neighbours (*Inst*. III vii 5). It must be efficient and useful (commentary on Numbers 4:4). Calvin therefore utterly condemns 'lazy good-for-nothings' (commentary on 1 Thessalonians 4:11) and talks about those who do not work as 'useless blocks of wood (commentary on Genesis 2:15 and Psalm 127:1).' More specifically on Job 7:2 Calvin contrasts the regular order of work with the irregular treatment of Job. He stresses the sense of order in the 'appointed time of work' of Job 7:1 rather than the reward, but the message is the same: Job accuses God of discrimination and inconsistency, because he has denied him a just reward.

To Calvin the difference is that even the worker who has a difficult job has at least the end of the day to look forward to ('it does not last forever'), whereas Job is 'without hope of delivery.' 'He who gets wages for his work, longs for the job to end, but as for me (Job) I have no rest nor release.' For Job, Calvin adds, his 'misery is excessive' in that he does not even know when it is all going to end. Yet Calvin also hints at what may reconcile Job and God or, in our terms, may possibly solve the puzzle of God's inconsistency mentioned at the beginning. He says that the problem with Job is that he wants to be his own judge and therefore to usurp God's authority.

This theme also reverberates in our New Testament reading. Jesus probably had Job's predicament in mind when he told the story of the eccentric owner of a vineyard who did not reward his workers according to work done. That New Testament reading (Matthew 20:1-16) is a parable which Jesus uses as an answer to a question of the disciples regarding salvation. He has just told them (Matthew 19:24) that it is more difficult for a rich man to enter the kingdom of God than for a camel to go through the eye of a needle. This disturbs the disciples no end and they therefore wonder whether anybody can be saved (Matthew 19:25). Jesus answers that question with: 'With men this is impossible, but with God all things are possible (Matthew 19:26).'

That answer does not sit well with the disciples either and they attempt to wrestle at least some hope for their own salvation. They hope that Jesus will at least recognize that some of their own decisions, efforts and values will find favour with God. Using Peter as their spokesman they suggest to Jesus, that their decision to forsake everything and to follow him must certainly give them preferential treatment, kudos and a guarantee for a place in God's kingdom (Matthew 19:27). Jesus confirms that indeed this will give them everlasting life (Matthew 19:28-29), but then rather enigmatically ends his little speech with: 'But many that are first shall be last; and the last shall be first (Matthew 19:30).'

This he follows up with our reading for today (Matthew 20:1-17) to elucidate that statement. But does the parable make it clearer? The parable is all about a strange owner of a vineyard who is obviously in a hurry to get a job done. He hires an increasing number of workers at various times during the day just to get it all finished before nightfall, but then pays each of them the same amount (one penny) he has arranged with the first workers at the beginning of the day.

This obviously makes those jealous who had been slaving in the searing sun and received no more than those who had been there for only one hour in the cool of the evening. They complain to the owner (who is God in the story): 'You have given those who have worked only one hour, the same as us who have suffered the burden and the heat of the day (Matthew 20:12).' Upon which the owner (God) replies: 'I have done you no wrong. Didn't you agree with me for a penny? Take what I owe you. I will give to the last as much as I gave you. Don't I have the right to do what I want with my own money? Is your eye evil because I am good?' And then he finishes the way he began the parable: 'So the first shall be last and the last first', adding as a further explanation: 'for many are called, but few are chosen (Matthew 20:13-16).'

The owner may be very generous, but he obviously plays havoc with market expectations of rewards being roughly equal to work done. In other words, if God is just, then harmony rather than conflict of the social order must be uppermost in his mind. To entertain unequal treatment smacks of eccentricity and obstruction, exactly what Job complained about in his answer to Eliphas. How then could we believe in a God who claims to have both the social order in mind, represents justice and yet goes against the grain of justifiable expectations? What does Calvin have to say about the parable?

His first reaction fits his favourite theme of modesty and humility in human relations. Those who were first, he says, 'have no right to boast or insult others.' Furthermore, they should not rest on their laurels, but 'should be spurred on to make progress', because 'indolence almost always springs from excessive confidence.' Implied in this interpretation is the idea that the spiritual life is different from earthly life. 'Christ observes a different order.' Yet this does not mean that the one is not relevant for the other: 'Only those are pleasing to God who labours for the advantage of their brethren.' Calvin thinks that Christ's intention is only 'to exhort all men to be modest, not to prefer themselves above others, but to willingly share with others the common prize.'

Calvin stresses God's goodness and love for all mankind when towards the end of his comments he observes that 'God bestows an undeserved reward on those who were called rather late in the day as he does not want anybody to fall short. 'He therefore solves our puzzle by suggesting that in God's kingdom there are no distinctions between late-comers and early arrivals, that the parable is an allegory and that it has little to do with an actual market place. The prize is salvation rather than merchandise or money for performance. Granted, but does that also solve Job's problem of social injustice (the wicked prospering and the good suffering)? Is it actually enough to put the blinkers on and assume that God's order is a blueprint only and that therefore we have to somehow accept the imperfect reality and cope with it as well as we can?

For a better answer we may have to return to Calvin's suggestion in his sermon on Job 7, where he suggests that Job's problem really centres on his assumption that he can be his own judge. To Calvin God's authority is at stake here. God must be independent of those whom he judges. He may like, even love, his servant Job, but Job is not the only pebble on the beach. Existence is more complex than what one individual may like to hear or what is happening to him. There is constant conflict between individuals, their peers and what society feels is just. Therefore like a good judge He must be above individual hopes and desires. He must have independent authority.

Yet if that were the case, Job could very well build a good case for himself. He could say that to be rewarded for what is to the advantage of the common good, by definition is good for God's blueprint for existence, his established order. That's why Job keeps saying that he wished he could meet God in court (Job 31:37) To solve our puzzle by referring to the need for a global authority and judge in order that justice will prevail for anyone and not just for a single individual gets us only so far. Admittedly the many conflicts in any society, leave alone our own diverse one, could do with a fair and impartial authority and judge.

Yet there is still an element of whimsy that worries Job and that one can certainly detect in our parable. By definition whimsy is contrary to God's character. Actually whimsy fits Satan's character rather than God's. You may remember that the whole Job story started as a bet between God and Satan. Satan puts all his money on Job losing his integrity, when all earthly securities are taken away. By contrast God accepted the bet, because he was convinced that Job would prove to be beyond basic reliance on earthly rewards and securities. Maybe that is the area where we should look for a solution, to our puzzle: the area where salvation (wholeness) is not anymore to be found in man's concoctions and fabrications, but in identification with the rarefied realm of God's kingdom. Actually that is where Job's story ends. It finishes when he actually meets God and re-discovers that through knowing God and experiencing His presence the real import of salvation is brought home.

That may also be the solution to the strange parable. Maybe that Jesus felt that the disciples who had forsaken everything should continue in their commitment, loyalty and faith mode, if the treasure of heaven was to be theirs. If that mode is taken too much for granted, or too much buried in tradition, convention and 'establishment' (organization), he seems to say, it may take them to the end of the queue rather than the beginning. Their place would then be occupied by the more recent arrivals, the prostitutes, the tax collectors, the losers and other battlers. The new converts: those who freshly discovered the treasure of God's offer of salvation and those who are still full of the miracle of it all, would now be first in line.

If that is the solution to our problem, and I think it is, it makes more sense than anything else I may come up with; it may also clear up the last few words of Jesus' explanation: 'for many are called, but few are chosen.' It may now dawn on us that salvation (wholeness) is offered to anyone (many), but that few are chosen. That means, I think, that those who accept the offer feel particularly privileged. Actually those who perceive the sense of wholeness the offer brings invariably also perceive it as something unexpectedly revealed to them. They accept it with gladness as something they have looked for all their lives and finally found. Salvation has now become a privilege that has little to do with their spasmodic effort. A sense of 'being chosen' accompanies the exultation.

The reward therefore of the parable means the gift of salvation, grace, faith. These have nothing to do with payment for work done, but Jesus uses the image of an employer to describe God as giver and provider and not as an example of good commercial practice. To Jesus salvation has something to do with identification with God, a transcendental and very personal source of order in a world that is not particularly orderly. And this salvation, grace and faith could in no way be achieved or appropriated by human labour or any other kind of work leading to reward. It is a gift.

To be chosen therefore means a sense of it being undeserved, rather similar to the workers who received a full day's payment for just one hour of effort. It is illumination not coming from within, but from without. It is not the outcome of human effort, or reward for hard work 'in the sweat of our brow (Genesis 3:19)' or the result of accumulated kudos from deprivation. It is a gift. Through the parable Jesus seems to say that only when salvation is presented as a gift rather than something humans produce, can the purity of order be guaranteed. The effect of purity as impinging on human disorder/sin/injustice will be diminished according to the lesser maintenance of its separation from the human scene. In other words, the more salvation is associated with gift and privilege, the better its purity can do its work as a counterbalance to Satan's disorder.

Yet that gift, or the gratitude resulting from it, has moral consequences. Those who experience the offer of salvation invariably also shed the very habits, patterns of immorality, sins, that in the past they were unable to battle or conquer. They have become the upstanding citizens society needs for its own integrity.

The enthusiasm and genuine sincerity at the early stages of charismatic movements is well illustrated by the revival meetings orchestrated by Henry Alline from 1775-1784 in Nova Scotia or the New Light evangelization on the Niagara Peninsula in the early part of the nineteenth century. The sense of calling by the Methodist circuit-riders approximately at the same time and the beginnings of the Salvation Army in the 1880s in Ontario similarly point to the effect of God's gift of salvation and faith to large sections of the population.

The converts at these occasions never claimed that the gift of grace resulted from changed behaviour. They always claimed that it was the other way round: changed behaviour was the result of their conversion. They all witnessed to the miracle of God's intervention in their lives. They all felt better for the improved niche they had now acquired in their community.

This was also Job's discovery when God spoke to him (Job chapters 38-42). Now he does not speak any longer about God being unjust and unfair. Now he is enveloped in God's mercy. Now he can accept his misery and misfortune. Now all that used to bother him has been put at a distance, relativized. Now his integrity which was almost destroyed has been restored. Or to say it differently: now salvation has become even more real than it had been ever before.

In summarizing my attempt to solve the puzzle of the eccentric employer Jesus tells us that wholeness (salvation) does not come about through earning rewards, but through accepting it as a gift from God. It is a privilege and therefore has the character of being especially selected or chosen for a particular individual. Yet it comes with a condition. Its bliss can never be ours unless we surrender our reliance on mundane securities.

Disorder, sin and injustice cannot be dispelled by a single stroke of the pen. A chasm separates 'pure order' from 'existential disorder.' The New Testament claims that Jesus bridged the gap and that he was and is the mediator. It was through Jesus that identification with God's pure order became a reality. That means that the believer can not only catch a glimpse but can represent as high a degree of salvation/integrity as one can hope for in this mortal life.

The parable has nothing to do with commercial reciprocity. It has everything to do with trust in the giver (God) and identification with His order. Yet that identification also has moral consequences. It means not just concern for our neighbour, but also identification with those standards and values that make for a healthy society. And this in turn means humility, understanding of others and accepting God's authority both for ourselves and for the common good. The common good requires that our labour is suitably rewarded and that workers not be abused.

CALVIN 25
The VIRGIN BIRTH

The Holy Spirit will come upon you, the power of the Most High will overshadow you. Your child will therefore be called Holy – the Son of God. Luke 1:35

The Bible is full of little puzzles. The virgin birth is only one of them. What are we to make of it? The Christian Church all through the ages has deemed it sufficiently important to incorporate it in the Apostle's creed: 'Conceived by the Holy Ghost, born of the Virgin Mary.' We have repeated this section of the creed hundreds of times. Does this mean that we actually believe it?

We know by now that sperm must fertilise the human egg for the birth of any human being to take place. Yet even here there is nowadays some doubt. According to an article in the papers last month Professor Ian Wilmut at the Roslin Institute near Edinburgh in Scotland suggests that he can clone humans from an unfertilised egg. After all he has done so successfully, as we all know, with Dolly the sheep. The process is apparently called 'parthenogenesis' which literally means 'virgin birth.' According to other articles in the newspapers, births of this kind can be expected next year in other countries.

The Bible itself assumes that Joseph is the father of Jesus. It is Joseph who is of Davidic descent and it is through Joseph that Jesus is legitimized as the Messiah. According to scripture the Messiah was to deliver Israel from its enemies and establish a kingdom greater than David's whose descendant he was to be (Matthew 22:42). Slowly, however, the Messiah (the Hebrew word for 'the anointed one', set apart for high office, Christos in Greek), became a religious rather than a political leader, a spiritual, rather than a worldly ruler. Jesus thought of himself as such a deliverer or saviour, a suffering servant.

To return to the puzzle mentioned at the beginning: if Jesus was regarded as the son of Joseph why then do we continue to repeat in the Apostle's creed that Jesus was conceived by the Holy Ghost, born of the Virgin Mary? Certainly Anglican Bishop John Shelby Spong feels that we should scrap the entire virgin birth idea. He was the Episcopal (Anglican) Bishop of the diocese of Newark in New Jersey, USA and wrote a number of books that propagate modernizing the creed. To him we are now beyond such primitive ideas which 'violate everything we know about biology' as he says on page twelve in his book 'Why Christianity must change or die.'

Yet in contrast with Bishop Spong I have no trouble with Jesus being 'conceived by the Holy Spirit and born of the Virgin Mary.' Why? Before answering that question I would like to lead up to it by having a good look at the lectionary readings for today.

There is first of all the Old Testament reading from 2 Samuel 7:1-16. It tells the story of King David who by now has conquered all his enemies, has established peace and prosperity for the people and thinks that it is about time to now also honour God who made all this possible. He therefore proposes to build something more substantial than a tent or tabernacle for Yahweh and asks the prophet Nathan for advice.

Nathan approves the plan, but then God appears to Nathan and tells him not to bother. The argument is that He (God) guided Israel quite satisfactorily in the past without all the extra brouhaha and that he does not need it now. He will continue to look after Israel anyway. His (David's) family, throne and kingdom shall be established for all time, forever.

The same sentiment is expressed in the section of Psalm 89 which we have sung together. It reiterates that God has made a covenant, contract, with the house of David that he will establish his posterity for ever and make his throne endure for all generations (verse 4). Moreover even if David's sons make a mess of things, He (God) may punish them, yet will continue to love them and be faithful to them (verse 33-37).

Traditionally both 2 Samuel 7:1-11 and Psalm 89 have been regarded as foreshadowing the Messianic Kingdom and that is why they are coupled together with the birth of Jesus as the promised Messiah in today's lectionary. Being in line with David's dynasty through Joseph the New Testament maintains that Jesus is the Christ, the anointed one. It is through him that the promise made to David has come to fruition.

Both 2 Samuel 7:14 and Psalm 89:26 call this descendant of David 'God's Son.' He is even called the 'first-born, highest among the kings of the earth' in Psalm 89:27. Yet that kingdom is also different, if we are to go by God's refusal to be too closely associated with the brick and mortar of earthly buildings. 2 Samuel 7 seems to foreshadow a heavenly rather than an earthly kingdom. The Messiah may be of the 'rod of Jesse (David's father)', but Isaiah (11:1) also calls him 'despised', suggesting that the kingdom is not concrete, but spiritual and therefore much more likely to be both misunderstood and controversial.

The New Testament closely follows the prophetic tradition of the Old Testament. It functions as the foundation and therefore legitimation of the old covenant. All the authors of the New Testament were shaping a new tradition but they were also steeped in the ancient understanding and interpretation of the Old one. To these authors Jesus represented a heavenly kingdom and as such was not in need of brick and mortar.

Therefore the passage of 2 Samuel 7:8 has been interpreted to mean that the Messiah will rise above and beyond the accoutrements, paraphernalia and machinery of earthly organisation. Jesus the Messiah, so the argument goes, has come in the humble guise of the son of a virgin. He did not appear as a pompous ruler, but as rejected by the world of the powerful. There was no room for him in the inn and his first bed was a crib in a stable.

Calvin adopts this traditional Messianic line. David, he says in his commentary on Psalm 89 was 'nobody, unknown and obscure … being the least esteemed of his father's children, in whose country cottage he held the humble office of a herdsman.' But then God elevated him above all others 'to the state of royalty' and gave him special status as the forerunner of 'Christ in whom alone, in the strict and proper sense, this everlasting duration is to be found.'

Calvin expresses an interesting view on the virgin birth in his commentary on Isaiah 7:14 where the prophet prophesies: 'Behold a virgin shall conceive, and bear a son, and shall call his name Immanuel (which means 'God with us').' He says that the prophet is here speaking about a virgin rather than a young woman because he wants to speak not about 'the ordinary course of nature, but (of) the gracious influence of the Holy Spirit.' This means, says Calvin, that 'virgin birth' in contrast with normal birth is used to highlight 'the greatness of the event.' Normally, he says, a virgin birth 'was revolting to the ordinary judgment of men.'

To Calvin the birth of Christ similarly shows God's intention to 'save them that believe by foolishness (1 Corinthians 1:21).' It tries 'the humility of faith or restrains the pride of the ungodly.' Only the proud, he says, 'deprive us of the knowledge of the inestimable secret which God has purposely hid from the wise and prudent, and revealed to the humble and to babes (Luke 10:21).' After all 'Christ is promised to a virgin in an obscure town of Judea.'

This leads us to our New Testament reading, Luke 1:26-38. Here we read that the angel Gabriel came not to the centre of Judaism, Jerusalem, but to an ordinary virgin, Mary, in an insignificant city in Galilee called Nazareth. She was to be married to Joseph of the house of David (verse 27). Mary was not particularly pleased with Gabriel's message. She was 'agitated' and no wonder. The angel announced that she was going to be the mother of 'the Son of the Highest' and that this son would be given the throne of his father David (verse 32) and that there would be no end to his kingdom (verse 33).

Therefore she asked Gabriel, how this could possibly be (verse 34) as she was still a virgin to which the angel replied in the words of our text for today: 'The Holy Spirit will come upon you, the power of the Most High will overshadow you. Your child will therefore be called Holy – the Son of God (verse 35).' Mary obviously was still worried about this strange announcement which went counter to the mores of her culture: single girls were not supposed to be pregnant before getting married. Therefore Gabriel says: 'Look at your cousin Elisabeth. Although she is much beyond childbearing age, she is expecting (verse 36). Nothing is impossible with God (verse 37).' This is enough for Mary. She resigns and says: 'I belong to the Lord, body and soul, let it happen as you say.'

Before we address ourselves to the issue at hand as to how moderns can continue to believe in the virgin birth, let us see what Calvin has to say about Luke 1:35.

He admits that this is beyond 'the common order of nature.' Like Zachariah (Luke 1:18) Mary initially confines 'the power of God within narrow limits', but then she accepts the boundless power of God and refuses to confine it to 'the level of her senses.' The crux of the matter therefore becomes that the biblical authors want to express Jesus being both a human like all of us, but also the 'sinless son of God.' They do this by bringing in the Holy Spirit as the 'essential power of God, whose energy is manifested and exerted in the entire government of the world as well as in miraculous events', as Calvin says. This 'heavenly generation has separated (Jesus) from the ordinary rank of men.'

Calvin sums it up as follows: 'Though Christ was formed of the seed of Abraham, yet he contracted no defilement from a sinful nature; for the Spirit of God kept him pure from the very commencement: and this was done not merely that he might abound in personal holiness, but chiefly that he might sanctify his own people. The manner of conception, therefore, assures us that we have a Mediator separate from sinners (Hebrews 7:26).'

On verse 37 (about God doing the impossible) Calvin suggests that if our faith is confined to what 'we are able to comprehend' or 'to what our sense receive' it is airy-fairy. By contrast, if we can rise above these constraints on our faith (as Mary did according to verse 38) a solid faith will bear results and 'have effects.' What these effects are, Calvin does not spell out. However, it is a safe bet that he has 'salvation (wholeness, integrity)' in mind.

In other words to Calvin the virgin birth is essential if one wants God to represent pure order as against man's disorder (sin). Denying the virgin birth is tantamount to eviscerating God's pure order to where it is nothing but a sugar-coating of a man-centred system of meaning. Denying the virgin birth is also denying that there is anything beyond human control of senses and reason.

Yet if Jesus is to be the mediator and saviour of man, then his earthly ties (descendant of David, of Abraham's seed) have to also be documented and given equal status. Jesus therefore is the synthesis reconciling the obviously impure, sinful state of man with God's perfection, pure order and sinlessness.

In this scenario God's authority, love and forgiveness are essential elements. They are all part of raising man above self-centredness and are the death of self-idolization.

Calvin's view of God's purity over against man's impurity therefore is our first answer why the virgin birth is to be maintained as an integral part of our confession of faith. God's pure order is dragged down into our disorderly, man-centred world, unless we accept it through faith as sufficient unto itself. At the centre of existence is an anomaly. Our longing for, and need of, a vision beyond disorder of any kind is met by God's Holy Spirit. Right from the beginning Jesus was also of divine origin and this is what the virgin birth is trying to express. 'Nothing is impossible with God (Luke 1:37).'

Yet there are two other reasons why I personally have no trouble repeating Jesus being born of the Virgin Mary when I confess my faith. The second one has to do with the biblical view of sexuality or libido as it is called in the psychological literature. When I read and interpret scripture I often put on my sociological rather than my theological hat. In contrast with theologians who traditionally leant more heavily on philosophical canons of logic and overt meaning, social scientists are more likely to be sympathetic to the latent meanings. By this I mean that anthropologists, psychologists and sociologists search for explanations that lie below the surface and are more likely to be hidden rather than obvious.

Doing this with our virgin birth topic I see a deep gap between man's animal origin and its prerequisite of physical survival through procreation on the one hand and his capacity to deny this origin through self-denial allowing for society and culture to come to full bloom on the other hand.

All we see around us, our standard of living, our capital, our democracy, our scientific endeavour and division of labour are only possible because at some stage in the past our ancestors learnt that postponing gratification and disciplining raw instinct could have major evolutionary advantages. Religion was always at the forefront of advocating and strengthening that advantage.

I cannot think of any religion, whether primitive or modern, which has not in some form or other canalized libido. By this I mean that religion has either surrounded libido with proscriptions or prescriptions in order to safeguard tribal, family or social systems. Surviving religions have often gone further. They have sublimated the libido and thereby turned it from enemy to ally: for instance, the Catholic Church believed that its priests could concentrate better on their calling and vocation, if they stayed celibate.

Our Bible is a beautiful example of this sublimation. From its physical base, love (eros in Greek) became transfigured into love, friendship or affection between members of the clan, family, army unit, or community (filia in Greek). This meant a natural affection for those with whom one had much in common and with whom one had a bond of friendship. This in turn became further sublimated or universalized into God's love (agape in Greek). The latter, agape, is exemplified in Christ's love also for the rejects, the ugly , the despised, the mentally deranged, the battlers, those who cannot cope, rather than only for those for whom one had a natural bond of friendship.

The virgin birth in our text is therefore a good example of the elimination of the physical base of libido in order to allow for its sublimation into agape represented by the Holy Spirit, the emotional or faith aspect of the trinity or the love of God. Paul's remark (1 Corinthians 7:9) that it is better to marry than to burn with vain desire is another example of the practical endorsement of canalization of the libido, even if, as Paul also suggests, control or sublimation as we would call it now leads to the 'agape' that God has in mind for Christians.

Yet as the Catholic Church is presently experiencing, the celibacy of priests may indeed be the path to libido sublimation, but the libido is of necessity a strong instinct not that easy to control. One can only be understanding and observe with tragic sympathy that a certain percentage of its clergy has not been able to cope with the rigorous demands of celibacy.

But there is a third reason why in contrast with Bishop Spong, I personally have no trouble with repeating in the apostle's creed that I believe in Jesus conceived by the Holy Ghost, born of the Virgin Mary. The virgin birth compels us to distance ourselves from the idea that symbol is inferior to fact. Why should it be? Haven't humans outgrown the faith in fact as something glorious that can stand on its own feet without interpretation? Hasn't the gospel and our experience of the living saviour, the Lord of life, shown us that in Jesus we meet the altogether 'other?' And isn't the 'other' enlarging our existence beyond what you and I make of that existence if we refuse to open ourselves to the wonder and miracle of God coming to man? Aren't our ancestors' and our own horizons extended when we let Jesus into our lives?

If that is the case the virgin birth points to a symbol rather than a fact, lifting us to a glimpse of God who expects submission rather than control, humility rather than pride, faith rather than reason. The virgin birth points to an enduring aspect of life surpassing the momentary. The virgin birth symbolizes the reality of the Holy Spirit that according to our text overshadows the Virgin Mary. It is the Holy Spirit that has since time immemorial facilitated the vision that has made man more than his animal instinct.

There is a dialectic or symbiosis at the heart of existence. The virgin birth is like a parable. It points to something valuable in life. It is not to be trivialized or prematurely resolved by what we insist is so-called 'reality.' What we define as 'reality' is always interpreted. It does not exist without interpretation. Christians insist that Jesus, the Messiah, the Christ, the anointed one of the lineage of David, is eternally alive not just as an abstract model to be emulated, but as someone walking next to you and me, whether we want it or not.

It is this living presence of Jesus and the Holy Spirit for all times which the virgin birth is attempting to highlight.

Conclusion: (1) The virgin birth is the Gospel's way to point to a supernatural dimension of life. God's pure order and wholeness (salvation) can only affect the disorder and fragility (sin) of our human existence if we leave it on its own. Bending it to what we want it to be or limit it to what we can understand will only destroy that dimension.

(2) The virgin birth is a sublimation of our libido and denies our libido its place as a central determinant for living beyond which there nothing more important. The virgin birth is not less important than our urge to procreate. Through countering the libido's physical dominance sublimation opens up the world of social systems and cultures and unshackles its hold on our soul and psyche.

(3) The virgin birth restores the symbol to its legitimate place in human history and denies the exclusive hegemony of fact and reason at the centre of history. It points to a less obvious, latent truth, below the surface of the way things appear. Therefore humble adoration rather than usurping the place of the Holy Other is a more promising path on the evolution of existence.

CALVIN 26

THE LAMB OF GOD and THE TREE OF LIFE

Then he showed me the river of the water of life, sparkling like crystal, flowing from the throne of God and of the Lamb down the middle of the city's street. On either side of the river stood a tree of life. Revelation 22:1-2

Our readings for today have two themes:(1) God's global perspective (God's concern for all nations); (2) God's partisan participation in the battle between good and evil, saints and sinners (God representing order in the battle with the satanic forces of chaos). Let us take each of these readings, one by one.

(1) First Psalm 67. It is one of the thanksgiving Psalms thought to be composed by David. It thanks God for a bountiful harvest, but it also deals with God's reign and just treatment of nations. It asks God to be gracious and 'to make his face shine upon us' (verse 1) and to make his saving power known to all nations (verse 2). In other words, God is the source of inspiration not just for David, but for the nation and the entire world

The next five verses continue this universal perspective. God is described as both judge and guide for all people on the planet (verses 3-5), but also the one who has provided a good harvest (verse 6), blessed his people and therefore must be feared until the ends of the earth (verse 7). And by 'fearing God' the author did not suggest that people should be afraid of God, but should stand in awe of him, seek his inspiration and the source of motivation.

God is here portrayed as the protector and guide for the individual and the social good. He is thought to promote justice and order not just in one culture and society, but in the entire world, however much societies and cultures might differ one from another. They all need 'God's saving power', that is to say, they all need integrity, or righteousness as the older translations call it, if they are to survive as individuals, nations or groups of nations.

The problem is, of course, that individuals may clash with other individuals, that groups within nations may be at loggerheads with one another and that nations may quarrel amongst themselves, with sometimes disastrous consequences for their own chances of survival. In other words, order can easily turn into disorder. The Bible usually associates these sources of conflict with Satan and the sources of healing with God. That is certainly the case with our New Testament reading, Revelation 21:22–22:5.

(2) What does it say? Before we come to that, let us first look at the context.

The Book of Revelation is a strange book. It is not exactly popular with preachers. Calvin does not use it much. It is full of mysteries, strange visions and images. Yet its major theme has always had a strong appeal to an age of war and rapid change. It speaks about a world in which satanic forces appear to have the upper hand, vanquishing what is good, orderly and peaceful. Yet it also maintains that God's kingdom will win out in the end. It is at hand. God, who in the first verses of the Bible (Genesis 1:1-5) creates order out of chaos, or light out of darkness, will continue to do so until the very end of time.

During World War II people in the German-occupied countries, such as the Netherlands flocked to the churches where sermons and lectures were given on the Book of Revelation, mainly because it dealt with Christians martyred by the military might of the Roman Empire. People saw parallels with their own suffering, their country being overrun by Nazi Germany. The Book of Revelation gave people hope because it spoke about the total defeat of the anti-Christ which to their way of thinking was identical with Nazism.

Yet even within Germany, Revelation was very popular in certain circles. One of them was an old guard on the third floor of the Magdeburg Prison where I was serving a sentence for undermining the German war economy. He was an old man in his sixties and had been in prison work all his life. He had never been a Nazi and did not even pay lip service to the Hitler worship around him. He was kind to all prisoners. The other guards treated him as the village idiot, but he was no fool; no prisoner could take advantage of him and there was no corruption or false dealing with food when he was around.

He was a pious Lutheran and usually went around the cell block with a well-used Bible. He expected the return of the Messiah any day and loved to talk about the city of God as graphically described in the Book of Revelation: streets of pure gold and the fruits of the tree of life with The Lord and the Lamb of God on the throne.

Every day he came to visit me, ostensibly to inspect my cell, but actually to practise his little sermons on me. I had several debates with him which usually finished with him having the last word. Strangely enough, this was not because I felt compelled to pay homage to his authority – he was much more secure than any of the other guards – but because through listening I seemed to get the full benefit of relaxation and edification I felt after his visits. I was enthralled that there were Germans of his calibre around.

He never discussed Nazism, politics or even the war. To him the gospel and the Lord on his throne in Revelation were the great news. I did not agree with his visions. Yet to me they became signs of something very precious: a soul at peace with himself, a solid trust in God's plan for the world, a mental calmness which I had not been able to muster.

THE LAMB OF GOD and THE TREE OF LIFE

The Book of Revelation was obviously written at a time when the Roman Emperors had begun to be worried about the appeal of Christianity and the refusal of Christians to worship the emperor and the state. In very colourful language the latter are described as harlots and the beast with seven heads plainly refers to the seven hills on which Rome was built. Satan and the Roman Empire were obviously one and the same.

The Book of Revelation was written towards the end of the first century AD. Revelation is the Latin word for what in Greek is called Apocalypses, both meaning disclosure of what is hidden. And what is hidden and will be revealed is God's firm control, in spite of the suffering and affliction of the martyred believers. In the future there will be no corruption, no evil, no persecution and no death.

John, the author of Revelation is not likely to be either the disciple of Jesus or the gospel writer, but a Jewish Christian from Asia Minor. His Christian beliefs and repudiation of emperor worship had gotten him into trouble with the Roman authorities and he was therefore exiled to the island of Patmos in the Aegean Sea where even now tourists can visit the grotto where he is supposed to have written his visions.

John was actually lucky to be exiled rather than executed. The Roman Emperor at the time Domitian (51-96 AD), like his predecessor Nero (37-68 AD) made a habit of murdering the followers of Jesus, Nero in 62 AD because he accused Christians of setting fire to Rome, Domitian during his reign from 81-96 AD because he wanted to restore the old standards and conduct of Roman religion. In 64 AD both St Peter and St Paul had been martyred and towards the end of the century many of their followers had been similarly dispatched.

Our reading for today starts at chapter 21:22. It bluntly says that in the New Jerusalem, the city of God, temples were not necessary anymore. Normally they may be pointers to God, but because the satanic forces have now been conquered, 'the Lord God the almighty and the Lamb' rule without obstruction. Therefore, anything to do with religious organization and organized ritual is now downgraded. The verse seems to tell us that order now has conquered chaos. Light has so much overcome darkness that both chaos and darkness have vanished from the world. Therefore perfection, salvation, wholeness, integrity and righteousness do now exist without their opposite, imperfection, sin, corruption, disintegration and inequity.

It is often in the sectarian segments of our culture that mundane establishments are down staged and the heavenly perspective is highlighted. In those circles the organism is usually contrasted with organization. What unites Christians, they say, is the exuberance of the Holy Spirit, not formality. The joy of redemption, they say, is central to what they are all about. They contrast conviction with hypocrisy, fervency with prudence, ecstasy with indifference.

They therefore appeal more to those who are marginal to society than those who are comfortable in the prevailing arrangements of power.

They therefore like the description in verse 23 of God's city not needing 'sun or moon ... for the glory of God gave it light, and its lamp was the Lamb.' In Revelation John uses the idea of Jesus as the Lamb of God numerous times. To him Jesus is not the power hungry conqueror, but the innocent, crucified, saviour. He is, as the thief crucified with him testified, the man who had done nothing wrong (Luke 23:41)' in contrast with those who did the crucifying, the political (Roman) and religious establishment (Sanhedrin) of the time.

The idea of the Messiah as the Lamb of God has a venerable history. It goes all the way back to the prophet Isaiah who depicts the Messiah as a lamb, led to the slaughter, sacrificed for men's sin (Isaiah 53:5-7). And long before Isaiah, blameless lambs (Leviticus 23:12) were used as substitutes for human transgression (Leviticus 14:12 ff.) Is then this picture of Jesus as the 'lamb of God' an outdated remnant of ancient Hebrew religion?

No, it is not. Sacrifice has always been, and still is, a clarification of priorities. It is a form of commitment. Freud thought of civilization as a sacrifice of primitive impulses. Sacrifice improves devotion to the sacred cause. And in our instance of Jesus being the lamb sacrificed for men's sin and it being the core of the communion service, is a solemn way of reinforcing God's control of order and his conquest of disorder (sin) by means of the highest form of sacrifice, giving one's life for the sacred cause.

Yet Jesus as the Lamb of God is also God's warning to the world in general and Christians in particular, that man-made security is not the end-all of existence. John's apocalyptic visions and his constant use of the picture of Jesus as the Lamb of God, tells me that there is more to life than the harsh reality of survival of the fittest and man's ardent attempt to hide behind a seemingly impregnable wall of power, wealth and mundane securities.

It tells me that the very vulnerability of the lamb has its own peculiar potency and authority. It tells me that the apparent absolute power of the military might of the Roman Empire had its own weaknesses. It tells me that the obvious powerlessness of the Christian martyrs, so familiar to John, had its own strength. After all the subsequent spread of Christianity all over the globe at the expense of Emperor worship was based entirely on the blood of the martyrs as the seed of the Church.

The image of the Lamb of God and its importance for the author of Revelation has another aspect. It points concretely to the close association of Jesus with other vulnerable, often rejected members of our society. The gospels give us many examples of Jesus actually pointing to harlots, beggars, foreigners, such as the Samaritans, and tax collectors as closer to God than the arrogant pillars of society, the rich and the powerful, the rulers and those dominating the major social institutions. He seems to say that the vulnerability of the losers and the social failures may bring them closer to God's saving power than the proud and the successful.

Ever since, the Christian Church has been sensitive to the underprivileged and disadvantaged. Christianity has always strongly assisted and helped those who had fallen by the wayside, who had and have a raw deal.

The image of the vulnerable and crucified Lamb of God has contributed much to the inclusiveness rather than the exclusiveness of western societies.

And still there is on the global scale the real danger of the rich getting richer and the poor getting poorer. Or to say this differently, our concern for the underdeveloped countries, where families have to live on one dollar a day is decidedly smaller than our concern with maintaining our own high standard of living. In any country the establishment, often supported by religion, has almost absolute power as compared with the marginal, those at the bottom of the heap.

I vividly remember how appalled I was by the 1944 Christmas service in the unheated hall of the prison with hard labour in Halle, Germany. As all Sunday services this one too began and finished with the Hitler salute. The sermon too, as always, was lavishly sprinkled with references to the Fuehrer, God's protection of the nation, heroic soldiers dying unselfishly for a free Germany, and the messianic responsibility of the Reich.

The sermon was nothing but warmed-up Nazi broth. More than half the prisoners were foreigners, most of them political. Yet the chaplain insisted on nailing his Nazi colours to the mast. All we seemed to hear was the bubbly foam of a Nazified Christianity.

Where was the universality of the Christian Church? Strangely enough it was there in the readings about the suffering servant in Isaiah and about the birth of Christ from Luke. It seemed to whisper to me that the suffering Messiah born as a defenceless infant in a hostile society was at one with other marginals such as us.

Over against the sermon, the readings seemed to preach that salvation was not with the establishment (Nazi or otherwise) but with the poor of heart who had put their burden on Christ, the powerless, defenceless Lamb of God, sacrificed for our sins. This was the unexpected consolation in an otherwise inconsolable, self-destroying world.

The image of the Lamb of God, sacrificed for the sins of the world, is therefore not just an ancient idea built on ancient, out-dated symbolism of a primitive society. It is pertinent for any culture that aspires to be inclusive. The image of a vulnerable (yet blameless lamb, Leviticus 23:12) evokes both the idea of sinlessness/perfection and Christian sympathy and understanding of all who feel rejected by society at large.

The final verses of Chapter 21 (verses 24-27) continue to depict an ideal world, where the lamp of the Lamb of God provides the light 'by which all the nations walk, and the kings of the earth bring into it all their splendour (verse 24).' In this city of God and his Lamb, disorder, corruption, persecution and injustice have been completely banished. Satan (here identified with the Roman Emperor and its murdering of the Christian martyrs) has been definitively defeated. So much so that that there is no further need for securing the city walls: 'The gates of the city shall never be shut by day – and there will be no night (verse 25).'

In this ideal world where there is no oppression by the occupying Roman forces, killing wherever they can find Christians, the nations of the world will bring 'their wealth and splendour (verse 26).' And because Satan, his falsehood, his corruption, disorder and injustice have now been conquered (actually do not exist anymore) nothing 'unclean' or any person who does not accord with the values, norms and beliefs of the Lamb of God are barred from the city of God. Only 'those who are inscribed in the Lamb's roll of the living', in other words, those who confess their faith in Jesus as saviour and who follow his injunctions for living, are citizens of the city of God.

Yet, as Calvin indicates (*Inst.* I xiv 14-15), Satan is also a 'roaring lion (1 Peter 5:8)', representing injustice, 'opposing the reign of integrity.' He sows 'the tares in order to corrupt the seed of eternal life (Matthew 13:28).' 'Truth he assails with lies, light he obscures with darkness. The minds of men he involves in error; he stirs up hatred, inflames strife and war, and all in order that he may overthrow the kingdom of God, and drown men in eternal perdition with himself.'

Chapter 22, the last one in the Book of Revelation and the last one in the Bible, begins (verse 1) with a picture of 'the river of the water of life, sparkling like crystal, flowing from the throne of God and of the Lamb.' It is not stagnant, but sparkling and flowing. God's spirit is a life-giving spirit. It is feeding those who are thirsting for fulfilment. It is cleansing the robes of the believers to make them immune to satanic influences.

The next verse (2) introduces another well-known picture. 'On either side of the river stood a tree of life (with leaves that) serve for the healing of nations.' The tree of life can already be found in the beginning of the Bible. Genesis 2:9 introduces both the tree of life and the tree of knowledge in the middle of the Garden of Eden. In Genesis 3:22 the tree of life makes those who eat its fruit immortal and Adam is driven out of the Garden of Eden to prevent him using it for a meal.

THE LAMB OF GOD and THE TREE OF LIFE

To Calvin the expulsion from paradise and from eating from the tree of life was God's way of teaching Adam 'to become weary of his pride that he might learn to embrace true humility.' Adam, he says, 'not content with his condition, had tried to ascend higher than was lawful.' God 'resolved to wrest out of the hands of a man that which was the occasion or ground of confidence, lest he should form for himself a vain hope of the perpetuity of the life which he had lost.'

Isaiah (61:3) also uses the tree symbol. The humble, the broken-hearted, the captives, the mourners shall be called trees of integrity/righteousness. These are the people who Calvin calls 'those in whom the justice of God or good order shines forth.' From this he draws 'universal doctrine, namely, that there is no other way in which we are restored to life than when we are planted by the Lord.'

John too, regards the tree of life as a symbol for wholeness, integrity. It guarantees the very fulfilment humans are craving for. It derives its efficacy from being the source of meaning and order. Yet that order is not produced by humans, the producers and enablers of meaning. It is derived from the throne of God and the Lamb. Its efficacy depends on its being given rather than independently created.

Verses 3-5 reiterates John's vision that disorder has now vanquished. God's servants worship God and the Lamb and see him face to face (verse 4). There is now 'no more night, nor will they need the light of lamp or sun, for the Lord God will give them light; and they shall reign for evermore (verse 5).'

To sum up our readings for today: John's vision in Revelation transcends the disorderly world of persecution and corruption. The satanic forces represented by Emperor Domitian are being replaced by the city of God. A river of crystal waters 'flowing from the throne of God and the Lamb (22:1)' symbolizes this new world. John calls it the 'river of life.' This river feeds the tree of life. It is the foundation for humans for building existence. It can withstand all the storms of life. It is the word of God, the only source of security when everything else fails. It is the deepest source of one's serenity and integrity.

CALVIN 27

THE BEGINNING and THE END

I am the Alpha and the Omega, the first and the last, the beginning and the end. Revelation 22:13

Psalm 97 anticipates the picture of today's New Testament reading. God is the king of the universe. He is the Alpha and the Omega, the first and the last, the beginning and the end, as Revelation 22:13 describe him. He encompasses all that exists. He is like the first and the last letter of the Greek alphabet, the bookends that sustain all that is in between.

The psalmist begins (verse 1) with describing the earth. The coasts, islands, clouds, mists (verse 2), the fire (verse 3), the lightening-flash (verse 4) melting mountains, all point to 'The Lord of all the earth' (verse 5). Yet God is not only the creator of the universe and therefore above the idols and images worshipped by others (verse 7), he is also on the social rather than the physical level, a God whose integrity/righteousness extends to global justice (verses 6-8).

It is this global justice which Calvin (in his commentary on Isaiah 61:3) equates with 'good order', both concepts (justice and order) constituting the essence of God's plan for the world, that we also find in Revelation 22. Closely tied in with God's righteousness/justice/integrity is 'the Lord's love for those who hate evil (Psalm 97:10, also Revelation 22:11). Psalm 97 finishes with associating the righteous with light rather than darkness. The author of Revelation does the same in chapter 21:24 ff.

The last chapter of the last book in the Bible is an actual description of a world in which the satanic forces have been overcome and eliminated. God's order is altogether different from man's order. In the city of God all evil will be banned. The prophets, of whom the author, John, is one, are the messengers of God and their prophecies are on the point of being fulfilled (22:6-11).

John insists on his prophetic heritage. He mentions prophecy as much as six times in today's reading. A prophet in the Hebrew tradition was not just a preacher foretelling the future. Above all he was God's mouthpiece and as such usually not very popular. After all God often rebuked leaders and sometimes the entire nation. They were apostles of change in contrast with the priests who typically consolidated establishments and defended the status quo.

John's vision depicts an ideal world in which all that is so obviously oppressive (the Roman Empire and its power to inflict worship of the emperor), all that is evil and filthy (verse 11) have been overthrown. The Lord will intervene radically and what is more, to John the situation is so clearly intolerable that the Lord will come any time. He will recompense 'everyone according to his deeds (verse 12).'

Then follows our text for today, where the Lord says: 'I am the Alpha and the Omega, the first and the last, the beginning and the end (verse 13).' In other words God envelops all of life to those who believe and belong to his city. He guides and protects them. He provides the contour of meaning for them. He puts their existence in an eternal context. He guarantees their integrity, wholeness, salvation, from the beginning to the end. His justice will prevail. They will be nurtured by the tree of life (verse 14).

By contrast 'outside are dogs, sorcerers and fornicators, murderers and idolaters, and all who love and practice deceit (verse 15).' They will not be allowed to enter God's city. They have been written off in God's books. They therefore cannot obtain righteousness, integrity and wholeness. They failed to take the opportunity to live life to the full. They have missed both their chances and their ultimate destiny.

John finishes the Book of Revelation by insisting that Jesus has provided him 'with this testimony for the churches (verse 16)' and that nothing should be taken away or added to it, failing which 'the plagues described in this book (verse 18)' will be heaped on the culprit. Also 'God will take away from him his share in the tree of life and the Holy City, described in this book (verse 19).'

So far in our summary of the readings for today we have followed the smooth transition from the physical universe to the social one. After all that is the way the authors of both Psalm 97 and Revelation 22 think. However, are patterns of order actually so harmoniously intertwined? And if they are not (as I think they are not – they actually clash quite violently sometimes – personal advantage often conflicts with the social good), it must be crucial for us to find out where God stands. Does he favour the one over the other? And if not, how can we understand him covering or, more likely, reconciling, both.

After all, the religious segment of our culture is not exempt from conflicts of this kind. The priestly and the prophetic side in our Jewish/Christian/Islamic heritage have fought life and death battles on this issue: Jeremiah was stoned to death, John the Baptist decapitated, Jesus was crucified, Stephen was stoned to death, and Mohammed would have been killed if he had not managed to escape to Medina in 622 AD, and Calvin to Paris in 1533 AD. And all this happened because a powerful priestly establishment felt threatened by profoundly critical, but often powerless prophets, who were convinced that God spoke through them. Although they were usually powerless, scripture backed their legitimacy through incorporation in its pages.

Jesus recognizes the full impact of this conflict between kinds of order. Luke 13:1–5 tells the story of the conflict between the physical and the social order.

People came to Jesus and told him about the Galileans whose blood Pilate had mixed with their sacrifices (verse 1). Were they greater sinners than anyone else in Galilee (verse 2)? Jesus says: 'They were not (verse 3).' Eighteen people were killed when the tower fell on them at Siloam (verse 4). Again Jesus says that they were not guiltier than all the other people living in Jerusalem, but then adds: 'unless you repent, you will come to the same end (verse 5).'

The implication of the story is that to Jesus accidents, such as earthquakes etc., should not be linked to God's punishment for individual or social misdeeds. People should not feel guilty about them. In other words, accidents or natural catastrophes may be destructive and therefore destroy order, yet they are different from moral, ethical, misdeeds that people should feel guilty about, such as stealing, lying, adultery, murdering, envying, etc.

Both catastrophes and sins break down order and create disorder. Yet the physical order is different from the social order. If God is the creator of heaven and earth and light out of darkness as the first few verses of Genesis on the first pages of the Bible maintain, then the order that God rescues from chaos is different from the social order that God wants to safeguard by discouraging the trespasses of the Ten Commandments.

Societies and individuals may badly need the consolation, comforting and understanding of prayer when natural catastrophes or death strike, but they are different, Jesus seems to say, compared with the disorder resulting from thwarting and contravening social values and norms. By contrast repentance, penitence, forgiveness, etc. are called for when the social order is imperilled. Sin is linked to an endangered social order. Salvation is linked to a strengthened social order.

Yet that social order needs more than mere awareness of its necessity for human survival. What the city of God (as depicted in the last chapter of Revelation) adds, is the conviction that it and the tree of life flowing from the throne of God and the Lamb of God are superior to, actually conquer, the forces that Satan commands. They break down, while God's forces build up.

Conviction is the right word here, as faith in what God rather than Satan stands for is central. Salvation, wholeness and integrity are hardly ever achieved by the rational argument, but usually by emotional contagion. That's why John in the last chapter of Revelation (22:17) comes back to the importance of the Holy Spirit. 'Come forward you who are thirsty; accept the water of life, a free gift to all who desire it.'

Faith therefore is the crucial prerequisite for repentance. Faith is also, as Calvin has it in his 30 page chapter on the subject in the *Institutes of the Christian Religion,* inseparable from repentance which, as you may recall, Jesus said was a necessity to avoid premature death. Why? Repentance is only necessary when one feels guilty. If this is a necessity, as Jesus implies, what should one feel guilty about? Obviously it is not the catastrophic events mentioned in Luke 13.

Calvin says that repentance is not only inseparable from faith, but is also produced by faith. He insists that faith is primary. To him it is not individuals feeling guilty about something and then projecting the need for forgiveness on a fabricated external source. Why is Calvin so adamant about the one way direction from faith to repentance and not from repentance to faith?

Faith is the all-important link between God and humans. The latter learn to think in terms of God's expectations. Without the faith relationship humans are thrown back on themselves. And since no one can exist without being influenced by his surroundings or his social environment, human behaviour is of necessity strongly affected by families, upbringing, communities, schools, peer groups, churches, friends, relatives, etc. Without God all these expectations become man-centred and therefore narrower than they ought to be.

However, through faith in God or Jesus, the Lamb of God as we read last week in the reading from Revelation, humans learn to look at themselves and the world around them the way God sees it. And if God promotes global justice and global order, then from that point of view, much is wrong with tension, conflict, war, distrust, injustice, corruption, evil, sin, pride, etc. on all these various levels where expectations are important to us as individuals. Then we learn to be concerned not just about these faults and imperfections in our immediate environment, but also in our region, our nation and the world at large.

Faith therefore is elemental. Faith links us to God's view of things and imprints it in our hearts. I remember how in 1954 when Ruth and I arrived at Union Seminary at the heart of bustling, hard-nosed, dog-eat-dog world of Manhattan in New York we felt surrounded by Christian charity, goodwill and concern for others. Not just on the part of other students from all over the United States but from all over the world, but also by faculty, all living within the seminary walls. It was faith in action rather than in theory.

That is also the way Calvin sees it. To him humans are never without a certain amount of disorder in their personal lives, but also and primarily in the individual's relation with his family, society, culture or any other form of order. He calls that sin. Repentance therefore means apologizing for that disorder. For Christians the apology is directed to God, the epitome of order, the provider of salvation or wholeness. The faith relationship with God is the only link with him. Through his life and sacrifice Jesus Christ has shown the way to repair and strengthen that relationship and therefore Christians ask for pardon in Jesus' name.

This also means that ideally the concrete form of repentance should always be translatable in terms of the contribution, or lack of contribution, a particular item of order or disorder makes to the patterns of order mentioned above. We can test this by taking each of the various values and norms mentioned by Calvin in his chapter on repentance and trace their effect on the various units of social organization.

It is easy enough to think in terms of individual sins, trespasses and shortcomings. But are we also responsible for global mishaps and conflicts, such as ethnic cleansing in Kosovo or Uganda and Burundi? There is very little we can do about it, is there? Yet from God's global point of view, it goes definitely against the grain of the global justice and order that both our readings for today attribute to him. Maybe that it is our task to also repent for the kind of world, we as human beings have made and are making of planet earth. Or on a more national level, it may be our task as Christian believers to repent for injustices perpetrated by the rich on the poor, or the powerful on the powerless or to repent for the blind eye we cast on the perpetrators of social injustice and discrimination.

Calvin 'enumerates seven causes, effects, or parts he thinks belong to repentance', as mentioned in 2 Corinthians 7:11. In his first letter to the Christian community, in Corinth, St Paul accused it of party divisions and ignoring a case of incest. They had repented and in the second letter Calvin comments on the seven positive effects this repentance had. Each of these seven effects can also be traced more generally to the contribution they make to increased group integrity.

The first one is *carefulness* which Calvin describes as the care and attention to 'completely disentangle oneself from the chains of the devil and keep a better guard against his snares, so as not afterwards to lose the guidance of the Holy Spirit.' Obviously care for others has also a positive effect on the bond of any unit of social organization to which the individual belongs. Care gives humans the sense of belonging they need for their security and wellbeing.

Next Calvin mentions *excuse* which to him does not mean 'defence, in which the sinner escapes the judgment of God by either denying his fault or extenuating it', but an apology 'to obtain pardon.' An apology clears the air and therefore ideally allows for closer integration of any group, family or fellowship for which the apology is meaningful, or even necessary, to repair disunity.

The third component of repentance is *indignation* which to Calvin occurs when the 'sinner expostulates and is offended with himself on recognising his perverseness and ingratitude to God.' This relates to the degree of honesty and feeling of the 'sinner' when he or she repents. St Paul praises the Corinthians for these and the other sentiments constituting their repentance for the wrong they had done.

The fourth consequence of repentance is *fear*. Calvin explains it as 'the fearful severity of the divine anger against sinners.' In other words, the Corinthians feared that they had not met God's expectations about the behaviour of Christians and by repenting and mending their way their faith relationship with God had grown and so had their communal integrity.

Desire (to Calvin 'as they had dreaded punishment on receiving Paul's admonition, so they eagerly aimed at amendment') is the item which led to augmented common endeavour. So is the sixth item *zeal* (to Calvin 'everyone, with great fervour of zeal, aimed to give evidence of his repentance'). This too would naturally lead to a greater sense of common participation.

The last consequence of repentance, *revenge*, (to Calvin 'the wickedness which they had countenanced by the connivance and indulgence, they had afterwards shown themselves rigorous in avenging') similarly belongs to the ever so many sentiments (Calvin calls them 'affections') that are implied in repentance as cause or effect. They reinforce or weaken social cohesion, the bond that keeps various patches, patterns or pockets of order together.

To recapitulate our argument so far: in Psalm 97 we were reminded of the beauty of God's creation. The coasts, islands, mists, the fire, the lightning-flash melting mountains introduce the moving poem. But then at the end the author moves to the social rather than the physical order also under God's dominion. Here he introduces God's integrity, righteousness extended to an orderly system of global justice.

Then we looked at the first and the last page of the Bible and our text which deals with God representing order in the face of chaos, the Alpha and the Omega, the beginning and the end. But then we asked the awkward question: 'what order are we talking about?' and discovered that there are all sorts and patterns of order which may be, and often are, at loggerheads with one another.

We looked at one of these discrepancies in Luke 13:1-5, and found that guilt had nothing to do with these physical events, although they too came under the rubric of God's close association with any order. If God represents, as our text implies, all-encompassing, all-comprehending order, expressed in him being the Alpha and the Omega, the beginning and the end, then Jesus actually says that we are talking about a different kind of order. Guilt feelings and repentance refer to a social rather than a physical order and both are fundamentally different.

Then again we looked at our reading for today and found that repentance should also include more than individual shortcomings and sins, such as the kind of national or global disorder that conflict with God's justice and order. We also looked at the solution that Jesus offered in Luke 13:5 by looking in more detail at the seven causes and need for repentance and translated these items to their practical social effect.

Yet there are other fundamental differences between patches, patterns, of order that we could look at and which makes us wonder how God could still be the Alpha and the Omega, the beginning and the end and straddle all these varying pockets of order. Let us mention one more: the deep discrepancy between the individual and social integrity or wholeness.

One does not have to dig very deeply to discover that the Bible is actually full of descriptions of conflicts of this kind. The prophet Nathan accuses King David of stealing Bathsheba, the wife of Uriah the Hittite. David then repents (2 Samuel 12:13). King Ahab wants to buy Naboth's vineyard. When he refuses to sell it, Jezebel, Ahab's wife, cooks up a plan to have Naboth killed. She hires two scoundrels who falsely accuse Naboth of cursing both God and king. Naboth is stoned to death and Ahab now has the land. God speaking through the prophet Elijah strongly condemns the shenanigans and tells Ahab that he will die a gruesome death on the very land he has so deviously acquired. Ahab is now extremely sorry and asks God for forgiveness. This is granted and the gruesome death is postponed (1 Kings 21:1–29).

In the New Testament flesh (sometimes associated with personal integrity) is often contrasted with spirit (sometimes associated with social integrity). For instance Jesus accuses his disciples of a 'willing spirit', but 'weak flesh (Matthew 26:41).' St Paul contrasts his carnality with his spirituality: 'In my mind I am God's willing servant, but in my own nature I am bound fast, as I say, to the law of sin and death (Romans 7:23)'.

Conclusion: God is indeed the Alpha and the Omega, the beginning and the end, the first and the last, represented by God, Jesus the Lamb of God and also the Holy Spirit. We will celebrate the latter next week (Pentecost and the ecumenicity it implies). It is through faith that Christians have attempted to meet God's expectations and through the ages have incorporated in their day-to-day living their concern for others, close by and far away.

They have never fully succeeded. Therefore repentance is crucial for all Christians anywhere. Therefore it is also essential to never neglect the prophetic emphasis we find in Revelation 22:19 (the third last verse in the Bible): 'should anyone take away from the words in this book of prophecy, God will take away from him his share in the tree of life and the holy city described in this book.'

CALVIN 28

JESUS: REFUGEE or KING?

… an Angel of the Lord appeared to Joseph in a dream, and said to him: 'Rise up, take the child and his mother, and escape with them to Egypt, and stay there until I tell you.' Matthew 2:13

Has it ever happened to you that you sing a hymn and then wonder whether you actually believe it? Yet you sing it anyway, because everyone else does. Or you sing it because you like the tune?

At Christmas time we sing again and again that Jesus is king, but isn't the picture we have in our mind of Jesus anything but a king? Look it up in your hymn book. Hymn 224 begins 'Joy to the world. The Lord is come; let earth receive her king.' Or Hymn 227: 'Hark! The herald angels sing, glory to the newborn king.' Or Hymn 235: 'Angels from the realms of glory … worship Christ, the newborn king.' Or Hymn 239: 'As with gladness men of old … hallelujahs to our king.' Or Hymn 240: 'O little town of Bethlehem … and praises sing to God the king.' And these are not the only ones.

A king? Yet born in a stable? And crucified at the end of his life? What is so regal about a stable and a cross? Our Westminster Confession also refers to Jesus as prophet, priest and king, as does the other Christmas Hymn we have just sung (218: Unto us a boy is born! King of all creation) But the third verse goes as follows:

> Herod then with fear was filled:
> 'A prince', he said, in Jewry!'
> All the little boys he killed
> At Bethlehem in his fury.

And didn't Pilate ironically write an inscription to be fastened to the cross saying: 'Jesus of Nazareth King of the Jews?'

Similarly, today's story is anything but typical for a king: Joseph and Mary escaped to Egypt to prevent Jesus from being one of the children below the age of two in Bethlehem to be slaughtered at the behest of Herod who was mortified by the idea that a baby from that town would usurp his throne? As we all know, Herod was a cruel individual, dead set on keeping power at any price. And this included murdering some of his relatives and offspring.

And so Mary, Joseph and Jesus had to flee to Egypt and become refugees in a foreign land, inevitably relegated to the bottom of the social ladder. Everywhere refugees are marginal people at the lowest rather than the highest rung of the pecking order. Often they can only save their lives by abandoning their homes and communities where they were respected and comfortable.

Yet saving their lives comes at the cost of having to learn another language, having to adjust to a different culture, to change one's taken for granted rules of behaviour, adopting different ways of acting and reacting. And the older the refugee the more difficult it is to fit in the new environment. As we all know youth comes with flexibility. Old age comes with hardening of the arteries.

In 1533 Calvin became a refugee. He saved his life only because his students helped him escape Paris while the bailiffs were at his door to arrest him for heresy. He became very aware of the danger of non-conformity and the need for flexibility. Interpreting today's reading about Jesus' escape to Egypt Calvin wonders why God did not protect Jesus from Herod and the exile and then concludes: '… it teaches us, that they act improperly who prescribe to God a fixed plan of action.' By implication Calvin thinks that predestination and order in human affairs is not man's prerogative, but God's. Order is in God's rather than human hands. The problem in human affairs is often that what is order on one level is disorder on another.

In 1960 Dr Visser t'Hooft, Secretary General of the World Council of Churches asked me to write a book on the sociology of migration and religion in preparation for the 1961 conference on that theme in Leysin, Switzerland. It was good to be in the USA at the time. Like Australia, the United States is built on the experience of immigrants, exiles and refugees. And I discovered very soon how vast the literature was on the pain of exile and how vast and widespread the refugee problems of adjustment were not just in Bonegilla in Australia where I had been chaplain, but even more in other parts of the world, such as the Soviet Union and Germany where persecution had been endemic. In my academic work ever since I have concentrated on the necessity of identity and the problems of adjusting to a different one.

Jesus' experience as the young child of refugees in Egypt must have made him particularly sensitive to the suffering caused by the history of Jewish exile in Babylon and the rejection of the Hebrew prophets. After all, the long recorded tradition of marginality had even then become the core of Jewish identity and is reflected in both the Psalms and the Books of the Old Testament prophets. The more marginal the Jews became, the more they cherished their identity. And isn't that experience of marginality of individual, family and nation the exact opposite of the royal experience of a king at the top of the social ladder?

There is a long established Israelite tradition, enshrined in the Old Testament, of God the loving, redeeming, deliverer of people's suffering. Our Old Testament reading of Isaiah 63:7-9 testifies to that.

The exiled Israelites have now returned and found their land and temple in ruins. They have learnt what it means to be foreigners in a strange land. They suffered immensely from that experience. Yet it also widened their vision. It taught Isaiah (56:6-7) that even the oppressors did not fit into a neat black/white pattern. He learnt that God's kingdom extended beyond cultural boundaries and that foreigners should be welcomed, 'for my house shall be called a house of prayer for all people.'

A good example of the pain of exile is Psalm 137 which begins:

> By the rivers of Babylon we sat down and wept.
> When we remembered Zion.
> There on the willow-trees
> we hung up our harps,
> for there those who carried us off
> demanded music and singing,
> and our captors called us to be merry:
> 'Sing us one of the songs of Zion.'
> How could we sing the Lord's song
> in a foreign land?

Calvin describes the calamity of exile as being so deep that not even 'all the luxuries of Babylon could tempt the Israelites to forget their native inheritance.' Losing their ethnic identity and their corresponding suffering they equate with 'the deserved chastisement of God.' Being cut off from the worship of God, 'they felt that they were torn from the inheritance of promise.'

Yet Calvin was also aware that the exile enlarged their vision and that their very suffering brought them closer to God and to an understanding of what God was about. The experience of the exile taught the Israelites, says Calvin that 'the children of God, wherever they have lived, have always been like strangers and foreigners in the world.'

In other words, according to Calvin, the exile had a twofold effect on Israel: (1) Their tears of loss made them more humble and penitent and (2) it made for a better understanding of God's universal concern: 'at the time before the exile the worship of God was confined to one place, but now the temple consists of wherever two or three are met together in Christ.' Still on the issue of exile leading to widening one's vision: It happened to me and some of my Dutch friends while being a guest of the Gestapo in Germany during World War II for what the secret police called 'undermining the war-economy.' Yet the imprisonment also cured my black/white thinking. I owe both my increased respect for the Christian faith and even my physical survival during my incarceration to an old Lutheran German guard and a fellow German prisoner who organized a soft job where brains rather than brawn were required.

How can we reconcile the picture of Jesus as a refugee with the similarly scriptural emphasis on Jesus as king?

The solution lies in checking the Bible for what is actually meant by the kingship of Jesus. It may be something quite different from our understanding of a king invariably occupying the highest position in the land.

The best way to do this is to look at our other New Testament reading for today, the parable Jesus told about the marriage feast in Matthew 22:1-14. It is all about a king who was rejected by the very people whose sovereign he was. You remember the story.

The king in question gave a marriage feast for his son. He drew up a special list of highly placed people and sent his servants to invite them, but they had all sorts of excuses: they were kept too busy with their farms or their business. Some of the invitees even treated the servants shamefully and killed them. And so the king decided to extend the invitation to anybody the servants could find. This time the wedding hall was filled with guests. But when the king entered the hall, he saw a man without a wedding garment. Then the king said to the attendants, 'Bind him hand and foot, and cast him into the outer darkness. There men will weep and gnash their teeth.' And then he added: 'For many are called, but few are chosen.'

To Calvin the servants of the king are represented by both the prophets of the Old Testament and later Christ and the apostles (Matthew 22:5). Those who rejected the invitation and 'exercised their cruelty', he says, were affected by a 'universal disease that every man is led away by his desires in consequence of which all are wandering in various directions.'

The kingdom of heaven, the parable says, does not consist only of those who have arrived, the powerful, the 'nouveau riches', those who have made it, those who are at the top of the social ladder. On the contrary, they are the ones, like the rich young man (in Luke 18:18–27), who had done everything right in life. He had kept all God's commandments. Yet his wealth had gone to his head. It was more important to him than God's invitation to join his kingdom, for that is what the wedding feast of the parable is all about.

And therefore God (the king in the parable, whose invitations were rejected by the establishment) also invites the nobodies, the battlers, the great unwashed, the riff-raff, the roughnecks, the prostitutes, the tax collectors, the undesirables, the losers. In other words the rejected king now invites the rejected as well. The kingdom of heaven is altogether different from the kingdom of man, Jesus appears to say. It is inclusive rather than exclusive.

It includes those who cannot get it all together, the broken-hearted, the un-loved, the newcomers, and the sufferers, the refugees, who still have not learnt the locals' ways of acting and reacting, who still speak broken English. Jesus can sympathize with them, because he himself was a refugee.

The king of the parable is also the rejected king, whose invitation of salvation, (united with him at the joyous occasion of the wedding party) is of lesser importance than the pursuit of our businesses and other, narrower interests. Are we so much occupied with the affairs of this world, that we cannot see the larger picture? Our narrow concerns may occupy so much centre stage in our lives, that we squeeze all the joy of the wedding party in the parable out of our perspective.

Aren't our stressful and anxious lives often the product of our narrow concern with our private feelings? We hold on to them like grim death as we are wrongly convinced that this is the only realistic thing to be preserved. And therefore we actually take God's invitation, God's offer of salvation, God's love, God's pity and sympathy as less important than our own self-concocted, self-fabricated search for happiness and fulfilment. The invitation of the parable is for celebration and union with the one who calms our fevered brow, offers salvation and a sense of participation and belonging taking the place of our marginality, alienation, loneliness.

The parable also contains a warning. Even the losers cannot unconditionally enter the kingdom or the wedding party. There is a condition. One has to wear a wedding garment. By this Jesus meant that one can come (wherever we are in the human pecking order), provided our worldly cares have not taken precedence over the joyous anticipation of being invited to God's party. Even our sins can become so precious, Jesus implies, that one cannot let go. In God's heavenly kingdom salvation is primary. It is not found in whatever tickles our senses or gives us a thrill. Salvation is letting God take over.

Only when we are prepared to let God take over can we enter the joy of his party and his presence. One may have to be prepared to confess one's sins and sense of separation, one's imperfection, rather than hold on to them. One has to have a strong desire to be made whole, saved and united. If not, the parable says, the wedding guest is not welcome. He will be thrown out into the utter darkness of existence, where one's teeth gnash. Jesus is always very realistic about the world around us. Even the losers cannot unconditionally enter the kingdom or the wedding party. There is a condition. One has to wear a wedding garment. And by this Jesus meant that one may come wherever one is in the human pecking order, but one has to be prepared and sufficiently motivated to join the joyous occasion of God's presence. One has to be prepared to confess one's sins, one's lack of wholeness, and one's imperfection. One has to have a strong desire to be made whole, saved and united with God.

If not, the parable says, the wedding guest is not welcome. He or she will be thrown out into the utter darkness of existence, where there is gnashing of teeth.

There is no other choice. Either we are at the centre of the universe or God is. If we are at the centre of our narrow universe, we are doomed, engulfed by our self-imposed darkness, where one's teeth are gnashing. Yet when we accept God's invitation leaving the self and our wallowing in confusion and meaninglessness at the door, we enter the light and the joy of the wedding hall.

Jesus is king not because he has joined the overbearing, the haughty, the powerful, or the conquerors but because he has joined the humble, the powerless, the suffering, and the rejected of this world. Therefore he is also a refugee in a world where wealth, power and cleverness seem to determine one's place in the human pecking order. To be a king, today's Bible readings tell us, is to take stock of basic motives. Salvation, our sense of wholeness, is closely bound up, the Bible warns us, not with earthly power, but with the heavenly sort.

Then the temptation to be at the top of the pecking order is sometimes more dangerous than to be relegated to the bottom. Over-estimation of the self is usually a more severe handicap than under-estimation. Yet there is danger in either extreme. To join God's wedding party and to adopt the garment of joyful anticipation of celebration rather than selfish calculation of how to get to the highest rung on the ladder of the human pecking order seems to be Jesus' advice in the parable of the wedding feast.

That is why it is appropriate to celebrate the coming of Jesus as both king and source of authority and also as an exile who shows us that salvation is to be found in God's rather than man's kingdom.

CALVIN 29
ROOTS and ROOTLESSNESS

As it had no root, the seed withered away. Matthew 13:6

Today is Calvin's birthday. He was born exactly 496 years ago, 10 July 1509 in the town of Noyon (Northern France). He grew up in a staunchly Catholic home with three brothers and two sisters. His father was a highly respected lawyer. His mother's piety inspired the entire family. He was solidly educated in the Roman and Greek classics. Even in his early twenties he acquired prominence as leader of the Protestant party in Paris.

In 1533 he had to flee for his life when the Catholic hierarchy discovered that he was the evangelical ghost-writer of the inaugural speech of his friend Nicholas Cop recently elected as vice-chancellor of the University of Paris. He eventually landed in Geneva, Switzerland, where the Reformation had taken hold, but again had to flee that town when the city rejected the discipline he had helped to institute. Yet in 1541 the authorities begged for him to return. The city had enough of the prevailing loose morals and longed for the stability of former days.

Now under Calvin's strong influence, Geneva began to attract French Protestants persecuted by the Catholic authorities. The latter burned at the stake anyone sympathetic to the reformers' cause. Calvin himself had witnessed such an execution of a close friend and it left him with an intense hatred of the Catholic Church of the time. Yet Calvin never denied his roots and upbringing in a pious Catholic home. It is shown in his life-long admiration of the church fathers and in their interpretation of scripture.

The increasing flow of Huguenots fleeing France, the impressive reputation of the newly established Calvinist University drawing students from all over Europe as well as Calvin's towering intellectual and theological influence (reflected even in the Jesuit's curriculum) shifted the balance of power on the Genevan municipality from the local Libertines to the Reformers. Yet Calvin was not offered citizenship until 1559.

All these horrible experiences and his constant ill-health (migraines, pleurisy, consumption, gallstones, and arthritis) did not seem to affect his enormous output and his Christian convictions. When he died on 27 May 1564 at the relatively young age of 54, the entire city of Geneva mourned as if a national calamity had struck it. His comments on today's readings are a testimony to the founder of our Presbyterian and Reformed heritage.

Calvin's life, upbringing and particularly his experiences of having to choose between life and leaving his country must have affected his concern with roots and rootlessness. After all one is not usually aware of the values, norms, ways of acting and reacting unless one is thrown into a new environment where different values, norms, ways of acting and reacting prevail. Does that show in his interpretation of scripture? Let us see whether his handling of today's Bible readings is influenced by his personal experiences.

Our Old Testament reading comes from Genesis 25:19-34. It tells the well-known story of Jacob and Esau. After waiting twenty years, Rebecca, Isaac's wife finally conceives. But all is not going well and she asks the Lord why she is in so much trouble. And God says (verse 23) that there are two nations struggling in her womb, and that her first-born (who happens to be Esau) will serve his twin (Jacob). This goes against the prevailing rules. Calvin therefore thinks that by inverting the order, God 'distinguishes the spiritual from the carnal seed.' And so it happens that Esau sells his birthright for a bowl of soup (verse 33) because, as Calvin says, 'being deprived of the Spirit of God, he relishes only the things of the earth.' Calvin thinks God prefers spiritual rather than carnal roots.

The deeper, spiritual roots are universal. By contrast the shallower, carnal roots are local and coloured by local, ethnic and national differences. This is also true for today's other readings. We may take God's universality for granted, but numerous biblical incidents, such as the exodus from Egypt, the Babylonian exile, the despair of the persecuted and martyrs, deepened the human understanding of God's transcending cultures, civilizations and personal predicaments.

The other, Old Testament reading for today, makes a similar point. It comes from Psalm 119:105-112 which we have sung together. It makes the point that God's word is a 'lamp to our feet (verse 105)' illuminating our path through life. Yet the life of the psalmist is severely afflicted (verse107), so much so that his life is continually at stake (verse 109). Being rooted in God's instructions (verse 111), however, is more important to him than being 'deprived of all other things, such as riches, honours, comforts and pleasures (Calvin's comments).'

Our New Testament reading from Romans 8:1-11 similarly stresses the substantial and essential rather than the superficial and the transient. To Paul Jesus Christ represents the former, or as he writes in his epistle to the Ephesians (3:17): 'Rooted and grounded in love, may you be strong to grasp with all God's people, what is the breadth and length and height and depth of the love of Christ.'

To Paul the new spiritual principle of life in Christ lifts him out of the old vicious circle of sin and death (verse 2) or as Calvin comments: 'the trembling consciences of the godly have an invincible fortress, for they know that while they abide in Christ they are beyond every danger of condemnation.' Paul equates the carnal mind with death and the spiritual mind with life and peace (verse 6). Calvin too links peace with happiness, felicity and integrity. Yet that integrity (or righteousness) is not man-made but God-given (verse 10). It is as Calvin has it:

'a celestial gift', not man's understanding of obeying 'reason through their own will, but such as God rules through his Spirit.' In other words, to have one's roots in Christ is the equivalent of having grasped the fullness of life, although Calvin warns: 'the children of God are called spiritual, not on the ground of a full and complete perfection, but only on account of the newness of life that is begun in them (comment on verse 10).'

The theme of roots versus rootlessness is fully developed in Christ's parable of the sower and the seeds (Matthew 13:1-9 and 18-23). God (the sower in the parable) sows the seed (the Christian message of salvation), but most of it goes to waste and cannot take root. Some of it falls on the footpath (verse 4) where the birds come and eat it up. Wickedness, depravity, lack of humility and persecution, Calvin says, prevent the seed from growing.

Some of the seeds fall on stony places where they initially take root, but then wither away. These Calvin compares with 'too many of this class in our own day, who eagerly embrace the Gospel and shortly afterwards fall off; for they have not the lively affection that is necessary to give them firmness and perseverance. ... For if the word does not fully penetrate the whole heart and strike its root deep, faith will want the supply of moisture that is necessary for perseverance.'

Thirdly, the seed sown among the thistles represent those who hear God's word, but it is choked by worldly cares and the false glamour of wealth (verse 22). Calvin adds pleasures of life, covetousness and anxieties of the flesh to the thistles, but then sombrely concludes that 'there is scarcely one individual out of ten who attempts to cut down the thistles, leave alone root them out.'

Yet not all the seed is wasted. Some of it falls into good soil (verse 23). They are the ones 'in whom the word of God not only strikes its roots deep and solid, but overcome every obstacle that would prevent it from yielding fruit', says Calvin. They are the people who become models for others, thereby enriching and edifying those with whom they work or live. The good news of salvation is then spread and produces hundredfold or maybe sixty fold or thirty fold fruits.

What do our Bible readings have to say to our time? Is the quest for roots as relevant today as it was in ancient days? Is Calvin's experience of being uprooted and finding his spiritual foundation in Jesus Christ relevant for today's world?

The New Testament readings certainly show that Jesus did not have his head in the clouds. He did not expect his message of salvation to be unopposed or to have an easy passage. His hearers and disciples were certainly not likely to be all dedicated followers bearing hundredfold fruit, strong in the faith, persuading acquaintances, friends and relatives that God's kingdom was the answer to their quests and their questions and fitted their desires for living life to the full. And that certainly is as true today as it was in Palestine 2000 years ago.

Now too we want to make up our own minds based on our experiences in the workplace, the kinds of motives and aims that others around us have. Now too there are multiple ideas, notions, perceptions coming to us from television, the radio, the paper that somehow we have to absorb, convert into a workable unity. The world around us seems to be crowded with disparate, unrelated pointers to disorder rather than the order God and Jesus represent. Don't they point to the loss of roots in our present world?

In this confusing culture around us, survival seems to require that we do our own independent selecting. One has to be both stubborn and diplomatic to safeguard one's identity and sense of wholeness. And yet in the parable of the sower and the seeds, Jesus tells us that all this selecting has to be left to God. God does the selecting rather than us mortals. He is the sower; we are the soil for the seed to grow or not to grow. We are the selected.

Isn't all this rather strange? Life around seems to have programmed us to choose and determine what in this sea of influences we will adopt and what we will let roll over us like water off the duck's back. What is more, our basic instincts seem to drive us to the conclusion that we ourselves have to select which approaches, views of life and conceptions we should take seriously, if we want to remain sane and fit in the web our society and culture have woven around us.

And yet the gospel tells us today that is not the way to go. It actually warns us that unless we let God do the selecting and choosing, we will not meet our destiny and the ultimate purpose of being here at all. It warns us that all this self-selecting leads nowhere and that our job is to become like the receptive soil in the parable.

The parable actually goes further. It explains in detail what will happen if we don't go in that direction. It says that we are likely to become like the seed fallen on pavement, picked by birds or being destroyed by manipulating, depraved individuals and aggressive characters. It cannot germinate and we become easy pickings.

Our lives sometimes tend to become as hardened as the asphalt on which the seed is falling. And there may be some very good reason why we have to steel ourselves to survive in this dog-eat-dog world around us. Surrendering or joining rather than beating the system seems to be almost the only way out. Not leaving it to our instincts and leaving the guiding and selecting to God seems folly.

Yet secretly we know that the parable is right. We instinctively know, don't we, that the hardened soul's route is not the way to go. We do not want to become unreceptive, unloving individuals, Machiavellian operators, or ambitious manipulators who cut a path of destruction on the way to the top, empire builders, rich charlatans.

And so we recognize both in ourselves and others, the various soils advancing or hindering God's kingdom. We may feel the exhilaration and excitement of being touched by the Holy Spirit and catch a glimpse of what God's word is all about. Or we may get a heart-warming sympathy for Jesus.

Yet the faith is sometimes not long lasting and does not survive the day. The soil is too shallow and our conviction not strong enough. Shallowness may hide insipid tolerance and only an appearance of conformity. Yet the Christian gospel requires depth, constancy and durability, all necessary to withstand the darkness on our path and pilgrimage of life.

And then there are the thorns in your and my life choking the best part of our Christian soul: our sins, rationalizations of conduct that actually cannot pass muster, thoughts that do not particularly fit God's expectations, white lies getting us out of trouble, taking a vacation from God.

Now we can defend all this by pointing to the rootlessness of our society and our culture. How can we help not being chameleons in a society that encourages living on the surface, not rocking boats, fitting with fashions of speaking and behaving of people with standards lower than the ones we ought to have?

Yet both the Bible, and Calvin's interpretations, point to the ray of hope and the conviction of faith flowing from God's word. It tells us that in a rootless world we are not left alone with our personal and our society's predicaments, sense of being lost and the shifting sands of desperation and depression.

Calvin's experiences as a fugitive from his native environment seem to have helped him to deeply understand individuals, such as Jacob, David and Paul. They too had to delve deeply below the superficialities of life and culture to find the depth of soil for God's seed to germinate and to discover that God's word transcended civilizations, local customs and languages.

The Bible also tells us that in Jesus Christ we have a saviour who has conquered the world. Not all the seeds of the sower are consumed by birds of prey, swallowed by shallowness and choked by the weeds of empty promises. Some of the seeds have fallen into good soils and taken firm roots.

As Paul says, these roots are in Jesus Christ (Colossians 2:7). Through him our rootlessness has been suspended. In the community of believers, the Church, the fertile soil of faith has become the recipient of the message of salvation. The Holy Spirit has locked in our hearts an exuberant sense of calm and serenity, because God has put in these hearts the invincible fortress of grace.

CALVIN 30
FREEDOM from OPPRESSION

Jesus went about doing good and healing all those who were oppressed. Acts 10:38

The great Scottish reformer John Knox was born in 1505 in the village of Gifford near Harrington, in East-Lothian, 16 miles East of Edinburgh, where he went to the excellent grammar school. Knox attended the universities of Glasgow and St Andrews. Here he learnt all about the works of Augustine and became accomplished in Latin, Greek and Hebrew. He was ordained a Catholic priest around 1530, but soon became an enthusiastic follower and bodyguard of the learned reformer George Wishart.

Wishart was burnt at the stake for his Protestant beliefs and Knox had to be restrained from sharing a similar fate. He became the Protestant minister in St Andrews where in 1547 he was captured by the Catholic authorities. He endured nineteen months of galley-slavery on French ships that permanently affected his health.

Through the intervention of the English government he was released and became a minister of the Church of England, where in 1552 he was involved in producing *The Articles Concerning an Uniformity in Religion* which formed the basis of the Thirty-nine articles of Anglicanism.

Knox became one of the six chaplains to King Edward VI. However the latter was succeeded by the devout Catholic Queen Mary, who in her short reign, managed to burn at the stake more than 300 heretics, such as Thomas Cranmer and Hugh Latimer. Knox saw the writings on the wall, decided that England had become too hot under his feet and went to Europe. Here he accepted a call in 1555 to the refugee English congregation in Geneva, established by Calvin. Four years later he returned to Scotland. Here Protestantism became the national religion in 1560 with Knox as leader and minister of St Giles in Edinburgh.

Queen Mary of Scotland, however, was a staunch Catholic and made the life of Knox and other reformers rather miserable. She disliked him for being too plain-spoken and not enough of a smooth-tongued courtier. Knox became involved in many controversies with her, so much so that he had to take refuge in St Andrews not once, but several times.

He survived all these calamities and escaped and died in Edinburgh on November 24, 1572. He was buried in an unmarked grave in the graveyard of St Giles. He left behind a young second wife, Margaret Stewart with her three daughters (the first wife, Catherine Bowes had died and had two sons with him). He wrote extensively and it would be interesting to see how these horrible experiences of persecution coloured his and his mentor Calvin's biblical interpretations. In a letter (20 January 1555) from Calvin to Knox he commiserates with him as 'being pulled violently from your country.' They are likely to take to today's readings as ducks take to water. Both the Genesis reading of Jacob's exile and Romans 8 are very relevant for the alienated and stranger in a hostile environment. What do they have to say?

Our Old Testament story is all about Jacob being sent away from Beersheba because his mother, Rebecca, did not want him to marry any of the local women. Rather practically she said: 'If you do that, my life will not be worth living (Genesis 27:46).' And so we find Jacob in foreign territory in Luz, where he had this strange dream of a ladder to heaven and the Lord God telling him that He would give the land to him and his descendants and that He would protect them. Jacob then called the place Bethel (house of God), because this is where he had met God. Calvin interprets this event to mean that exiles (Esau to Calvin is a rival and reprobate from whom Jacob had to flee) may be at a great disadvantage and even in danger, yet 'be blessed by God (Genesis 28:10).'

God rescues and consoles the alienated and exiled, through the link with heaven, or as Calvin has it: the ladder represents 'the covenant of God founded in Christ. … It is Christ alone, therefore, who connects heaven and earth: he is the only Mediator who reaches from heaven down to earth (Genesis 28:12).' To Calvin exiles or foreigners show God's supernatural power. 'God rescues his servant (Jacob) at a critical moment', says Calvin. To him 'the ladder is the medium through which the fullness of all celestial blessings flows down to us, and through which we in turn ascend to God.' God to him is no longer taken for granted. God rescues, saves actually.

Psalm 139; 1-12 is also one of today's Old Testament readings. We have sung it together. It celebrates God's penetration of all existence. What is hidden to humans is transparent to God. Humans cannot escape from His Spirit, nor can they flee from His presence (Psalm 139:7). Or as Calvin has it: 'God cannot be deceived. … God is independent of our words (because) he knows the heart.'

Calvin also says that David, the author of the Psalm, thinks that 'it is folly to measure God's knowledge by our own' and that actually 'to conceive of God like unto ourselves is most condemnable.' In other words, the oppressed, the perplexed and those to whom life has given a raw deal, such as Jacob, David and the reformers find in their religion, prayers and worship a God who is the complete 'other.' Freedom from their oppression is represented by God whom they have encountered personally. They have personally experienced ('in their hearts' as Calvin says), God's protection and His gift of faith and capacity to cope with adversity. God lifts them above their predicament and perplexity and thereby liberates them from that predicament and perplexity.

That's why God's knowledge is 'beyond comprehension (Psalm 139:6).' God is quite different. He is the opposite of adversity, darkness (Psalm 139:12) and disorder. The darkness of the night cannot 'cover our sins.' Security is to be found in God's grace rather than in man's 'false apprehensions', as Calvin has it. Or as Knox similarly says in his commentary on Psalm 6: God calls the elect from the 'deep dungeons of despair' to the light of his glory.

In the same way our reading from Romans 8:12-25 can be summed up as an escape from existential suffering (verse 12), freedom from oppression, spirit of slavery and fear (verse 14), frustration (verse 20), shackles of mortality (verse 21), groaning of creation (verse 22). By contrast all this points to the 'splendour which is in store for us (verse 18).' Paul is writing here not to people who have arrived, well-to-do citizens, but to a community of foreigners, both Jews and Gentiles, who felt the pain of oppression, rejection and discrimination. Here too all their hopes are founded on Jesus as their saviour.

The Gospel reading comes from Matthew 13:24-30 and 36-43. It is the parable of God sowing the good seed, but Satan (the 'evil' one, or 'the enemy' verse 27) sneaks in at night and sows weeds among the wheat (verse 25). His servants then want to pull out the weeds, but God feels that it is better not to disturb the wheat and 'to let them grow together till harvest and then tie the weeds together for burning and collect the wheat for storing in my barn (verse 30).'

Calvin sums up the purpose of the parable as helping the godly not to lose heart when they feel oppressed by the corruption all around and within them. Human nature may be 'a mixture of good and bad' and 'absolute purity may nowhere to be found', but the harvest at the end of time will see 'all things restored to regular order.'

Even the church may 'be burdened by the reprobate' (Calvin uses this term as synonymous with what the parable calls 'weeds' or 'the evil ones'), 'hypocrites' and even 'the polluted dregs of society', but 'the stumbling blocks will be removed' and the 'sons of God, now covered with dust ... will then shine in full brightness, as when the sky is serene, and every cloud has been dispelled.'

To Calvin 'the life of the godly is now hidden and their salvation invisible, yet it consists in hope. Christ properly directs the attention of believers to heaven, where they find the glory promised to them.' To Calvin the church is on 'a pilgrimage' and the believers are 'pilgrims' guided by the light of heaven while enjoying the freedom of the redeemed.

How relevant are today's readings for us living in the twenty-first century?

The gospel has no illusion about humans. It depicts in our parable a grim world in which there is little purity and a lot of evil and disorder mixed with goodness and order. Perfection only exists in heaven. Yet it is not irrelevant. It provides a frame of reference in which sin, or breakdown of whatever leads to disorder, is contrasted with salvation, integrity or whatever leads to order.

In Calvin's interpretation the parable is a pointer to Jesus Christ as redeemer and saviour. And that means that this grim world and our place in it is redeemable, can be liberated for all those who follow him. We may be oppressed by our anxious attempt to liberate ourselves, but then the parable shows that we cannot lift ourselves up by our own boot straps. The liberating force does not reside in the self, but on the contrary in the surrender of the self.

Yet that imperfect world which you and I inhabit is also rather impervious to change. And it must occur to all of us, I am sure, that there is so little we can change. We are bound and shackled to our past, our upbringing, our lost ideals, our missed opportunities.

Even our Christian faith is moulded and embedded in the structures of this imperfect world. Maybe that is why Jesus in the parable warns us not to expect too much from immediate action (the servants suggesting to pull out the weeds before they can do more damage). Expecting everything from immediate action may obscure the larger picture and assumes that we can distinguish too readily between weeds and wheat.

Still these oppressive burdens can be put aside when we let ourselves be grasped by the promise of Jesus, that those who follow him 'shall have the light of life (John 8:12).' It is this light that frees us from all oppression whether caused by others, originating from within ourselves, linked to our upbringing or other events that have shaped and are still shaping our very being.

It may be that Jesus in the parable had Job in mind. The latter made the mistake of wanting to be his own judge rather than leave it to God to do the judging. Jesus himself said: 'Judge not and you will not be judged (Matthew 7:1).' We seem to naturally crave for the clarity of black/white thinking. Yet there is in our world much greyness. It always astounded me to discover how much good, understanding, concern for others and altruism there was in my fellow prisoners in Gestapo camps and prisons in World War II. Or to bring this up to date, how much Christian humility and love for Christ and respect for the Holy Spirit there is sometimes amongst alcoholics, drug addicts and the mentally disturbed in our society.

The parable teaches us that, however oppressed and anxious we may feel there is a light at the end of the tunnel of our pilgrimage. It is this light that liberates and lessens our darkness. It is this light that frees us (Romans 8:21) from the shackles of our mortality. It also teaches us that in Jesus Christ we have a mediator or a ladder to God and the heavenly kingdom. Ascending that ladder and leaving our burdens behind gives us the vision necessary to live life to the full.

CALVIN 31

PREDESTINATION or ELECTION?

… to those who love God, who are called according to His Plan, everything that happens fits into a pattern for good. Romans 8:29

Calvin's worldly hero was someone whom he more than respected. He came close to worshipping him. He actually called him 'saintly' in his comments on one of today's readings. This hero was born in the little town of Tagaste on November 13 in the year 354 AD and died at the ripe old age of 75 on August 28, 430 AD (1575 years ago) in Hippo Regius 65 miles west of Carthage on the northern coast of Africa.

The father of this hero was an influential pagan. By contrast his mother, Monnica, was a devout Christian. He became a well known teacher of the Latin and Greek classics. In his youth he was known for what in his *Confessions,* he calls 'carnal corruptions' and 'illicit pleasures' which produced a son with a young mistress when he was only 17, but these stopped abruptly after his spectacular conversion in 386.

From here on his faith sustained him during the most tumultuous of times. The barbarian Germanic, Vandal tribe, itself driven southward by the, if anything, more barbarian Huns, overran most of the Roman Empire and penetrated as far as the North African coast. They were actually at the gates of the town when this hero of Calvin died. Some of you have probably guessed his name already. He is Augustine, Bishop of Hippo.

Calvin was a voracious reader. He also had a phenomenal memory. He must have read all Augustine's voluminous writings and so Augustine became by far the most quoted of all authors. There were no serious disagreements between Augustine's and Calvin's theological opinions. They also shared similar biases. Both were affected by the latent rational individualism of the classics and this shows in their treatment of predestination, one of the topics in today's reading of Romans 8:26-39.

Augustine with Calvin and Knox following paid much attention to predestination and wrote extensively about it. To Calvin (*Institutes of the Christian Religion* III xxi 5) predestination is what God 'has fixed with Himself, what he wishes to happen to each individual.' That is also the way Augustine thought about predestination (*De Praedestinatio,* chapter VIII). Similarly John Knox, founder of the Church of Scotland, defined predestination as the 'immutable decree of God which determined what is to be done with every human' in his tome on the subject.

Yet in the Bible the idea is hardly ever used. Paul only mentions it in today's reading of Romans 8:30 and in Ephesians 1:5, 11. In Ephesians predestination relates to the destiny of Christians to be God's sons through Jesus Christ. Here as well as in Romans 8:30 it is the equivalent of election.

What then is the theological difference between predestination and election? Predestination as used by Augustine, Calvin and Knox tends to closely and exclusively associate it with God's ordering of each specific human life. By contrast election in the Bible is more widely linked with God's ordering in general, whether personal or social.

Election means, as it says in Roman 8:30, to be called, elected; chosen by God to accomplish His purposes. Faith is a crucial element in the way election is used in the Bible. It is, as all of us are no doubt aware, like loyalty, love, affection an emotional rather than rational idea. Paul also thought much less in terms of the individual and more in terms of the social, such as God's choosing, electing, the nation (Israel), and the community of believers (the Church).

Today's Old Testament reading (Psalm 105:1-11) testifies to that social aspect of election. The Psalm starts (verse 1-2) with thanking God for all his wonders and the orderly arrangement of all that exists in the world around us. Calvin in his commentary on the Psalm (verse 5) speaks about God's design, which he says could not come about by mere chance. God encourages his people to 'make his deeds known in the world around (verse 1).' After all He is a global, universal God and the believers must spread the good news about His whole-making, loving, concern for His entire creation, not just individuals.

Yet God also has a specific relation with a specific nation, Israel. This is expressed in the covenant (verse 8-11) between God and that nation. The binding link (verse 10) of the covenant is the faith, the tie of loyalty binding God to Israel and Israel to God. It hinges on mutual acceptance, mutual affection and commitment, not just reason.

This does not mean that we must downgrade the importance of the individual. The social, ethnic, element of the covenant depends largely, if not entirely, on the hold it has on the faith and the beliefs of individuals. The stronger the hold on individual hearts and motivation, the healthier and more exuberant God's kingdom, or the invisible Church, will be. This is what today's New Testament reading of the parable of the mustard seed and the yeast is all about (Matthew 13:31-33 and 44-52).

Jesus says here that the growth of faith of individuals is essential for the spread of the good news of the gospel. Individuals may not be the exclusive carriers and missionaries of the message of salvation (the community of believers has this responsibility as well), but without those believers becoming God's personal mouthpiece, the mustard seed would not grow and the yeast would not have its rising power.

And yet the harmony between individuals and the social should not overshadow their differences or the contrast between ego and superego, the self and community. We are reminded by all four authors (Paul, Augustine, Calvin and Knox) that individuals can be like preying beasts, their sins obliterating the very bond that binds individuals to the protection of one's community, encouraging self-denial rather than self-assertion, humility rather than pride, peace rather than conflict, understanding rather than brute force, peace rather than war.

Election has a very powerful effect on the individual. Like Paul, both Augustine and Calvin had experienced conversion. All three felt in their bones that this experience was not their doing, but God's. God had elected, called them. Therefore anything that took God's initiative or God's separateness away was heresy to them. Or to say all this differently: the efficacy (and social effect) of God, the Orderer, as Augustine called him in *The City of God* (book xix, chapter 13) depended on Him being contrasted with the actual existence on earth which was always a mixture of disorder and order, evil and good, sin and salvation.

Election therefore is central to all three of them. So central in fact that it colours their thinking, preaching and writing. Salvation by faith alone is the basic theme in the thinking and believing of Paul, Augustine and Calvin, but all three are also adamant that this faith, however central it is to the covenant in both the Old and the New Testament is secondary to election. Calvin makes this very clear in II iii 8 of the *Institutes of the Christian Religion*. Here he quotes Scripture and Augustine (whom he calls 'holy', and whose 'authority is justly of so much weight in the Christian world') to back his point that faith (which he equates with the 'heart' or motivation) proceeds from election.

The reason is clear. A vision of pure order is an essential prerequisite for a civilization and a society. This vision contributes to self-maintenance. It also contributes to coping with devastating change. It dramatizes the separation of order and chaos, but also dramatizes the perpetual interaction between them.

The Bible from the very beginning to the very end insists that God is doing that very thing. He represents unadulterated order (wholeness or salvation) in a world where on all possible levels disorder (Satan, sin) is obvious. Without commitment (faith) to that order, any community is less likely to survive. So both strict separation (election, God's rather than man's initiative) and commitment (faith in God's hegemony or rule) need one another, but the first (election) has priority over the second (faith).

But let us return to Scripture, Romans 8:26-39 and Matthew 13:31-33, 44-52. Paul may insist on God being separate, yet in Romans 8:39 he also insists that nothing in creation can separate us from His love. How can we maintain this strict separation of God and humans as a central facet of the Bible and then in other parts, such as today's Bible sections read 'that nothing can separate us from God's love (Romans 8:39)?'

I want to repeat what already has been said before. The Old Testament reading of Psalm 105:8-11) stresses the importance of the old covenant between God and Israel. The New Testament or the new covenant enlarges on that vision and says that in Jesus Christ we have a link with God. He is the mediator. It was through his sacrifice on the cross that our sins, all the disorderly elements in human existence were not fatal any more. Through the Holy Spirit and our response through faith we are invited to be participants in God's kingdom.

And the good news of today's parable is that like the tiny mustard seed God's power ultimately prevails, or as Calvin has it in his commentary on Matthew 13:47: 'Our God is the God of order, and not of confusion, (1 Corinthians 14:33) and therefore, recommends to us discipline; but he permits hypocrites to remain for a time among believers, till the last day, when he will bring his kingdom to a state of perfection.'

Yet perfection and unadulterated order are a vision and a future promise. The reality of a mixture of disorder and order are all around us. Paul testifies to that when in Romans 8:22 he says that 'the whole created universe groans in all its parts as if in the pangs of childbirth.'

Nevertheless there are even now glimpses of God's order all around us, to which not only Paul, but also Augustine and Calvin bear witness. The lack of perfect order is brought out most clearly in Augustine's writings where he speaks not only about God representing the frame and regulation (forma et modus) of order but also about 'evil as the corruption of order.'

Yet he also mentions degrees of order (*De Natura Boni Contra Manichaeos*, book 4, chapter 3). He seems to suggest that there are different kinds of order harmoniously intertwined with one another. Yet true to his rational individualistic bias, he does not go as far as modern social scientists do when they suggest that these different kinds of order may also be in conflict with one another: the social system may not always accord with the personality system, however strong the integrative, reconciling push.

In other words one may dissolve the dilemma of defending predestination as an exclusive personal, rational concern, if one links predestination or God's order also to non-personal, emotional concerns. Paul contrasts the flesh with the spiritual, man as preying beast with social restraint. Individuals interact with other forms of order, such as a communal one which may go counter to individual wholeness.

This means practically that we have to modify our view that each individual is wholly and entirely determined by God. God's order is wider than puny me, my family, my nation or even my universe. God's loving hand is indeed stretched over all these. God is even 'above every order', as Augustine reminds us (*Contra Manichaeos*, iv 3) Yet God's wider order cannot be suspended just to provide us with what we think we deserve in an ideal world where the good is always rewarded and the bad punished. Have you ever thought what a chaotic world we would have, if everyone would get what he or she thinks he or she deserves?

Today's New Testament reading also includes Matthew 13:47-50 where Jesus compares the kingdom of heaven with a net let down into the sea, in which fish of every kind were caught. Then the good fish was collected in pails, but the worthless was thrown out. And then Jesus adds: 'That is how it will be at the end of time.' In final resort, God's order will prevail, but until then (as we have also read in Romans 8:22) 'the created universe groans in all its parts.'

However, as soon as the function and the necessity of God's perfection, pure order, all-encompassing love, salvation bestowing are not only mentioned, but also believed in, what is left for man's free will? Endless controversies and debates have existed throughout the history of Christianity. Today's Scripture readings have a definite answer to that controversy. It says explicitly that indeed God's independent, ordering authority is beyond question. Yet it also says that Christians are partners in a covenant which requires active participation through growth in faith, growth in humility, growth in love and self-denial. It is up to Christians to allow the mustard seed to come to full maturity and the yeast in the dough to fully rise.

How can we tie today's readings together? What have we learnt from Scripture and from Augustine and Calvin's interpretation of Scripture? How relevant is it for our daily living, thinking, experiencing?

From Psalm 105:1-11 and from Calvin we learnt that God represents and orders the universe. Yet God is not just an Orderer (as Augustine calls Him), separate from a disorderly existence, He also has a covenant with a specific nation (Israel) or the Church in the New Testament. Through election and faith humans are linked with God's order or God's essential being. He deals with order, salvation, the good, and wholeness in a world where Satan sows disorder, sin, evil and confusion.

Election, as we have learnt from Romans 8:26-39, is God's way of calling individuals from the confusion, disorder, sin of human existence (or its 'groaning', as Paul calls it in verse 26) to the serenity, peace of mind and calm of the kingdom of heaven. Yet we have also learnt that God's plan extends beyond the individual's life as Calvin and Augustine tend to do in their interpretation of predestination in verse 30. The Bible provides copious examples of conflict between social and personal order. Yet both are part of God's order. The kingdom of heaven is God's plan for minimizing the conflict.

Our last reading, the parable of the mustard seed (Matthew 13:24-30 and 36-43) tells us that God's kingdom is expanding because God's order minimizes this conflict between self and the non-self, because believers respond to God's expectations and so contribute to the larger order of God's kingdom.

And yet an over-emphasis on the collective/social can lead even more than an over-emphasis on the individual/personal to perversity and universal injustice. Not just Hitler's utopian dream of the Thousand Year Reich, but also the 50 million victims of the Stalinist Gulag and, as we have just learnt last month, the 70 million slaughter and butchery of Mao Tse Tung's regime teaches us that an over-emphasis on the collective are even worse than an over-emphasis on human rights. The parable of the mustard seed shows that the faith of individuals, such as you and I, are just as pivotal for the building of God's kingdom as is its opposite, our collective obedience to God's plan for the world, as our text from Romans 8:29 suggests. It is the moving balance between these two opposites (the personal and the collective) which comes closest to what I think God has in mind for our existence.

How relevant is all this is for our day-to-day living? It is best expressed in Hymn 519 (*SCH*): Who is on the Lord's side. It tells us that God's victory is secure. Verse three says that the conflict may be fierce, but God's unchanging truth makes the triumph sure. We may be soldiers in an alien land (verse 4), but we are called and chosen. Or to say it all with Romans 8:38, in spite of all, overwhelming victory is ours through him who loved us: 'there is nothing in death or life, in the realm of spirits or superhuman powers, in the world as it is or the world as it shall be, in the forces of the universe, in heights or depths – nothing in all creation that can separate us from the love of God in Christ Jesus our Lord.'

CALVIN 32

BEING CHRIST'S LETTER

You are an open letter of Christ which we ourselves have written, not with pen and ink but with the Spirit of the living God. Our message has been engraved not in stone, but in living men and women. 2 Corinthians 3:3

Exodus 34:25-35 gives a fascinating account of the face to face meeting of Moses and the Lord. God had been very angry with the Israelites for worshipping the golden calf (Exodus 32:35), but Moses persuaded the Lord to forgive them and instead make a covenant (Exodus 34:10). He would promise to be their only God and they would promise not to worship the gods of the natives (verse 15).

And so it happens. Moses 'stayed with the Lord (on Mount Sinai) forty days and forty nights, neither eating nor drinking and wrote down the words of the covenant on the tablets of stone (verse 28). When he descended from Mount Sinai, he was not aware that the skin of his face shone because he had been speaking with the Lord (verse 29).'

This awe-struck the Israelites so much that Moses put a veil on his face. Calvin explains that these events showed that their 'minister was invested with angelic glory in order that the majesty of the Law might be indubitable.' Calvin then wonders why 'Moses could have borne the brightness of God's glory, whilst the people could not bear the rays which shone from his face?' He solves that problem by suggesting that 'the difference between them was caused by their original 'departure from God' in contrast with 'Moses' conference with God and bearing the marks of God's terrible power.'

In our New Testament reading (2 Corinthians 3:1-18) Paul returns to the story. He explains (verse 14) that Christ cancelled the old covenant and that now all believers in Him are 'transfigured into his likeness' and that therefore the veil has been lifted permanently for the Corinthian faithful. They are all now 'an open letter of Christ' because the Spirit of the Lord reigns amongst them (verse 17).

However before we turn to the meaning and relevance of being Christ's letter, let us stay a while longer with this obvious, awe-inspiring, change in the appearance of Moses. It must have had a critical effect on the authority Moses enjoyed amongst the Israelites. He not only got away with accusing them of idolatry, but actually inspired an entirely new interpretation of their tribal purpose in a foreign land.

Thanks to God's spirit having this momentous and visible effect on Moses, his leadership had become total. He became the bright conduit of 'God's glory', as

Calvin called it, adding that he now 'bore the marks of God's terrible power.' So much so, that nothing could separate him anymore from that death-defying moment when he met God on Mount Sinai.

Paul carried that same Spirit right to his own martyrdom in about 67 AD in Rome. And, of course, in doing so he followed in the footsteps of the many prophets before who were persecuted for their faith, including Jesus' death on the cross and John the Baptist's decapitation. They were similarly to Moses smitten by the encounter and engagement with God and so swallowed up by the Holy Spirit, that it negated, strongly eclipsed, any fear of death and mortality.

And let us not forget the many martyrs of the Christian faith ever since. I am thinking about the 300 Christians, following Calvin's teaching in England who Queen Mary burned at the stake in her short reign, a fate that the founder of the Church of Scotland, John Knox only managed to escape by fleeing to Europe. But I am also thinking about the more recent examples of charismatic leadership (because that is what we are talking about here) amongst the Indians in Ontario (Canada) and the Maoris in New Zealand.

Ganeodiyo or Handsome Lake (1735-1815) lifted the Iroquois out of a morass of decadence after a visit from three celestial visitors. Sobriety and industry had to take the place of drunkenness, gambling and idleness, not because these values were good in themselves, but because the omnipotent, omniscient, creator god, the Great Spirit, or Hawennyeyu, demanded it. Handsome Lake's anti-white faith inspired large sections of his people into an effective tribal force which has continued into the present day.

Tahupotiki Wiremu Ratana (1873-1939) had a visit from the Holy Spirit in 1918 instructing him to become the mouthpiece of God, to unite the Maori people and turn them to Jehovah. This vision had quite a sobering effect. He gave up drinking and began to heal the sick and crippled. His fame spread rapidly to all parts of New Zealand and henceforth the movement became thoroughly inter-tribal. He gave the Maoris pride in their descent and faith in their belonging to the faithful remnant (morehu).

However let us return to our New Testament reading for today, 2 Corinthians 3:1-18, where Paul explains that God has made a new covenant with Christ's followers. That covenant is not anymore written on stone, but on the human heart. The veil has been lifted: God does not work indirectly anymore. He works directly. The Christians in Corinth therefore are his letter.

There had been a controversy in the Christian community of Corinth. The dispute was about leadership. Should it be Apollos, Peter or Paul? There had also been instances of moral laxity. But these issues had been resolved. As Calvin explains, not anymore was Paul accused of being 'excessively fond of publishing his own exploits' or of 'indulging immoderately in commendations of himself.' Not any more was it necessary to exchange testimonials (2 Corinthians 3:2), because he and the Corinthian Christians were united in their common faith in Christ.

Christ was their letter and both Paul and particularly the Corinthians were mere instruments of God's Holy Spirit. The letter was not a cold distant script written on stone as were the Ten Commandments. No, it was engraved in living men and women (2 Corinthians 3:3). Or as Calvin puts the words in Paul's mouth: 'So long as you shall remain Christians, I (Paul) shall have recommendations enough. For your faith speaks my praise, as being the seal of my apostleship (1 Corinthians 9:2).'

Paul then continues to expand on all Christians (both men and women) being an open letter of Christ. He sharply distinguishes between Jews and Christians. The former focus on the Law of Moses, the latter on Christ (verse 14), who has liberated humans from the restrictions of the old covenant (verse 18). And that meant, Paul says, that the veil which Moses put over his face (Exodus 34:34) whenever he conveyed God's messages to the people, is now superfluous. In the new covenant Christ is the bond. His Spirit directly affects humans. And he means all humans, not just one ethnic group, the Jews. The Christian church is universal.

Calvin elaborates on this newfound liberty or men's souls now set free. 'Let the soul be connected with the body, and then there is a living man, endowed with intelligence and perception, fit for all vital functions. Let the soul be removed from the body, and there will remain nothing but a useless carcass, totally devoid of feeling.' And still on verse 17, Calvin calls Christ 'the universal soul (who) quickens us by the life-giving influence of his Spirit.'

That Spirit is tied to 'grace' or 'charisma' in the Bible. Moses, Jesus and Paul were typically charismatic individuals. Their influence was wide and infectious. They attracted through their enthusiasm and living faith large audiences, followers and disciples. The Bible is the depositor and fount of that charismatic spirit. It is, as Calvin describes it, 'life-giving', transcending the ages and as relevant today as it has ever been.

How can we translate to our day and age Paul's declaration that Christians are open letters of Christ? Paul moves quickly from an actual letter of reference (verse 1) to a letter that is intrinsically an expression of a personal relationship (verse 2) to, even more abstractly, a letter that actually represents, stands for (verse 3), the people to whom it is addressed.

Let us ask ourselves three questions (or answers to those questions) under three headings: (1) Do we, Christians as the Corinthians, represent clear, decipherable, messages from God or are we big black blots, as though Christ is writing on blotting paper? (2) Are we non-descript in the eyes of the outside world, empty sheets of paper that have nothing to say to the age? (3) Are we letters that curl around and write their scripts rather than letting Christ do the writing?

(1) Are we, church-going Christians, cold business letters or do we present a more personal letter to the surroundings, where we live and work? Business letters invariably attempt to profit in some way or other from the relation with the person or the business to which the letter is addressed. They are usually formal. Most of the letters I get in the mail every day are of that sort. They are not unimportant, because they give me the information I need to keep our company viable.

Yet they are definitely not personal. By contrast, the letters, or nowadays phone calls, we receive from friends, relatives, children or grandchildren are different. They may be about practical things, but in between the lines we perceive concern, affection, love, and understanding. This is what Paul had in mind when he called the Christians in Corinth 'open letters of Christ.' Are we as a Christian congregation that kind of a letter?

Of course the church is also an organization and as such it has to deal with finances, jobs to be done, tasks allocated, membership rolls kept, grounds maintained, leadership exerted. Yet Paul meant that in a Christian organization there also is a strong bond of charity, a concern for one another, surpassing down-to-earth matters, going beyond ties of taste and status.

Jesus spoke about this in Matthew 25:34-36. 'Come, enter and possess the kingdom that has been ready for you since the world was made. For when I was hungry, you gave me food; when thirsty, you gave me drink; when naked you clothed me, when I was ill you came to help, when in prison you visited me.'

(2). If in tomorrow's mail you were to receive an envelope with an empty sheet of paper you would say: 'So and so has made a mistake.' Well, the Church has sometimes been called a historical mistake by our adversaries. Christians are compelled to prove them wrong. This must be done through showing that Christian integrity, salvation or wholeness is more than stereotyped affability or a mildewed platitude, a tradition for which the Sunday morning has been set apart. Do we Christians have something to share with a world lost in its own emptiness?

Almost all of us have been baptized. That means that our sheet of paper may be empty, but still has a letterhead. Christ has put his stamp on us through baptism. The first important step has been taken. Yet it has to be followed up, if we want to avoid the world outside dismissing us as non-descript, of no consequence.

(3) Have you ever seen something as absurd as a letter curling around and writing its own message? Yet that is what people outside the Church call 'reality', nothing exists that cannot be explained in terms of its own inherent structure. And even

within the church there is the danger of us being just a club for the internal religious pleasure of its membership, sufficient unto itself.

However the Church does not primarily exist because you and I have economic, social, and also religious needs. Certainly trusting the Lord gives us the serenity to face the day. Yet the Bible never talks about 'religious needs.' Particularly the prophetic strain in Scripture is often not congenial to any of our needs as we feel them. God challenges our sins and the social disorder for which we are responsible.

The Word of God may not suit everybody. Is your letter one that curls around and writes its own message, rather than is receptive to Christ's writing on you, even when this writing is not particularly convenient?

Where does all this leave us?

If we are at all realistic, we have to admit that we fall short of being Christ's letter as described. We are often more like a cold business letter, an empty sheet of paper, chameleons, adjusting ourselves to other's expectations, blotting papers with big black blots rather than clear, distinct writing, letters that curl around to absurdly write our own message.

Humanly speaking we belong in God's waste paper basket with all the other dismissed, discarded, bits of paper. But that is where the Corinthians also belonged. Didn't Paul also speak about their 'horrible infamies', 'sects', divisions, quarrels, jealousy, selfishness, fornication?

How then can he also call them Christ's letter? Certainly the answer is that they repented. Yet more importantly, both Corinthians and us are not letters of Christ, because we deserve that title, but because God has refused to put us in the wastepaper basket, but has put us on his writing desk. We are 'declared', as our text says, to be Christ's letter, in spite of our deficiencies. God has not left us to our own devices, but has come down to us in Jesus Christ.

Being Christ's letter does not only mean living up to an impossibly high standard, but above all, it means living by a sure promise, a saving promise, a covenant that God has established in Jesus Christ. And living by that promise will make us Christ's letter.

CALVIN 33

JESUS in the WILDERNESS

There is a voice that cries: 'Prepare a road for the Lord through the wilderness, clear a highway across the desert for our God. Isaiah 40:3

Do you have favourite Bible passages? I do. I particularly like the ones from Romans 8, where Paul writes about nothing separating Christian believers from the love of God. I usually quote those in hospital visits or at funerals. Today's reading from Isaiah (40:1-11) is another popular one. It speaks about God comforting the oppressed. You probably remember that one from Handel's Messiah, but also from the Gospels quoting John the Baptist announcing the coming of Jesus as the Messiah redeeming Israel.

Isaiah addresses himself to the Jews as exiles-to-be in Babylon. Their suffering will come to an end. They will return home. God will prepare the way. He will make the wilderness into a smooth highway (Isaiah 40:3). To Isaiah life is like a wilderness, but God will level the path through it and make it smooth.

Calvin explains this passage, as he says, 'metaphorically.' To him and to John the Baptist who quotes this verse from Isaiah, 'an exceedingly disordered and ruinous crisis is lifted to a banner of joy.' The wilderness represents 'the depravity of our nature, the windings of a crooked mind, and obstinacy of heart', but prepares for 'true self-denial and obedience.' To Calvin the wilderness of life will be tamed in the same way as the exiles will return to Jerusalem. God always 'takes care.'

The gospel is the good news of liberation, redemption. Its chief message is one of 'comforting the oppressed.' It is the comfort of returning to one's home after long periods of absence in a foreign country, such as Jerusalem for exiled Jews or Geneva for Calvin when its citizens had gotten sick of his reproaches and had thrown him out in 1538. In a wider sense it is the church as the refuge from life's wilderness. The job of the prophets is 'to support believers in adversity that they may not faint or be discouraged (Calvin's commentary on verse 1).'

And of course there was enough 'adversity' in the history of the Jewish race to be a lasting source of reference. The exodus from Egypt comes to mind as full of dangers, escapes from oppression, persecution, hunger and pain. Not the least of the dangers was blaming Jehovah (the actual source of rescue) for all the hardships and disasters inevitably trailing the journey of what was essentially a nomadic tribe.

Moses was the first of the prophets warning against the easy way out of trouble and projecting solutions on visible, concrete, close at hand, idols such as a golden calf. He retreated into the wilderness to meet Jehovah, to refurbish inspiration and to be filled by the Holy Spirit enabling him to lead a recalcitrant nomadic tribe to the Promised Land.

Commenting on the verses Isaiah 40:3-6 of today's Old Testament reading Calvin insists that only inspired 'boldness and clearness' will meet the demand for rescue from the predicament of the Israelites travelling through foreign, hostile lands, feeling alarmed and insecure.

Calvin: '(P)rophets ought not to mutter in an obscure manner, but to pronounce their message with a distinct voice, and to utter boldly and with open mouth whatever they have been commended to declare. Let everyone, therefore, who is called to this office constantly remember and believe, that he ought to meet difficulties of every sort with unshaken boldness, such as was always manifested both by prophets and by apostles.'

'Woe to me', says Paul, 'if I do not preach the gospel: for necessity is laid on me (1 Corinthians 9:16).' Therefore Calvin commenting on verse seven and eight (people are like withered grass enlivened by the Spirit of God which will stand forever) insists that the job of prophets is 'to drag humans into the presence of God' to prevent them from 'indulging in false confidence and places of concealment.'

And says Calvin, don't think that God is speaking of foreigners only. No, God is talking about the people of the book, Jews and Christians, 'for the Jews might have thought that they were more excellent, and held a higher rank than other men, and that on this account they ought to be exempted from the common lot.' No, nothing is further from the truth. And he therefore adds: 'we are nothing but in God.'

All this leads to our New Testament reading Matthew 4:1–11 where Jesus too, like Moses retreats to the wilderness. Here too the wilderness is the place where one meets God. Here too the wilderness is like the witches' cauldron of the unconscious where we are confronted with our own horrifying dreams so much part of daily living and human experience.

It is the place where Jesus meets the devil who tempts him with the easy life of self indulgence and illusions of power (verse 1). It is the place where our loneliness and self-deception are revealed for what they are in stark severity. It is the place where we cannot hide any longer behind a facade of shallow chit chat and idle titillation. The wilderness is like a pathless jungle of creeping vines and nightmare sounds. Yet it is also the place where Jesus meets God.

John Knox, the founder of Presbyterianism and the Church of Scotland left few sermons, commentaries and theological dissertations behind. However his comments on our New Testament reading are available in the five volumes of his works. The significance of Matthew 4:1-11, he says, lies in Christ being like us. He fought the same battles we are fighting. He goes so far as to say that God fights our battles for us: 'tribulations and grievous vexations of body or mind are not signs of God's displeasure with the sufferer', but that God cares for us. In other words, God prepares a road through the wilderness of existence.

The wilderness is also the place where the wolves of destruction reign. It is the place where all the carefully built securities and certainties of life are all of a sudden suspended, where even our faith seems to dissolve into airy nothingness. It is the place where the wild beasts roam shaking our carefully preserved comforts of safety, where demons attack us, leaving us in a crumbled heap of terror and despair.

All this is presented to us in the shape of Satan, the devil, in today's reading. Knowing that Jesus had fasted for 40 days and was very hungry, he tempts Jesus first by suggesting that if he is the Son of God he should tell these stones to become bread (verse 3). Jesus then quotes Deuteronomy 8:3: 'man cannot live on bread alone but lives by every word that comes from the mouth of the Lord (verse 4).'

The implication is that God is not in the business of upsetting nature for the sake of one person's whim. More importantly, God is interested in man's unique spirituality as compared with the physical needs he shares with the rest of creation. To regard bread, or any nourishment, as more important than the life of the spirit goes against the grain of God's intention for the human race.

Yet spirituality on its own is not enough. It can be too egocentric and too exclusively concerned with personal feelings. It must also be shared with others, constantly repeated and compared with alien forces if it is to be relevant. Paul in 1 Corinthians 14 is quite explicit at this point. He says that individual spirituality, as it is expressed in feelings of personal ecstasy or speaking in tongues just will not do, unless it is also interpreted (verse 28) and builds up community (verse 6). 'For the God who inspires is not a God of disorder but of peace (verse 33).' Only when it is shared with the community of believers can it survive the powers obstructing its delicate and transcendent quality. And that is where the next temptation comes in.

The second temptation (Matthew 4:6) similarly stresses God's transcendent, spiritual quality rather than His arbitrary ability to suspend the law of gravity (an essential part of His universe) just for the sake of showing off His power. The devil suggests that Jesus throw himself down from the parapet of the temple to illustrate God's capacity to rescue His son. Jesus again uses scripture to counter the devil's intention (verse 7): 'You are not to put the Lord your God to the test (Deuteronomy 6:16).'

God is not going to subvert the elaborate structure of his own edifice. Jesus also represents the soul or essence of humanity as God intends it to be in the fullness of time. Calvin in his commentary on the temptations in the wilderness calls Jesus 'the universal model of all the godly.' And this means that humans must take His will as final in contrast with their own idolatrous ego-centric, narrow, concept of humans who are constantly creating golden calves to substitute for His authority which they are required to obey rather than control.

The third temptation similarly deals with Satan's misunderstanding of God's global intent. Here the devil promises Jesus all the kingdoms of the earth provided he 'falls down and pays homage to him (verses 8-10).' Satan assumes here that God is nothing but a miserable autocrat competing with him for absolute power rather than the one who relativizes power and allows Jesus to serve and be actually crucified for man's redemption.

The third temptation also brings up the point that, over against Satan, Jesus represents the delicate balance between social fit, conformity (Jesus' emphasis on serving rather than being served – Matthew 20:28) and human rights (the history of the prophet's insistence on criticizing social organization and resisting establishments leading to Jesus' crucifixion).

Did you see the recent television program on the psychology of the suicide bombers? They were discovered to be typical products of immigrant or refugee families who still had not found their bearings in what was to them, an alien culture. Their response to the predicament was total surrender to fanatical groups subverting that culture, according to the psychologists interviewed for the program.

In other words losing one's life for the sake of the subverting cause was believed to be a laudable supreme sacrifice. Actually this means surrendering to a narrow cause, such as personal power or the destruction of the opposition. The third temptation warns against this usurping of God's power and the elevation of Satan instead. Calvin calls this 'overleaping the boundaries which God has prescribed' instead of 'preserving the order of nature and the lives of God's creatures.'

Commenting on the third temptation, Calvin says that it is Satan encouraging Jesus to 'indulge in a foolish and vain confidence – to neglect the means which are in his power – to throw himself, without necessity, into manifest danger and, as we might say, to overleap all bounds.'

All three forms of temptation make a major point: God's order is not to be subverted for the sake of one individual's whim, or more importantly, for the sake of radically changing nature, whether natural (the law of gravity), psychological (indulging in sensation and propaganda to show one's superiority), social (maximizing power over others) or political (rebelling against the Roman overlord and lording it over other nations).

No, the three temptations make the point that God's order is, as our text says, smoothing the path through the wilderness of life, rather than arbitrarily subverting it to suit one individual's lust for dominance and power. It is very realistic and anything but utopian. Jesus' mission is not to fiercely and triumphantly play the all too human power game, but to guide his followers along the path of service, even if that eventually leads in his case to a cross.

The relevance of our text for today's world is plain. There are situations in life when bread for the soul is more important than bread for nourishment. In such situations morale, backbone and integrity (all part of spirituality) are more urgent than earthly power or material progress and gains. Or to put this differently: situations where giving one's life for God's global intentions and global peace are to be preferred over narrow, local or personal power and gains.

Power over nature may be an ingrained instinct, but it may also lead to erosion and even denial of man's eternal destiny. There is more to existence than capacity for military conquests. They may actually retard global peace because they promote the power of one nation over another. Power can serve satanic rather than a divine purpose. God's purpose for mankind is to smooth a path through the wilderness where chaos and Satan appear to have unchecked power and reign like unbridled brumbies.

CALVIN 34

IMPRISONED, YET FREE

Where the Spirit of the Lord is, there is liberty. 2 Corinthians 3:17

Today's readings and hymns are focused on God's Spirit. In Genesis 1:1-5 the Spirit of God moved upon the face of the waters or the formless abyss, 'shaping confused emptiness and an indigested mass thereby sustaining order', as Calvin has it, creating light out of darkness and form, stability out of chaos.

Psalm 29 the first part of which we have sung together, exalts the power of the Lord's voice. The Psalm finishes with the assurance that God blesses his people with peace leading to man's complete happiness, the freedom of a serene conscience. It teaches us 'to stand in awe of the majesty of God, and assures us that since his power is infinite, we are defended by an invincible fortress (Calvin).'

Then in Mark 1:4-11 we have read the story of Jesus being baptized 'and the Spirit, like a dove, descending upon him.' The dove is a symbol and a 'token of sweet consolation that we do not have to fear Christ who meets us, not in the formidable power of the Spirit, but clothed with gentle and lovely grace (Calvin).'

Finally in Ephesians 3:1-12 Paul writing from prison in Rome stresses the free access, trust and confidence of faith in God that allows him not to lose heart and face suffering. Instead of being discouraged by his persecution, Paul admonishes the Ephesians 'to promote the edification of all the godly' (Calvin).

Paul follows this admonishment as follows: 'I pray that out of the glorious richness of His (God's) resources He will enable you to know the strength of the Spirit's inner reinforcement – that Christ may actually live in your hearts by your faith. And I pray that you firmly fixed in love yourselves, may be able to grasp (with all Christians) how wide and deep and long and high is the love of Christ – and to know that love for yourselves. May you be filled through all your being with God Himself! Now to him Who by His power within us is able to do far more than we dare to ask or imagine – to Him be glory in the Church through Jesus Christ for ever and ever, Amen! (Ephesians 3:14-21).'

All our hymns mention in some form or other the freedom, liberating aspect of the Holy Spirit, the third member of the trinity. How are we to reconcile being both free and yet being a prisoner, as Paul was when he wrote the letter to the Ephesians? Maybe the theme of a recent film here in Canberra can help us to understand the paradox.

Merry Christmas (Joyeux Noel) is the best film I have seen in the last ten years. It tells the incredible story of German, Scottish and French soldiers climbing out of their trenches in the first year of the 1914-1918 Great War from which they have been shooting and killing one another, and celebrating Christmas together. The film is based on actual events. It makes the point that there is something in religion, music and sport that is stronger than national divisions and wars.

They sing Christmas carols, listen to a sermon from the Scottish chaplain, play soccer and are brought to tears by the beautiful singing of a Danish and German couple. They are all accused of fraternizing with the enemy and punished for their actions. The German and French soldiers are banished to other battle zones and the Scottish chaplain is severely reprimanded by his superior and sent back to Scotland. After all the war has to go on and be won.

The film is a beautiful illustration of the basic meaning of today's readings. They point to the reconciling and integrating power of faith in the vulnerable Christ child born in a humble stable in Bethlehem. To Paul, the strong faith in Jesus transcends the chains of the Roman prison from which he wrote this letter to the Christians in Ephesus. It (the faith) sharply contrasts with being incarcerated. To him the appalling conditions he finds himself in are overshadowed by the joy of his faith. He may be on the verge of execution and death, but he is grasped by an inner peace which he describes as complete freedom. It is well expressed in our final Hymn 110, verse 4 where Charles Wesley tells of his conversion experience as follows: 'My chains fell off, my heart was free.'

So with the soldiers, in the film, the appalling war conditions, the death-dealing in the mud of the trenches in France were overshadowed by the common Christmas celebration. It points to religion, play and music representing a global, universal, uniting element in existence momentarily outstripping its particular and tribal side. It sharply portrays religion in almost contradictory terms: liberating and yet also bound to and possibly even corrupted by, the all-embracing, powerful demands of nations at war.

Calvin captures the meaning of Christian freedom very well in his chapter on the topic in the *Institutes of the Christian Religion* (III xix). He makes quite plain what it is not. It is not hedonism, 'a cloak for lusts, to live sumptuously, delighting in feasting and dress, wallowing in the luxuries of one's house, surpassing the neighbour in splendour, hunting after new pleasures, immoderate desires, immoderate profusion, vanity and arrogance.'

No, says Calvin, it has more to do 'with learning to be content, whatever the circumstances may be', as Paul suggests in the letter to the Philippians (4:11-12): 'I now know how to live when things are difficult and I know how to live when things are prosperous. In general I have learnt the secret of facing either poverty or plenty. I am ready for anything through the strength of the One Who lives within me.'

In other words, to Calvin 'Christian liberty in all its parts is spiritual … giving peace to trembling consciences.' Or as he concludes in the last of his sections on Christian liberty: 'A good conscience is nothing but the inward integrity of the heart.' His argument centres on what it means to have a good conscience. He follows Paul's linking 'a good conscience, a pure heart and a genuine faith' in 1 Timothy 1:5.

What does Calvin mean by a good conscience and how does he relate it to liberty? To Calvin conscience registers what God reveals as right. It is God's voice within us to do right. The Holy Spirit liberates the conscience when sin pollutes and burdens it. The Holy Spirit cleanses the conscience or the soul as in baptism water washes away our sins or whatever separates us from God's Holy Spirit.

To Calvin the soul is the inspiring part of life. In his commentary on 2 Corinthians 3:17 he compares it with the vital functions of the human body: 'Let the soul be removed from the body and there will remain nothing but a useless carcass, totally devoid of feeling.' To Calvin Christ is 'the universal soul that quickens and emancipates the body from the servitude of sin and the flesh' and gives us 'the liberty and confidence which contrasts with bondage and fear' about which Paul speaks in Romans 8:15 and which Augustine stresses in his interpretation of that passage.

Yet to Calvin the soul is not just personal, 'the integrity of one's heart' or the centre of individual faith and feeling. To be liberating it also has to be sensitive to others. One's conscience must also embrace loving one's neighbour as oneself, if it is to fully liberate. Therefore Calvin quotes Paul where the latter counsels the Christians in Corinth to tolerate those amongst them who continue the pagan habit of consecrating food. One has to respect those feelings, he thinks. Yet they are part of the rules of law which Jesus relativised in the light of a larger, more liberating, attachment to the indwelling of the Holy Spirit.

Therefore Calvin insists 'to abstain from everything that produces offence, but with a free conscience.' He justifies this from Scripture (1 Corinthians 10:28) where Paul says: 'I myself try to adapt myself to all men without considering my own advantage but their advantage, that if possible they may be saved.' In other words the principle of tolerance is an important means to keep the lines of communication open with what Paul calls 'the weaker brethren.' On the one hand the gospel is quite direct and anything but vague and wishy-washy, yet on the other hand the Christian obligation of mission and Christian love may require a deep understanding of what motivates others.

How relevant is all this for our situation today? Aren't we all imprisoned in the imperfect world surrounding and within us? Aren't all of us affected by the tensions, anxieties, pains and hurts at work, at home and in society at large? And what about our inmost worries and insecurities and the ways we contribute to other people's unhappiness?

Yet the gospel says all this is redeemable. It is in Jesus that we have a saviour who guides us into that completeness that would escape us miserably if we try it on our own. It is that complete wholeness, or as the Bible calls it, salvation, which also liberates. Our faith and our trust lift us out of the swamp, quagmire of existence to the serenity of God's order.

A second source of relevance of our readings and Calvin's interpretation of what Christian liberty means stems from two observations Calvin makes about today's reading. The first one deals with taking the part too much for the whole and closely related to this is his second observation that specific items of the law so dear to the Jews rather than the Gentile members of his congregations should not have as high a priority as Christ, the Holy Spirit and the faith linking you and me to them.

On the first: Calvin (Galatians 5:14) quotes Paul (Romans 13:10) where the latter says that love fulfils the law and then goes on to say that loving one's neighbour as oneself is the part that should not be separated from the comprehensive first one, the whole or loving God. In other words the transcendental larger picture is a prerequisite for the effectiveness of the second one, loving one's neighbour as oneself.

To say this differently, cutting God out of the picture elevates the importance of the morality and law as such and sacralizes its cultural embeddedness. Similarly the Jewish insistence on circumcision, Calvin says, prevents the spread of the good news of the gospel to non-Jews. Therefore the Christian message has to be freed from its cultural setting. Through Jesus, God is directly accessible and in addition, tolerance of cultural difference is a necessity. This is why Calvin calls Jesus the author of our freedom (commentary on Galatians 5:1) and locates that freedom in one's conscience which to him is the human bond with God.

A third and final form of relevance of today's scripture readings and Calvin's interpretation has to do with the present, raging, worldwide, discussion about evolution and intelligent design. The liberty linked to the bird's eye view of faith in God is pertinent to that discussion as well.

In our Genesis reading, God creates order out of chaos. In the Judaic, Christian, Islamic tradition God is so much on the order side of the interaction with change that all through the Bible its purity has to be maintained at almost any cost. God is immortal, invisible, eternal, almighty. Yet the breakdown of that order is all around us, not just in the 2005 tsunamis and devastating earthquakes in Pakistan, but even more on the value and social level. Crime, tension in the workplace (cronyism, irresponsibility, personality clashes), at home (divorce, alcoholism, drugs) as well as personal, mental wellbeing (depression, breakdown, disharmony) all take their toll and have to be absorbed back in the order God represents and maintains as a beacon of hope and template of ultimate purpose and destiny.

But that is also what evolution is about. It is a constant, dynamic, interaction between integration and adaptation, fusion and fission, structure and process, heredity and variation, dark matter and dark energy, integration and differentiation, synthesis and analysis. It is here that Calvin's observation and accusation that the part is too often taken for the whole, is elementary and profound.

Religion deals with the largest possible frame of reference for living and it insists in all it forms on solid commitment, faith in that order to prevent things from falling apart. Life without God is like a can of worms without the can. It deals with commitment, faith, love, loyalty, all items for which there is little room in most scientific theories with the social sciences the likely exception. Yet the roomier religious frame of reference should also have a place for these scientific theories. And it does. Calvin's interpretation of the first five verses in the Bible fits the basic moving equilibrium underlying all sciences, physical, social, psychological. This is not just true for Judaism, Christianity and Islam. All religions can be studied as distilling order (or integration) from disorder (adaptation).

I am therefore advocating for the academic discipline of religious studies to closely interact with any other discipline dealing with evolution. Yet the difference between these two should not be ignored. I would like to defend with Calvin that the difference is a matter of the part differing from the whole and the former ignoring the items of faith, love, and commitment necessary for the larger frame of reference of academic study. And yet any academic approach is more partial than practicing of what it studies, if only because from the theological point of view it usurps God's place as standing outside and above the phenomena it deals with.

To sum up this sermon: Paul and Calvin following him think about Christian liberty as the God-inspired ability to be content under all circumstances. A good conscience, they think, is God's gift and frees Christians from being, and feeling, imprisoned in the anxieties, insecurities and worries of this life. Being enveloped by the Holy Spirit and God's love is an antidote to all forms of disorder. Our faith and the bird's eye view of existence provide Christians with the balance characteristic of the essence of evolution.

More importantly, our text, the Joyeux Noel film, the birth and crucifixion of Jesus, the freedom transcending imprisonment and embeddedness, sharply show that there are two strongly divided kinds of religion. The first one Augustine called the city of God, or the invisible church (Calvin). The second one Augustine called the city of man, or the visible church (Calvin). The first one transcends, the second one concretizes. And yet Jesus, the mediator between God and men, represents the miracle of the meeting and reconciliation of transcendence and concretization. Or more profoundly, Jesus represents the joyful message that order both has and will swallow up chaos and disorder.

CALVIN 35

SACRIFICING LIFE

There is no greater love than this – that a man lays down his life for his friends.
John 15:13

At the heart of evolution lies the instinct to perpetuate existence. One admires people clinging to life. Our entire health system is built on physical survival. No expense is spared to prolong life. Where would humanity be without the built-in urge to procreate? Suicide is unnatural. The main argument against homosexuality is that it does not lead to the elementary process of sustaining the race. All living things insist on doing so. We pray for the sick and the dying. Churches emphatically insist that life is sacred and that it should not be arbitrarily taken away.

And yet Jesus in our text today is saying that the greatest form of love is to lay down that life for one's friends. And where would any nation be if it weren't for its citizens being prepared to spend enormous amounts of money to defend borders? We feel it in our bones that our entire national identity would be at stake if it weren't for our soldiers being prepared to sacrifice their life for our national or even global security.

In other words the opposite of preserving our life at almost any price is incongruously countered by another principle of sacrificing that very life for preserving nationhood or global health and unity.

Actually that same principle is not just confined to the human race. We should not be overly convinced about our racial superiority! We have a mob of kangaroos on our property. Whenever we approach, the largest buck remains behind until all the females and the young ones have a chance to hop away. He is not afraid to endanger his own life by staying put and to ensure that the others are safe. He protects his mob. There are many examples in the animal kingdom of cooperation to ensure that the herd or the colony remains intact, even if this goes at the expense of personal survival. Ant colonies are examples of cooperation prevailing over the survival of the single ant.

Our text today specifies that love is a force for both social and personal survival. Of course it is built on a very physical foundation, such as attraction for the other sex. But then the horizons are widened to include loyalty and love for others, such as friends, neighbours, communities, countries or humanity in general. They are all good examples of the powerful influences of the non-personal or social on our existence.

But before getting too far, let us have a look at what the Bible has to say about sacrifice and how that fits not just with how Calvin treats the topic, but also how it links with the crucial Christian stress on the cross and its redeeming quality for our faith. In the process we may also discover how social science thinking about sacrifice in other cultures and religions may shed some light on our understanding of its biblical meaning.

In our Old Testament reading (Exodus 13:1, 2) we read: The Lord said to Moses: 'Every first-born, the first birth of every Israelite, you must dedicate to me, both man and beast; it is mine.' And that is why Abraham took his first-born, Isaac, to offer him as a sacrifice. But then (Genesis 22:12) we read that this was only a test. An angel of the Lord appeared and said: 'Now I know that you are a God-fearing man. You have not withheld from me your son, your only son.' And so a miraculously appearing ram was 'offered as a sacrifice instead of his son (verse 14).'

But then the prophets, such as Hosea (6:6) carry the symbolism further: 'Loyalty is my desire, not sacrifice, not whole-offerings but the knowledge of God.' Jesus adopts this interpretation of sacrifice (Matthew 9:12-13). The Pharisees accuse him of eating with tax-gatherers and sinners. He says: 'It is not the healthy that need a doctor, but the sick. Go and learn what the text means, 'I require mercy, not sacrifice.' I did not come to invite virtuous people, but sinners.' In other words not just loyalty, but also mercy, is regarded as more important than animal or material sacrifices in the New Testament.

St Paul adds spirituality to the list of items more valuable than lesser kinds of sacrifice. In his letter to the Philippians he thinks 'that all the good works of believers are called spiritual sacrifices (Philippians 4:18 as interpreted by Calvin, *Inst*. IV xviii 16).' The author of the epistle to the Hebrews makes it clear that Jesus became a sacrifice for man and made further sacrifices unnecessary, as Calvin insists.

Calvin develops a similar theme in his chapter on the Lord's Supper. He argues that the Roman Mass wrongly interposes the priest between God and the believers and writes that Scripture clearly teaches the priesthood of all believers. 'Christ is our mediator', he says. 'It is Christ, by whose intervention we offer ourselves and our all to the Father; he is our High Priest ... who 'has made us kings and priests to God and his Father (Revelation 1:6).'

Calvin agrees with Augustine when the latter says that 'it would be equivalent to Antichrist for any one to make a bishop to be an intercessor between God and man (*Inst*. IV xviii 10).' To Augustine and later, Calvin, the Lord's Supper is 'a commemoration, an image, a testimonial of that singular, true, and only sacrifice by which Christ expiated our guilt (ibid.).'

In parentheses: here Augustine and Calvin following him, strongly distinguish between the city of God, the invisible Church, Christianity as organic spirituality, on the one hand and the city of man, the visible church and Christian organization on the other hand. To Augustine and Calvin's way of thinking, the second is decidedly less sacred and therefore inferior, to the first.

Calvin links spirituality with sacrifice in the section (*Inst*. IV xviii 17) following the one just quoted above: '… even while the people of God were kept under the tutelage of the law, the prophets clearly expressed that under these sacrifices there was a reality which is common both to the Jewish people and the Christian Church.'

If Calvin had been alive today and had been able to consult, as he would have, the social scientific studies on the function of sacrifice in other religions he would have gone even further and suggested that the reality underlying sacrifice in any religion is to clarify priorities. As such he would also conclude logically, that this is true for any culture, whether ancient or modern, primitive or sophisticated.

That priority in the case of our Old Testament reading of Abraham being prepared to obey God through thick and thin is also central to our New Testament reading and Calvin's emphasis on the Eucharistic (praising God) meaning of the Lord's Supper that avoids what he calls the 'fatal vortex' and the 'execrable spiritual whoredom' of denying 'the royal priesthood of all Christians by the interposition of the priest where only Jesus could possibly be.' Calvin insists that only Christ is the mediator between God and man (*Inst*. IV xiii 17-18) and no man, including, ordained priests, could usurp that function.

How relevant is all this for our day and age or for each of us personally? Anything to do with sacrifice of animals is rather foreign to us, isn't it? Even the more transcendent, symbolic interpretation of this kind of sacrifice as expressed by the Old Testament prophets seems rather strange now. And how are we to understand the central event in the New Testament, Jesus' sacrificial death on the cross for our sins?

I want to defend the idea that it is more relevant than appears at first sight. For one, already in the Old Testament story of Abraham preparing for the ancient and repulsive offering of one's first born, the Bible emphasizes that here God was testing Abraham. It says that Abraham's faith in God was more relevant than any actual sacrifice whatever its concrete base.

The story stresses that faith in God (obeying Him) is the pinnacle in the hierarchy of priorities. It fits with what any sacrifice in any age and religion is and was essentially about. It is also relevant for our Christian conviction that God represents the essence of order in society. And what is more relevant than that for all human beings?

And how are we to think about Jesus dying for our sins? How relevant is that in our day and age? This concept is obviously built on the familiarity of any society in the first century AD whether Roman, Greek or Judaic, with sacrifice and altars, originally the places where the victim was slaughtered and burnt.

I would like to answer these two questions under three headings.

(1) The first one is historical/sociological. Jesus saw himself as the representative and protagonist of a long line of prophets reaching all the way back to Moses, Isaiah, Jeremiah, Hosea, John the Baptist. They all suffered from being rejected by the establishment of their historical period. They were the critics of idol worshippers (Moses) or royal abuses and corruption (Nathan, Elijah) or the Roman and the Sanhedrin establishment (John the Baptist) and suffered severely from being rejected, persecuted and even killed sometimes. Jesus' crucifixion and death on the cross can therefore be interpreted as punishment for being in a long line of the 'stirrers of Israel.'

Following this line of argument the sins for which Jesus died are the social corruptions and injustices of his time. His death on the cross is then not only the revenge of those who defended the corrupt status quo but also Jesus' personal sacrifice to safeguard a healthier, saner, just society in which the powerless were no longer rejected but accepted and redeemed.

(2) There is a second way of looking at the relevance of the drama of crucifixion and resurrection for our day and age. Jesus' death on the cross underlines the crucial importance of his God-given integrity or righteousness. It therefore has and can strengthen the same sentiments and conviction in his followers.

It highlights the personal wholeness or salvation, preserved at all costs against the odds of a hostile, non-believing, corrupt, sinful environment. Sins break down social cohesion, communal wholeness. Yet there is also the burden of one's individual guilt (jeopardizing personal wholeness) that has now been taken away and has restored the individual to private integrity.

In the Old Testament the projection of sin on the scapegoat was well understood both on the social and private level. Jesus taking our sins away safeguards our wholeness or integrity as embodied in God who is love and order. In other words, faith in God is the vital link in this process of salvation, wholeness. The Holy Spirit is an important chain in that link. It enables, cleanses and therefore realistically makes God pivotal in the hearts of humans.

Jesus dying on the cross is the epitome of sacrificial love. It takes away sin from one's individual life. It contrasts with the suicide bombers' attempt to pursue a national (anti-Israel, or anti-American) cause, however sympathetic one may be with their attack on hedonism and consumerism. The Christian emphasis is on deep understanding, empathetic suffering with all humanity, the despised and rejected as well as people who rely entirely on the narrow, and proud establishment power of those who think they have arrived. The resurrection summarizes the ultimate victory over sin, as is particularly foreshadowed in the last chapter and the last book of the Bible (Revelation).

By contrast the beginning of the Bible still depicts the process of order being rescued from the clutches of chaos. In the Book of Revelation that process is now accomplished. God's kingdom has prevailed over Satan's realm.

(3) For the third way of looking at sacrificial love as reflected in Jesus' death on the cross and the resurrection we have to go back to our text. It stresses love as the definitive cause. Together with loyalty, commitment, faith it is the capping stone of creation. It is the force binding individuals, families, communities, nations, and the entire world. It spans the world, as is expressed in Psalm 98 which we have sung together and is also on the lectionary for today.

If that love is exclusively attached to an individual, local or national identity (as it is in the case of the suicide bombers, sacrificing themselves for the destruction of Israel or an opposing sect – Sunnies or Shiites) this narrow commitment destroys the very, global, mankind-straddling, faith and commitment God has in mind for humanity. It has then moved into Satan's kingdom. Christian love and faith are inclusive rather than exclusive.

The world as we realistically perceive it is a constant, moving, balance, equilibrium, between order and change of that order. The Bible sides emphatically with order, God's, side, as over against the disorder, or sin, as represented in Satan. Our Hymn 'Who is on the Lord's side' (Hymn 519 in the Scottish Church Hymnal) exactly expresses that sentiment.

CALVIN 36

SEPARATE, YET TOGETHER or the TRAGEDY and TRIUMPH of DIVERSITY

And God, who can read men's mind, showed his approval of them by giving the Holy Spirit to them, as he did to us. Acts 15:8

Today's Old Testament reading from Ezekiel 20:32-44 is a personal predicament. What hat do I put on? If I put on my academic hat, I am duty bound to speak about Ezekiel's idols as legitimate, understandable, and even necessary, marks of specific cultures. On the other hand, if I put on my hat as an evangelical Christian, I have to treat these idols as undesirable competitors for the Christian faith. And as I am fully committed to the latter, I cannot very well approach the former without prejudice. At least so it is generally assumed.

Yet I think I can resolve the dilemma without doing a grave injustice to either the academic or the evangelical Christian point of view. However you may have to wait to the very end of this sermon for this to become clear. In the meantime, of course, to think in terms of two diverse, contrasting, approaches is uncomfortable, to say the very least.

Let us have a close look at our Old Testament passages. All through the book Ezekiel crusades against idols and idolatries. He sees them all around. Similarly to Jesus being upset by the commercial exploits in the temple, so God speaking through Ezekiel despises what he calls the pollution at the heart of Judaism. In verse 39 of chapter 20 he actually prefers out and out idolatry (which means rejecting Yahweh) to amalgamation with other gods, invariably called idols.

Out and out idolatry Ezekiel also finds in the countries surrounding Jerusalem. In the same chapter 20 he rails against the Egyptians united under their rulers revered as gods. Even more he accuses his fellow exiles in Babylonia of being seduced by the local deities. Calvin observes in his comment on 20:8, that this is understandable and not even surprising as 'slaves tend to contract the pollution from superstition to gratify their owners.'

No, says Ezekiel, in the verses following, compromise is not in God's vocabulary. He alone is the one who guided Israel in the past and will do so in the future (verse 42). It is a matter of all or nothing. He alone determines Israel to be his preferred nation, in spite of their 'wicked ways' and 'their corrupt doings.' He alone, without help from the gods of the surrounding nations (all idols in his language) will be Israel's guide, comforter and supreme head, uniting the nation under his benevolent and loving authority.

Calvin's comments on Ezekiel 20:32–44 are the last of the sixty-five daily lectures on Ezekiel he gave at the University of Geneva which he had founded in 1559 and which had become an instantaneous, world famous, success. Calvin never finished the lectures on the remaining twenty-eight chapters and died a few months later of tuberculosis (27 May 1565). Calvin has some interesting comments on these last 12 verses of Ezekiel 20. Being himself an exile from Catholic France he deeply understands the hardship of the Israelites being banished from their country and carried to foreign Babylonia. In verse 33 he has just commiserated with the 'miserable captives' and their temptation 'to throw off God's yoke and mingle with the profane nations (Babylonia).' Yet 'uniting with the rest of the world and avoiding the hatred of mankind in consequence of their religion' is not what Yahweh's plan is for them.

No, Yahweh insists on keeping his covenant with Israel through thick and thin. He does 'not suffer them to be snatched away from him, just as a master fetches back his fugitive slave; or like a prince who might destroy the perfidious and rebellious, yet only chastises them that they may groan under a hard slavery', says Calvin.

Or, to use another example, Calvin insists that this chastising and suffering following in its wake has a purpose. It may make for 'perverse bondage', he says. How? Would not all this chastising and suffering alienate from, rather than bond his people to, God? After all isn't God supposed to be almighty and omnipotent? And why is it perverse? Or is this maybe a textbook example of sadomasochism, getting false satisfaction from pain, punishment or suffering?

Perhaps Calvin attempts to express what I prefer to call an example of 'symbiotic bondage.' This means bonding two separate entities (in our case clashing Israelite and Babylonian ethnic groups) each strengthened by separate cultures and their different gods. In other words separate ethnic cultures which also have to live together, therefore bond and adapt to one another. Consequently they are pressured to mitigate and even reconcile their different sacred beliefs.

Yet this also means that in the give and take of social contacts, the conquering nation has all the cards and the conquered, enslaved, ethnic group, such as the Jewish exiles in Babylonia, has none. Or to say this differently, Ezekiel's constant idol bashing is essentially a strong and necessary defence of endangered Jewish identity in the light of an unequal power struggle between conquering and conquered, master and slave.

Yet in spite of the unequal power struggle, the powerless, subjugated, can still use to their advantage the conqueror's need for social and religious conformity and integrity of nation and exiles. After all even the powerful, conquering enemy can never be comfortable with the snake of potential rebels at its bosom. Consequently there often arises a mutual search for, and understanding of, what both have in common. And what they have in common is almost always transcending and relativising the concrete differences of acting and reacting, norms and values and stressing the more abstract religious ideas. Both are more likely to agree about values such as humility, kindness to others, the unity of faith, etc. What they have in common are almost always not specific, culturally specific ideas, but commitment to more transcendent themes, such as immortality, eternity, wholeness, salvation or even commitment as such.

Perverse or symbiotic bondage therefore is the inevitable concomitant of diverse ethnic groups living together (the actual meaning of symbiosis) and under pressure to reconcile their religious (the actual meaning of bonding) orientations. Yet this reconciling process has to fight an uphill battle ('perverse' according to Calvin as it goes against the actual meaning and function of reconciliation). In other words symbiosis is perverse because it combines both bondage and separateness.

The by-product of this reconciling process (the tragic necessity of a deeply anchored and entrenched system of sacred beliefs being under pressure to adapt) is also a higher level of global understanding of God's cosmic intentions for the planet (the triumph of overcoming too much diversity of a dangerously divided world). God's global order is somehow connected with the partial breakdown of that order so that the former, global order can both adapt and survive. If this is the case we may have an example here of the essence of evolution as the symbiosis of conservation and adaptation for the well-being of both.

Whatever the case, Calvin is actually using the founder of Presbyterianism in Scotland, John Knox's suffering as 'perverse bondage' when the latter was captured by the Catholic French fleet from his refuge in the Reformed Castle of St Andrews in Scotland in July 1547 and compelled to serve as galley slave. Calvin, still in his comment on Ezekiel 20:33, compares the Lord as 'a master seeing that he cannot obtain voluntary obedience from his slaves, he compels them to the galleys, or other laborious works, until they become half dead.'

Continuing with verse 36, Ezekiel quotes the Lord freeing his people in the past from 'the wilderness of Egypt.' But, Calvin insists, this freedom had its own 'disagreeable consequences.' He suggests quite similarly and realistically that future liberation from the Chaldean or Babylonian yoke does not necessarily lead to a bed of roses. Or, as Calvin says in his comment on liberty in verse 39 'that it is in vain to worship God by halves', meaning that the desperately hoped for freedom similarly requires God's 'strong hand' in order that salvation can be understood as what it is supposed to be: wholeness, integrity lifted to a more sustainable level.

Calvin's profound insight into the relevance of God's strong hand in order to rescue and distil order from the stark realism of all-pervasive physical, social, individual disorder is also obvious in his comment on Ezekiel 20:44. Here God says that he has to rescue, (honour), his name when confronted 'with your wicked ways and vicious deeds.'

Calvin interprets this to mean that 'our salvation' relates 'to a debtor and creditor account': God is not 'in the slightest degree indebted to us' when we 'diminish his glory ... and despoil ourselves of that inestimable privilege which the Prophet now commends.' I take this to mean that God's hand of order has to be all the stronger the more pervasive the breakdown of the physical and social unity appears to be.

This in turn leads to the plus and minus thinking that undergird most, if not all religions, whether primitive or modern. What do I mean by plus and minus thinking? The best way to explain this is to use the example of the Inuit in my *Faith and Fragility* book on religion and identity in Canada (p. 24):

> The souls and the spirits, the deities and the myths, the taboos and the shamans, the magic words and the rites of passage together built a world which made a stronger whole out of various forms of endangered integrity. These forms might consist of the unity of nature and society, or of the community as such, or of one's body, but in all instances religion provided the plus which fitted in with the minus (or potential minus) of their fragility.

To transfer this 'plus/minus thinking' to Ezekiel and Calvin: God's strong hand (verse 33) is the plus balancing the minus of the endangered Israelite integrity or bondage The very idolatries which Ezekiel so strongly attacks and his preference for 'out and out idolatries' over a wishy-washy amalgamation of culture-bound religious organizations are ever so many pointers to the tragedy (or minus) of the embeddedness of all religious organizations in their cultural milieus and their human fabrications and concoctions. Yet it contrasts sharply with the triumph and transcendent quality of God's 'strong hand' and global intent (a plus).

This kind of thinking and interpreting is also basic to our understanding of our New Testament reading of Acts 15:1-11. Before going into these passages, it may be useful as a prologue to say something about doctrinal bickering. After all this is what this section is all about. I am sure that hardly any of us in church today feels that doctrinal bickering has much use. All of you justifiably feel that religion has to do with integrity, unifying sentiments, bonding, as indeed the derivation of the word 'religion' suggests. The Latin verb 'religare' means 'to bind together.' Or to say this in terms of our plus/minus thinking: aren't disputes about doctrine divisive (a minus compared with the plus of our faith in Jesus as our saviour)? Aren't ecclesiastical fights the worst of all conflicts?

Well, today's reading of Acts 15 is an example of doctrinal bickering that had quite positive consequences and changed the progress of Christianity for good. How?

A major split occurred within the early Christian community. The controversy was not just minor and had become fierce (Acts 15:2) The Jerusalem Christians insisted on keeping things in the old way. That meant circumcision as a prerequisite for admission. Others could not be saved (Acts 15:1). But the Gentile Christians represented by Paul and Barnabas felt that this was an undue requirement. They felt that the Holy Spirit inspiring the congregations outside Judea, had made this injunction unnecessary. To them it was 'provoking God to lay a yoke on the shoulders of these converts which neither we nor our fathers were able to bear (Acts 15:10).'

And so 'the apostles and elders held a meeting to look into the matter (Acts 15:6).' The upshot of it all was that Paul and Barnabas won the long debate, their main argument being as follows: 'And God who can read man's mind, showed his approval of them by giving the Holy Spirit to them, as he did to us (Acts 15:8).'

Ever since, Christianity has spread through foreign lands, whereas Judaism has remained an ethnic enclave to this very day. Circumcision (essential for the Jews) became a symbol for removal of the flesh allowing the Holy Spirit to become the centre of motivation and inner life (for the Christians, Philippians 3:3), as our text suggests.

Calvin uses this controversy in his comments on 1 Corinthians 14:34-36 by stating that 'it does not necessarily follow, that Churches that are of later origin must be bound to observe, in every point, the institutions of the earlier ones, in as much as even Paul himself did not bind himself by this rule, so as to obtrude upon other churches the customs that were in use in Jerusalem.'

In other words, as in Calvin's interpretation of Ezekiel's concern with ethnic religions representing diverse cultures, so here too perverse or symbiotic bondage follows doctrinal divisions. The bridge (bond) between these divisions is to perversely and symbiotically separate the elect from the reprobate, salvation from sin, the sacred from the secular, pure order from disorder, God from the economic, political, scientific structures now free to follow their own secular paths. Yet these separate spheres must also unite to some extent what otherwise would fly apart, like a can of worms without the can.

All this is much more relevant than you may think. Historically and theologically it is a faithful following of Calvin's (and behind him Augustine's) deepest interpretation of Christianity. Academically, however, it also strongly maintains that dispensing or at a minimum, downgrading, idols as a useless and unfashionable concept is unlikely to take us very far. Our age must stress global understanding and tolerance for the sake of even token peace. And yet that very global peace depends more than one realizes, on a global commitment to supra-cultural ends.

Global warming, nuclear proliferation, genetic manipulation, infinite tolerance, moral confusion, are all basic issues in the entire world and not just in our little corner of it. They all harbour potential pitfalls as well as potential enrichment for the expression of our human responsibility to Yahweh, God, and Allah to not just prevent global destruction, but also to heal and save the world. It may be our Christian duty to redefine the concept of idols and to resurrect the religious, or more specifically Christian, point of view of idols. After all there are in our day and age numerous commitments which fall far short of these supra-cultural ends. Specific idols may have to be documented or specified as countering these supra-cultural ends.

The relevance of today's readings is that God's grace, the Holy Spirit, the offer of salvation through faith is straddling the globe. It is not confined to one nation, one ethnic group, one culture or even one narrow personal conviction. It is universal. The Christian vision may again and again be dragged down too much in the immediate here and now. It may be too much restricted to what our mind rather than our heart can fathom. It may obscure the vision of the city of God through sanctifying the city of man too much (Augustine). It may dim the splendour of the invisible church through too much attachment to its visible partner, the visible church (Calvin).

Our Christian vision is invariably shackled too much to what we humans can comprehend or want it to be. To make exclusive sense of our concrete existential predicaments, we may both underestimate and do an injustice to God's intention for our lives. And this may be our greatest sin that should be incorporated in all our public and private confessions! After all God has made us stewards of the global world and not just our national, ethnic or personal identity. And on this global level we don't seem to do a very good job at present!

The suicide bombers should be condemned because they commit the sin of associating God too closely to narrow ethnic boundaries, not unlike the circumcision party in our New Testament reading. God does not allow a compromise as also our Old Testament testifies. If God's order has to be sharply delineated from the existential disorder and kept separate to fulfil that function, it is essential that boundaries are firmly drawn rather than eroded.

Our text is quite explicit. What unites Christians (both gentiles and converted Jews in Jerusalem) is not outward, concrete, acts, such as circumcision or keeping specific food laws, but faith and spirituality. They may have the disadvantage of lesser concreteness and more transcendence, but then God whom we worship is also less visible than the idols of which Ezekiel speaks so volubly.

To counter ethnic diversity the Bible encourages not shallow common denominator tolerance of contrasting faith and beliefs, but actually suggests the opposite, commitment to, and faith in, transcendence, God's immortality, eternity, love, goodness, kindness, the Golden Rule, in other words, God's otherness. It is on this level that cross-cultural cohesion, integrity, wholeness can be achieved. It is also on this level that academic approaches to religion and evangelical, contextual theology can not only see eye to eye, but actually, symbiotically, support one another. I say 'symbiotically' because there is, and remains, a deep cleavage between analysis and synthesis, scrutinizing religion and being religious, committed.

The last verse two of Hymn 312 (Australian Hymnbook) sums it up beautifully:

> As thou in bond of love dost join
> The Father and the Son
> So fill us all with mutual love
> And knit our heart in one.

CALVIN 37

THE SIMPLICITY of FAITH

I am afraid that your thoughts may be corrupted and you may lose your simple devotion to Christ. 2 Corinthians 11:3

In the lane next to me at the Queanbeyan Swimming Pool yesterday a young man swam twice as fast as I could manage. I caught up with him in the dressing room where he had just finished a two-minute shower. I complemented him on his fitness and not wasting any water.

He said that he had done much weekend reading on global warming and the national carbon emission trading system. He felt that all of us should take it very seriously and discipline both our use of water and energy. He had read a recent survey showing that in the Canberra region greenhouse gas emission and water use was way in excess of the Australian average and even more in excess than in rural areas.

He had become intrigued, he said, by a television programme on carbon cops and intended to follow the couple which had halved their use of energy. 'Maybe', he said, 'that in the near future we all have to return to my grand-parents' life style on their property near Dubbo and the simple Christian living they had instilled in their children. How did I feel about it?'

I said that I agreed, and that I was preparing a sermon on a rather similar topic. I promised him a copy once I had finished. That is, if he was interested. He was polite enough to say that he was!

Our Old Testament reading comes from the book of Genesis, chapter 1:26-31. It is the story of God's intent to make humans 'in our image after our own likeness and letting them have dominion over the fish in the sea, and over the fowl of the air, and over the cattle, and over all the earth over every living thing that moves upon the earth (verse 26).'

Verse 27 then states that God actually did so and adds that he made both male and female humans. In the next verse (28) God blessed them and told them 'to multiply and replenish the earth and subdue it and have dominion over the fish in the sea, the birds of heaven and every living thing that moves upon the earth.'

The next three verses add God's gifts to humans of anything on the earth and then finishes (verse 31) with his satisfaction with what he had made. He gave himself a pat on the back and concluded 'that it was very good.'

Calvin has much to say about this first chapter in the Bible. He insists that before God took things in hand the earth was an 'indigested mass' and a 'disorderly heap' and asserts, that 'however confused it might be, it was (now) rendered stable, for the time by the secret efficacy of the Spirit.' To Calvin the order created out of chaos 'required the secret inspiration of God to prevent its speedy dissolution' and 'derived its strength from the Spirit as described in Psalm 104:30 as renewing the face of the earth.' Without the Spirit 'all things return to their dust and vanish away.'

Still on what precedes today's reading (Genesis 1:16) Calvin is aware that astronomers paint a different picture of the creation of the universe. Yet he insists that their science 'should not be reprobated or condemned', but feels that Moses (to Calvin the author of Genesis) 'was ordained a teacher as well of the unlearned and rude as of the learned (and therefore) could not otherwise fulfil his office than by descending to this grosser method of instruction.' In further comments on this verse Calvin again sides with the astronomers and 'dismisses the reverie of Plato, who ascribes reason and intelligence to the stars.'

On our reading of Genesis 1:26-31 Calvin is particularly interested in the meaning of humans being made in the image of God. It has nothing to do with 'corporeal' similarity nor with 'the admirable workmanship' of man's body or with man's 'vice-regency in the government of the world' although Scripture specifically refers to human dominion over 'every living thing that moves upon the earth.' To Calvin God 'appointed man lord of the world and expressly subjected the animals to him, because they, having an inclination or instinct of their own, seem to be less under authority from without.'

No, God himself is the regent. The 'chief seat of the divine image was in the human mind and heart.' 'In the mind perfect intelligence flourished and reigned ... and all the senses were prepared and moulded for due obedience to reason; and in the body there was a suitable correspondence with its internal order.' However this is how it was originally. But then the Fall interfered and now 'no part is free from the infection of sin.'

Today's Psalm is 116:1-9 where King David describes the deep trouble he is in. 'The cords of death bound me, Sheol held me in its grip. Anguish and torment held me fast (verse 3); so I invoked the Lord by name, Deliver me, O Lord, I beseech thee: for I am thy slave (verse 4).' The Lord obviously succeeded because in the next verse 5 God is lauded as 'gracious, righteous and full of compassion.' David then describes his feelings of relief: and attributes it to his private single-hearted faith: 'The Lord preserves the simple-hearted; I was brought low and he saved me (verse 6).'

David then exhorts his heart 'to be at rest once more (verse 7)' and concludes that 'The lord has rescued me from death and my feet from stumbling (verse 8)' and that from here onwards 'I will walk in the presence of the Lord in the land of the living (verse 9).'

In Calvin's commentary on Psalm 116, the footnote suggests that David's deep troubles were caused by 'the rebellion excited by his son Absalom.' Calvin is particularly interested in verse 6 as follows:

The psalmist 'accommodates the experience of God's favouring and fair preservation of the simple, that is of such as, being undesigning, do not possess the requisite prudence for managing their own affairs. The term rendered simple, is often understood in a bad sense, denoting persons inconsiderate and foolish who will not follow wholesome advice. But in this place it is applied to those who are exposed to the abuse of the wicked, who are not sufficiently subtle and circumspect to elude the snares of which are laid for them, in short, to those who are easily overreached; while, on the contrary, the children of this world, are full of ingenuity, and have every means at their command for maintaining and protecting themselves. David, therefore, acknowledges himself to be as a child, unable to consult his own safety, and totally unfit to ward off the dangers to which he was exposed.'

The New Testament readings start with 2 Corinthians 11:1-6. It begins with Paul's confession of attachment to the Christian congregation in Corinth. He was the one who had introduced them to Jesus which in turn lead to a strong bond between them and him (verse 2). But then in his absence other preachers had corrupted them and therefore he begged the Christians in Corinth to return to the 'simplicity that is in Christ (verse 3-6).'

Calvin explains that 'the simplicity that is in Christ means to keep us in the unadulterated and pure doctrine of the gospel, and to admit no foreign admixtures.' It is like 'a sacred marriage that must remain unimpaired and inviolable.' In other words there is something elemental, simple or single-hearted in the faith relationships that should not be squandered.

But that also means self-denial and Calvin devotes an entire chapter to this topic in the *Institutes* (III vii). He regards it as the 'sum of Paul's doctrine.' A frenzied desire, an infinite eagerness, to pursue wealth and honour, intrigue for power, accumulate riches, and collect all those frivolities which seem conducive to luxury and splendour ... are entanglements to be avoided (III vii 8).' The simple faith in God's blessing is the antidote to these satanic temptations.

The simplicity theme also dominates in our reading from Matthew 5:1-10, the so-called Sermon on the Mount. To Calvin the sermon is all about 'true happiness.' Yet that happiness has nothing to do with being 'free from annoyance, attaining all one's wishes and leading a joyful and easy life.'

No, by contrast, it has everything to do with 'placing happiness beyond the world and above the affections of the flesh.' Therefore 'to be poor in spirit (verse 3) means to be reduced to nothing in oneself and to simply rely on the mercy of God'; even 'mourning contributes to a happy life ... by seeking comfort in God alone' (verse 4). And of course Calvin's stress on humility in all his writings is also summed up in verse 5 where 'persons of mild and gentle disposition will inherit the earth.'

Integrity (verse 6) and 'taking a share in the afflictions of others (verse 7) leads to happiness. Purity of heart (simplicity) means having 'no sagacity to deceive the world (verse 8)' therefore leads to seeing God. Cultivating peace (verse 9) is typical for being a child of God. Persecution (verse 10) may lead to much suffering and rejection 'for the flesh cannot endure the doctrine of the Gospel; none can endure to have their vices reproved.' Yet the kingdom of heaven is the passport for those who endure.

Today's Bible readings can be summed up in a few sentences. God has charged humans with managing His earth. The management has one condition and that is simple, single-hearted faith in His order. Humility, modesty and child-like trust are the prerequisite for meeting that condition. Humans who seek that order within themselves or within their self-propelled activities will only get swamped by the polluted complexity of their social and physical environment.

How relevant is all this for our present situation? Let me answer that question rather personally. Twelve generations ago an ancestor, Joos Mol, was Mayor of Reimerswaal, the third largest town in the Dutch province of Zeeland. In 1584 he received a permit to hold consistory in the local church which meant that on that date the Reformation had taken hold in the town and that the community of believers had taken precedence over too much clerical domination.

The Calvinist strain has moulded my family ever since until my parents' generation. Until that time the ancestors worked hard and efficiently on their farms. They invested or salted away whatever they did not need for frugal living. My grandparents on both sides were elders of the local Reformed Church, but my parents became rather critical of religion because the Christian political party did nothing to counter the injustices perpetrated by landlords who had no qualms renting farms to those who were prepared to pay more rent without compensating the tenant farmers for the considerable improvements they had made on their land.

Yet my parents hugely profited from the ascetic Calvinist tradition of relatives on both sides of the family who had salted away the income of good years and rescued them from bankruptcy by lending them money to close the gap between rent owed and the dwindling income from milk and wheat during the 1930s depression.

The point I am trying to make is that the laudable Calvinist tradition of frugality, saving for the rainy day rather than wasting it on frivolities, has to be complemented by also actively encouraging a just social order. But it also meant that the savings resulting from frugality were to be used wisely. And this in turn meant profitable investments rather than private indulgences. Hence the spirit of capitalism.

It seems to me that this is exactly what is required at the present time: not squandering our resources and to be satisfied with simple living rather than chasing the diminishing returns of consumer products that seem to have also the purpose of showing off one's social status. Wasting energy obviously does not meet God's requirement to be good stewards of his planet. Good stewardship also means promoting justice and social order.

Simple faith, as our text suggests, is essential in that it strongly links believers with God's plan of order for this earth. Without that faith or frame of reference the human stewardship of the planet is ignored to the detriment of both its population and its intrinsic viability. Under that scenario humanity is very much like the prodigal son in the parable who soon discovered that when he got what he wanted he did not want anymore what he got.

One final point for the modem day relevance of our ancient Bible reading and Calvin's interpretations: the culture and the society handed down from previous generations should no longer be taken for granted. It should be carefully and gratefully preserved and handed down to the following generations, hopefully improved rather than neglected.

What do we pass on to our children and grandchildren? A philosophy of consumerism, indulgence, gluttony, revelry, intoxication, greed, sensuality and wantonness? Or moderation, sobriety and temperance? It is not just God's mandate in Genesis, but also the advocacy of environmental restraint by the young man in the Queanbeyan swimming pool which points to a global responsibility for those who have to build on the foundations we have left for them.

CALVIN 38
AUTHORITY and MINISTRY

(My servant) will not break a bruised reed, or snuff out a smouldering wick; he will make justice shine on every race, never faltering, never breaking down. ... Isaiah 42:3

Has it ever happened to you that you read your Bible and discover how, all of a sudden, rather uncomfortably, it speaks to you in no uncertain terms? I am not now thinking of the funny story of the beleaguered Christian who was perplexed about decisions he had to make and decided to go to the Bible for an answer. And so he opened it and read 'and Judas went and hanged himself.' He felt that this did not help him much and so he closed the Bible and tried again. The first words he came across were: 'Doest thou likewise.'

No, much more seriously, I mean that certain Bible passages don't allow you and me to escape personal application and confrontation. It springs to you unexpectedly from the pages.

It happened to me when preparing today's sermon and reading the Old Testament section of the lectionary for today, Isaiah 42:1-9. However I would like to more appropriately discuss the issue of personal embarrassment under the final, relevance section of this sermon.

As usual I prefer to start with careful listening to what the Bible readings say. Then bring in both Calvin's interpretation and social science reflection on both before launching on a discussion of their relevance for us today.

What then is the message of Isaiah 42:1-9? It is all about the mission of God's servant. In the Greek translation the word 'diakonos', or 'minister' in the Latin version, is used for what we call 'servant.' And by 'service/ministry' it is not only meant individuals, such as Isaiah, or any of the prophets, such as Moses, David, John the Baptist, Jesus, Peter, followers of Christ, but also the church, the nation, one's family. The servant theme runs through all lectionary readings for today.

The servant is chosen by God and has His Spirit bestowed on him (verse 1). He is quiet-spoken (verse 2). He is not aggressive, but will make justice shine on every race. He will not break a bruised reed, or snuff out a smouldering wick, he will make justice shine on every race, never faltering, never breaking down … (verse 3). He is guided by God to be a light to all nations (verse 6) and bring captives out of the dungeons where they lie in darkness (verse 2).

Calvin interprets the passages as foreshadowing Christ, the epitome of all God expects of his servants. Christ 'emptied himself, taking the form of a servant (Philippians 2:6)', so that he could be filled 'with the Spirit of God, in order to execute that divine office and be the Mediator between God and men (verse 1).'

No, the servant (Christ) comes 'without pomp or splendour, such as commonly attends earthly kings, at whose arrival there are uttered various noises and loud cries. No, that is 'not only for the sake of applauding his modesty, but first that we may not form any earthly conception of him; secondly, that, not having known his kindness by which he draws us to him, we may cheerfully hasten to meet him; and lastly, that our faith may not languish, though his condition be mean and despicable (verse 2).'

Calvin applies this to 'ministers of the gospel, who are his deputies (and) ought to show themselves to be meek, and to support the meek and gently to lead them in the way, so as not to extinguish in them the feeblest sparks of piety, but on the contrary, to kindle them with all their might (verse 3).' Calvin himself suffered from what he felt to be his calling as God's deputy, resulting in him being banned from Geneva in 1538, but recalled in 1541 when the moral laxity of the small town had become too much for its concerned citizenry.

Yet 'Christ will indeed be mild and gentle towards the weak, but will have no softness or effeminacy; for he will manfully execute the commission which he has received from the Father ... Christ's ministry, therefore, he testifies, will not be unfruitful, but will have such efficacy that men shall be reformed by it. This must not be limited to the person of Christ, but extends to the whole course of the gospel; for he not only discharged the embassy committed to him for three years, but continues to discharge the same embassy every day by means of his servants (comments on verse 4).'

Psalm 29 which we have sung together, is all about God revealing himself in nature. God's voice is in the thunder and the storms (verse 3). Yet it is also in the beauty of nature (verse 4). God speaks to us in the 'flames of fire (verse 2)' and in the earthquakes (verse 8) and the floods (verse 10). But he also provides people with the strength to endure all these calamities and 'blesses people with peace (verse 11).'

Calvin feels that all this is very relevant. As Christ's deputy and ambassador he has no qualms to denounce powerful establishments when they do not meet what he feels are God's expectations of service (ministers, deacons). Yet 'great men who excel in rank' have a disadvantage compared with us lesser breeds for whom it is easier to be 'reduced to order.' David (the author of Psalm 29 according to Calvin) wants to 'humble the princes of this world who being intoxicated with pride, lift up their horns against God', because 'they think that the power they possess is supplied to them from some other source than from the heaven' and therefore 'the great men of this world are wont to deprive God of the 'glory of His name (verse 2).'

After dealing with the corruption of the powerful, Calvin has it also in for those philosophers who 'weave themselves veils, lest they should be compelled to acknowledge the hand of God which manifestly displays itself in his works.' They 'are endured with sense and reason … and possess genius and learning, (yet) they employ enchantments to shut their ears against God's voice, however powerful, lest it should reach their hearts (verse 5).' 'Even philosophers who appeared to approach nearest to the knowledge of God, contribute nothing whatever that might truly glorify him. All they say concerning religion is not only frigid, but for the most part insipid (verse 9).'

No, Calvin concludes (verse 11), God 'blesses with peace, so that nothing is wanting to the prosperous life of the elect, and their complete happiness.'

The New Testament readings for today both deal with baptism and the Holy Spirit descending on those baptized. Matthew 2:13-17 describes Jesus being baptized in the Jordan by John the Baptist, who initially objected (verse 14) because he felt himself to be only a minor figure, a servant, but then is persuaded to go ahead anyway because it conforms to God's way (verse 15). Subsequently God's Spirit descends as a dove on Jesus (verse 16) and God proclaims him to be His son (verse 17).

Calvin interprets the event (comment on verse 14) to seal the servant character of Christ (Philippians 2:7), rising to the newness of life, mentioned in Romans 6:4 and to give an example of modesty. On the Holy Spirit descending in the shape of a dove (verse 16) Calvin thinks that the dove represents Isaiah's (42:2-3) picture of Christ as the one who does 'not cry, nor lift up, nor cause his voice to be heard in the street. A bruised reed shall he not break, and the smoking flax shall he not quench.' In other words, Calvin says the dove represents 'gentle and lovely grace' rather than formal and formidable power.

The other New Testament reading (Acts 10:34-43) tells the story of Peter's sermon inspiring the centurion Cornelius. God is not a respecter of persons (verse 34). In other words God has no favourites and does not discriminate between natives (the sons of Israel) and the hated Roman occupying force represented by Cornelius. Jesus Christ is the Lord of all (verse 36). God anointed Jesus with the power of the Holy Spirit. He did God's work by doing good deeds and healing the sick, but was crucified (verse 38). Yet God raised him from the dead (verse 40). Jesus was appointed judge of the quick and the dead (verse 42), following 'the witness of all the prophets' that every man who believes in Him may receive forgiveness of sins through His Name (verse 43). Subsequently Cornelius and those with him were baptized (verse 48).'

Calvin interprets Peter's sermon (verse 34) as Christ's Spirit transcending the exclusive Jewish dietary laws and the circumcision proscription. The Holy Spirit unifies by 'pulling down the wall of separation between Jews and Gentiles (Ephesians 2:14). 'God embraces the whole world … and the covenant of eternal life is common to all alike.'

Similarly God does not make other distinctions between humans such as individuals favoured because of their 'riches, nobility, multitude of servants, honour', or disfavoured because of their 'poverty, baseness of lineage, and such like things that make him to be despised (comment on verse 34).'

No, God's criteria are different from those of humans. God anointed his Son with the power of his Spirit (verse 38) and this means to Calvin that God's Spirit is universal and inclusive. In his comment on verse 35, Calvin stresses his central concern with 'the integrity of the whole of life' (or 'the rule of good life') which to him has two components: (1) godliness and religion, under which rubric he would put such items as faith and (2) the rules 'which men use among themselves' and which nowadays we would call social cohesion and belonging.

How can we summarize today's reading and Calvin's interpretations? First of all, following Christ means transcendence of ethnic peculiarities. Secondly, it means that instead of maximizing mundane authority and its rewards, Christians in general and ministers/deputies of Christ in particular, must seek ministerial/service-oriented power. Thirdly, only the servant-like stance represented by Jesus and those who follow him will lead to peace, reconciliation and integration on a global level.

The social science implications of today's Bible readings are obvious. A healthy society and a sane citizenry require both the stabilizing force of authority (e.g. God) and civic mentality of service. The balance between the two is constantly moving, as they are essentially opposed to one another. In other words they need one another. Yet too much movement in one direction rather than the other has been, and will also in the future, be disastrous for civilization as we know it. Traditionally all religions, whether primitive or modem, have been involved, not always successfully, in the symbiotic relation between the two. Therefore any society must nurture both authority and service to assist its survival.

How relevant is all we have read and heard so far? The first point is, of course, what is the personally discomforting note I mentioned at the beginning. You remember my saying that it sprang from the pages when I prepared for this sermon.

Next month I will be 86 and there are not too many left among you listening to me now in that age group. Like me they are closer to what my youngest daughter in Canada the other day called, our use-by-date. The time may well soon come that I will confront my Maker. And I could imagine the following conversation taking place:

God: 'In your ordination vows you promised to deputize for my son Jesus. Did you do that?'

Me: 'Yes, Lord, I have written 15 academic books about the understanding of religion. I have been the opening, key-note, speaker at two international congresses dealing with the study of religion; I have been international president in my chosen profession, the social scientific study of religion.'

The Lord: 'That was not my question. You were handsomely rewarded by the academic establishment for those achievements. Yet my son Jesus was crucified by the religious establishment of his time. You analysed religion and talked about it. By contrast my son and his followers lived the very commitment you only analysed.'

Me: 'Lord, you are right. I am arrogant and a miserable sinner. Have mercy on me.'

Upon which the Lord, hopefully will open the gate and say: 'Enter, you are forgiven.'

But there is another important source of relevance in today's scripture reading. It has to do with the contrast between the prevailing, almost exclusive, understanding of mundane authority and the implicit view of ministry as service.

The power of service or ministry obviously leads to a saner, more wholesome society than power for individuals to advance their own ego-trip or to re-assert their authority over others. At the bottom of almost all anti-religious literature, of which there is much nowadays, is the critique of religious organization or religion as it has allied itself with controversial ethnic, national or other groups. Yet the attacks are almost never levelled at religious figures such as Jesus, or any of the Old Testament prophets, such as Moses. Our society still looks for models to emulate, rather than mundane, publicity-seeking authoritarian figures.

All lectionary readings for today point to the central obligation not just of individuals, such as you and I, confessing Christians, but churches, families, nations to be God's servants or ministers. This contrasts sharply with the views of Calvin's contemporary Niccolo Machiavelli (1469-1529), living only a bit over 300 miles (about 500 kilometres, as the crow flies) to the southeast of Geneva in Florence, Italy.

He has been regarded as the father of modern political science, mainly because he wrote a book (*The Prince*), published in 1532, to get back into the graces of the ruling de Medici family which had arrested, tortured and imprisoned him. The book is a manual for any ruler on how to acquire and maintain personal power and authority with any means, however wicked. Religion is an important means to just do that, Machiavelli asserts.

Yet all our readings for today, together with Calvin's comments and modern social science show that this view is too narrow and excludes the very marginal people in any culture which God in Matthew 25:35 calls the hungry, the thirsty, the strangers, the sick, the prisoners (all powerless individuals). They too are part of a society. They too have to be incorporated and looked after, if that society is to be cohesive, united and congenial for everyone. And as such they have the power to avoid exclusion and division.

Peace, inclusion and reconciliation are the hallmarks of the servant which both Isaiah, Jesus, the early Christians and Christ's deputies and ambassadors regard as essential for restoring the bruised reed, the smouldering wick and above all for 'justice to shine on every race, never faltering, never breaking down', as our text in Isaiah 42:3 requires.

CALVIN 39

The HARMONY of FAITH

Is Christ divided? 1 Corinthians 1:13

Sixty-four years ago (the year is 1944, the last full year of World War II) I would have given the answer to Paul's question put in the first letter to the Corinthians, chapter 1, verse 13 with a resounding 'yes.' Christ was quite obviously divided. The Lutheran chaplain in the prison with hard labour (Zuchthaus) in Halle, Germany insisted on making the gospel relevant to his Nazi audience by equating the German conquests with saving civilization as God's global purpose. The gospel of salvation through faith in Christ was obviously shaped (made relevant for, determined by) what his audience needed or at a minimum wanted to hear.

Simultaneously in the same institution at the same time, my nine Norwegian friends (to a man serving heavy sentences for underground activities) held their visiting Norwegian Lutheran chaplain in highest esteem as he had managed to bolster their anti-Nazi convictions by getting permission from prison authorities to locate them together in a separate section of the prison. Here too the gospel of salvation through faith in Christ was made relevant for, determined by, what my Norwegian underground workers needed, or at a minimum wanted to hear.

Earlier that year in the middle of a typhoid epidemic an old guard daily visited my cell with a well thumbed Bible inspiring me with stories from the Book of Revelation pointing to Jesus ruling a world of golden streets with trees laden with delicious apples. He was an active Lutheran churchgoer and to him the gospel of salvation through Christ was made relevant for, determined by, the appalling prison conditions.

The gospel of Christ's redemption was obviously interpreted entirely differently for the Nazis, the Norwegian underground workers and the old evangelical guard. Christ was obviously divided according to what people wanted him to be in their specific, yet totally different, set of circumstances, the real threat of death hanging around both prisoners and their guards.

And yet Paul's answer to the question (is Christ divided?) is just as resoundingly: 'No!' The gospel of Christ's redemption is not divided, according to him, in spite of the leadership divisions in the Christian congregation in Corinth. Before attempting to solve the puzzle of my negative argument and observation compared with St Paul's positive optimism, let us first look at the lectionary readings for today after also giving a full hearing to Calvin's suggestions.

Psalm 27:1-9 is all about confidence in God and a sense of His presence in the temple. Verse one calls the Lord 'my light and my salvation' and therefore there is nothing to fear. He is 'the refuge of my life.' God also provides the temple 'to keep me safe beneath his roof in the day of misfortune; he will hide me under the cover of his tent (verse 5).'

Calvin stresses the importance of God as the 'preserver of our life' in verse 1. He thinks that 'all our fears arise from the terrors of death and that we are too anxious about our life.' 'We can have no tranquillity, therefore, until we attain the persuasion that our life is sufficiently guarded, because it is protected by his omnipotent power.'

But then he moves to verse four where the psalmist draws his strength from the beauty of the temple and addresses himself to those who rubbish the 'value of the sight of the external edifice' and the idea that 'God could be enclosed by wood and stone.' He feels that this is going too far. We live in 'very different circumstances from the ancient fathers, but … God still preserves his people under a certain external order and draws them to him by earthly instructions, temples still have their beauty, which deservedly ought to draw the affections and desires of the faithful to them.'

Then he strengthens his argument as follows: 'As the fashion of the temple was not framed according to the wisdom of man, but was an image of spiritual things, the prophet directed his eyes and all his affections to this object.' Yet, we can overemphasize 'the purity of holy things' and he therefore warns: 'The Word, sacraments, public prayers, and other helps of the same kind, cannot be neglected, without a wicked contempt of God, who manifests himself in these ordinances, as in a mirror or image.'

Our gospel reading comes from Matthew 4:12-23. It is all about Jesus selecting Peter and Andrew, John and James as his disciples. Jesus says he wants to make them 'fishers of men' (verse 19). All four of them were originally fishers. Calvin therefore assumes that Jesus suggests a change of occupation. Instead of gathering fish, they would from now onwards assist humans 'straying and wandering in the world as in a great and troubled sea, (to be) gathered by the Gospel.'

Calvin admires the 'ready obedience of the disciples who prefer the call of Christ to all worldly affairs.' He adds: 'The ministers of the Word ought, in a particular manner, to be directed by this example, to lay aside all other occupations, and to devote their selves unreservedly to the Church, to which they are appointed.'

Calvin also thinks that it is not accidental that Jesus selects 'rough mechanics – persons not only destitute of learning, but inferior in capacity, that he might train, or rather renew them by the power of his Spirit, so as to excel all the wise men of the world. He intended to humble, in this manner the pride of the flesh, and to present, in their persons, a remarkable instance of spiritual grace, that we may learn to implore from heaven the light of faith, when we know that it cannot be acquired by our own exertions.'

Yet this is not all. Calvin also is convinced that our Lord chose the unlearned 'not because they preferred ignorance to learning, as some fanatics do, who are delighted by their own ignorance.' No, he chose 'contemptible persons, in order to humble the pride of those who think that heaven is not open to the unlearned.'

The other New Testament reading is 1 Corinthians 1:10-18. Like the other readings it stresses the inclusivity of the gospel. Paul addresses himself here to the actual problem of leadership divisions in the circle of Corinthian Christians (verse 10-12). Then in verse 13 he draws attention to Christ being the unifying frame of reference. The next three verses explain that this unity is given concrete expression in baptism. Therefore Paul is grateful that he did not do much baptizing as their divisions would nullify the very basis for what baptism was all about (verse 14-16). Paul finishes with the good news of Christ's redemption as illustrated by his crucifixion and resurrection (verse 17-18).

Calvin accuses the Corinthian Christians of 'tearing asunder the true unity of faith. 'By contrast what they ought to do is love Christ and 'aim at promoting harmony.' He adds that 'the safety of the Church rests and is dependent on this harmony.' Christian unity is as important for the mind 'as the members of the human body are connected together by a most admirable symmetry (comment on verse 10).'

To Calvin ministers have an important duty. Good ministers must not be 'influenced by ambition, that man gathers disciples, not to Christ, but to himself This then is the fountain of all evils – this is the most hurtful of all plagues – this is the deadly poison of all Churches, when ministers seek their own interests rather than those of Christ (comment on verse 12).'

Calvin thinks that their divisions 'disfigured the simplicity of the gospel and (obscured) the pure and unadulterated knowledge of Christ (comment on verse 17).' Both simplicity on the part of the gospel and humility on the part of believers are the ever recurring elements in Calvin's comments.

How can we summarize our Bible readings? The Christian faith is the harmonizing link between the actual circumstances of existence and God's overarching, concern with that existence. It is like a string binding a loose package together. Yet if it is too exclusively tied to specific items, such as the wood and stone of a building, strong concrete commitment, attachment to the narrow bases of nationhood, personal ambition, physical/social wellbeing/survival, occupational status, any other sort of circumstance, it may improve its relevance yet simultaneously loose its potency and value. Then it usurps, takes away from, God's power. Then it digs its own grave of meaninglessness. Then it denies the wideness of God's mercy and love.

Is there any social scientific significance in our readings for today?

Yes there is. Societies, like individuals, have a built-in instinct for survival. It (survival) depends on marshalling all the available resources for cohesion, integration or salvation as it is called in the Bible. Traditionally religion has always been a major resource for accomplishing that very feat. That's why Calvin compares the symmetry of our physical bodies (also a product of the age-old process of integration) with the mind (comment on verse 10).

Yet the opposite, a break in that symmetry, synthesis or integrity is just as real. Our faith, God's love, understanding and concern battle the consistent breakdown of what holds us together, not just in the physical, but even more in the spiritual, immaterial, divine sphere of existence. The Bible calls that sin, or Satan.

Therefore St Paul almost naturally slides into emphasizing the cross in verse 17 of our reading of 1 Corinthians 1. This is to be expected. The cross represents to him the basic image of destruction of the very synthesis of what is represented in Jesus, God's infusion of integrity/order in humanity.

And just as natural and expected is the ultimate celebration of the defeat of the destructive (yet also sometimes 'adaptive') elements in cultures and civilizations. The stress on the resurrection of Jesus in St Paul's and Christian theology is therefore also an image of ultimate Christian optimism regarding that future. It is not just an intellectual apology for the centrality of the crucifixion and resurrection by Christians. It is much more the realistic and strongly experienced indwelling of the Holy Spirit.

Calvin's sense of academic/rational superiority (his innately held belief in the Athens perspective of individual rationalism) seems insufferable when he calls the 'unlearned' inferior and contemptible. But then he makes up for this by condemning the very pride of the learned in their learning and knowledge.

From the purely social scientific point of view situations or circumstances shape, determine healing, overarching, synthesizing interpretations. Therefore a picture of transcending and strongly believed in, order mitigates very real predicaments and other events.

Yet the poverty of the social scientific argument consists of its refusal to rise above the analytic posture. It confines itself to observing functions. It refuses to become non-scientific. It has to hide itself (to use terminology of Psalm 27, verse 5) in the tent of the sacred principle of objectivity, standing imperiously, overbearingly, beyond the human veil of tears.

The analytic posture divides (cutting up is the original meaning of analysis). By contrast synthesis combines; builds up (the original meaning of synthesis). This is rather similar to the gospel's stress on the crucifixion (cutting up Christ's body) versus the resurrection (restoring that body).

That's why, ages ago, in my *Christianity In Chains* book (originally called 'the shackled vision' published as long ago as 1969 by Nelson in Melbourne) I suggested that actual commitment is less idolatrous than merely talking about it, as we have to do in order to be acceptable to scientific establishments and its scientific canons of objectivity.

After all, both our social scientific establishments and my 1944 experiences, mentioned at the beginning of this sermon, seem to draw our attention to God's promise of salvation through faith in Jesus Christ into the not so pure concrete swamp of daily living and the so-called realism of the scientific enterprise.

Where does all this leave us? Did we resolve our puzzle of Paul's insistence that Christ is the unifying element in the specific Corinthian congregational divisions and my own personal 1944 experience of the contrasting, basically divisive, interpretation of the Christian gospel by the clergy?

Maybe that the answer lies in what follows today's reading of 1 Corinthians 1:10-18. Here St Paul speaks about the doctrine of the cross as sheer folly to humans, yet the power of God (verse 19). The doctrine transcends the teaching of the wise and the learned because it is limited to 'this passing age' (verse 20) or as we have expressed it 'local and present-day circumstances.' Isn't the whole issue of relevance of Christianity as expressed by the critics of Christianity and Bishop Spong on the wrong track, because it is not transcendent enough? Or because it takes the issue of Calvin's 'purity of holy things' not seriously enough?

Maybe that both the popular pro- and anti-Nazi chaplains, insisting on being almost exclusively relevant to the fervent hopes of their different constituencies were less in tune with the time and place spanning gospel of salvation than the old simple guard on the third floor of the Magdeburg Prison, despised by all the other SS guards for what they regarded as his, naive, outdated, evangelical convictions. After all the images of Revelation clearly pointed for him to God's salvation, integrity and wholeness eventually prevailing over man's puny, divisive, disparate and fractured world of 1944 Germany.

All this boils down to solving the puzzle mentioned at the beginning of this sermon. There may be awesome and, as Calvin calls them 'poisonous' divisions within Christian churches, illustrated by the actual differences in biblical interpretations. These differences may be thoroughly grounded in political, national and military conflicts and circumstances. They may even 'crucify' Jesus as he obviously stands in the way of human and religious establishments. Yet the gospel of the living, resurrected, Christ and the Holy Spirit unite what seems foolish (verse 21) to the world. More importantly it represents God's rather than human wisdom, because it harmonizes the faith.

CALVIN 40
HEAVEN, the HABITATION of ORDER

Eternal is thy word, O Lord, planted firm in heaven. Psalm 119:89

Have you ever thought about the Bible as occasionally an exciting detective story? Well today's text from Psalm 119:89 leads you to a very interesting one. Actually it is Calvin's interpretation that makes all of today's readings into a detective story. How? All readings are about heaven. And there is much in the Bible about heaven.

Calvin's exegesis of Genesis 1:16 (sermon 37) resolutely dismisses the creation story and its implied view of heaven as a location in the universe. To him the Genesis story shows Moses' obligation to do justice to his job of also enlightening the uneducated. But then Calvin goes on happily endorsing the astronomer's view of creation.

Yet if this is the case, Calvin's view of heaven as not a place located somewhere in the universe must be reflected in his interpretation of the numerous instances in the Bible where the heavens are mentioned. If it is not a geographic location, what else is it? What are its characteristics? In other words, do the Bible and Calvin explaining today's readings to us take heaven as a symbol of something else? This is our detective story.

Adopting the astronomer's view of creation must have had a strong influence on Calvin's thinking in our readings for today of Isaiah 55:1-13, Psalm 119:89-96, the ascension of Jesus in Acts 1:6-11 and the kingdom of heaven parables in Matthew 13:44-52. As usual let us follow this line of thinking by tracing (1) what the Bible says, (2) how Calvin interprets the passages and finally (3) how relevant all this is in light of present day social scientific thinking about religion.

Isaiah 55:9 compares God's thinking with heaven and human thinking with earth. Heaven here is decidedly not spatial or physical. It is the sphere where God dwells, where God is sovereign. The contrast is stressed in this verse. God's thinking is as broad and comprehensive as human thinking is narrow and limited.

Yet contrast does not mean irreconcilability. Jacob's dream at Bethel (Genesis 28:12) connects, reconciles, heaven and earth. Heaven here is God's dwelling place. It is the symbol for God's order and the ladder, Calvin suggests, is Christ, the mediator, 'who connects heaven and earth … through whom the fullness of all celestial blessings flows down to us and through whom we in turn ascend to God.'

Further, commenting on Isaiah 55:9, Calvin compares heaven and God with whatever is pure/infinite and earth and Satan with what is corrupt/finite. He says: 'Are men, who are corrupted and debased by sinful desires, not ashamed to compare God's lofty and uncorrupted nature with their own, and to confine what is infinite within those narrow limits by which they feel themselves to be wretchedly restrained? In what prison could any of us be more out rightly shut up than in our own unbelief?'

Psalm 119: 89 speaks about heaven in a similar way. The psalmist begins the section 89-96 with pointing to what supports him in all his troubles. It is God's word, the eternal, immutable, all-encompassing element that is secured in heaven. Yet it has also been planted in the earth and sustained all previous generations thanks to God's faithfulness and concern (verse 90).

Without this faithfulness the psalmist would have perished (verse 92). Yet he continues to depend on God's precepts which give him life (verse 93). And save him from destruction by evil men (verse 95), thanks to God's protection. Again the astronomer's view of creation stands its ground.

Calvin has a very interesting interpretation of Psalm 119:89. 'As we see nothing constant or of long continuance upon earth (the prophet) elevates our minds to heaven, that they may fix their anchor there. David, no doubt, might have said, as he has done in many other places, that the whole order of the world bears testimony to the steadfastness of God's word – that word which is most true. But as there is reason to fear that the minds of the godly would hang in uncertainty if they rested the proof of God's truth upon the state of the world, in which such manifold disorders prevail; by placing God's truth in the heavens, he allots it a habitation subject to no changes. That no person then may estimate God's word from the various vicissitudes which meet the eye in this world, heaven is tacitly set in opposition to the earth. Our salvation, as it has been said, being shut up in God's word, is not subject to change, as all earthly things are, but is anchored in a safe and peaceful haven.' In other words, heaven is where God's word and order are put out of reach to preserve their integrity.

Turning to the New Testament: what does the Bible have to say about the ascension and what does heaven mean here? Acts 1:6-11 tells the story. Jesus spoke to a gathering of the disciples (verse 6) who had asked him whether he would restore the kingdom to Israel (verse 7). Jesus answered that this was up to the Father (verse 8), but that they would receive the power of the Holy Spirit. Then Jesus ascended into heaven (verse 9). While they were still looking to heaven, two men in white apparel appeared (verse 10) and promised the disciples that Jesus would return (verse 11). Isn't heaven here the sky?

To Calvin 'it was only by his ascension to heaven that Christ's reign truly commenced.' and that 'his departure might be more useful to us than that presence which was confined in a humble tabernacle of flesh during his abode on the earth (*Inst.* II xvi 14)' Commenting on Acts 1:11 Calvin insists 'that we must not seek Christ either in heaven, either upon earth, otherwise than by faith; and also, that we must not desire to have him present with us bodily in the world; for he that doth either of those two shall oftentimes go farther from him.'

Still commenting on verse 11, Calvin regards heaven as 'opposite to the frame of the world; therefore it doth necessarily follow, that if he be in heaven, he is without (beyond) the world.' To Calvin it is the invisibility, otherness, of Christ which is essential rather than geographic location. Christ 'is spread abroad everywhere by the power of his Spirit, not by the substance of his flesh.'

The ascension of Jesus is reported not only in today's reading of Acts 1:6-11, but also in Luke 24:50-53 and in Mark 16:19-20 where Jesus is now seated at the right hand of God (verse 19). Calvin suggests that this 'is the same as if he were called God's deputy, to represent the person of God; and therefore, we must not imagine to ourselves any one place, since the right hand is a metaphor which denotes the power that is next to God. This was purposely added by Mark, in order to inform us that Christ was taken up into heaven, not to enjoy blessed rest at a distance from us, but to govern the world for the salvation of all believers.'

To Calvin the crux of the story is the stark contrast between the situation after the crucifixion compared with the one after the ascension. He describes it as follows: 'Every person would have thought that, by the death on the cross, Christ would either be altogether extinguished, or so completely overwhelmed, that he would never be again mentioned but with shame and loathing. The apostles whom he had chosen to be his witnesses, had basely deserted him and had betaken themselves to darkness and concealment. Such was their ignorance and want of education, and such was the contempt in which they were held that they hardly ventured to utter a word in public. Was it to be expected that men who were unlearned, and were held in no esteem, and had even deserted their master, should by the sound of their voice, reduce so many scattered nations into subjection to him who had been crucified?'

By contrast, after the ascension, 'the miracle of heavenly power was displayed', according to Calvin. So much so that in his opinion all miracles should be regarded as 'appendages of the word of God.' If this is not done, Calvin fears, 'God's holy order is subverted' or 'corrupt modes of worship are disguised.'

Calvin describes the situation after the ascension as follows: 'They went out and preached everywhere – men who but lately shut themselves up, trembling and silent, in their prison. For it was impossible that so sudden a change should be accomplished in a moment by human power; and therefore Mark (16:20) adds, 'The Lord working with them'; by which he means that this was truly a divine work.

Our final reading comes from Matthew 13:44-52. Here Jesus explains what the kingdom of heaven is all about. It is like a treasure hidden in a field. It is so precious that the man, who found it, sells all he has to buy the field (verse 44). It is also like a beautiful pearl (verse 45) again so precious, that the man who found it, sells everything to possess it (verse 46). Or the kingdom of heaven is like a net full of fish (verses 47 and 48).

Again it is not a physical location somewhere in the sky. Calvin is therefore justified in thinking about heaven as a symbol of something very precious: order, perfection, spirituality, goodness, etc. He stresses its hidden, invisible part. He says: 'The natural meaning of the words is, that the Gospel does not receive the respect which it deserves, unless we prefer it to all the riches, pleasures, honours, and advantages of the world, and to such an extent that we are satisfied with the spiritual blessings which it promises, and throw aside everything that would keep us from enjoying them.'

In his comment on verse 47 Calvin compares the kingdom of heaven with 'a net sunk beneath the waters, to inform us that the present state of the Church is confused. Our God is the God of order, and not of confusion (1 Corinthians 14:33) and, therefore, recommends to us discipline; but he permits hypocrites to remain for a time among believers, till the last day, when he will bring his kingdom to a state of perfection.'

Here our detective story finishes. Indeed Calvin remains consistent to the position he has carved out for himself in the exegesis of Genesis 1:16. Heaven is not a physical abode. It is more. It is where God is enthroned and that may be as close as the human heart.

Both in his treatment in the *Institutes* and in his interpretation of the biblical story of the ascension into heaven, the latter is described as a releasing and universalizing of the Holy Spirit. In other words, Christ's physical crucified body, the very strong impact He left on his team of disciples and followers, the deep sense of loss and defeat on those close to Him when he died on the cross, are now replaced by a very concrete, unifying, electrifying, Holy Spirit, emanating from Him and God the Father. It is this spirit which actually more than fills the gap of his physical absence.

So far our biblical exegesis and Calvin's comments have proved to be consistent with his endorsing the astronomers' views. What is the social scientific relevance? In the social sciences the search is for latent, hidden, rather than manifest, obvious, functions. Heaven represents the latent part of social functioning. Order, peace, perfection are all elements hidden in the phenomena we see with the naked eye. Yet unless they under-gird our thinking and acting, unless they are our basic frame of reference, our social system drowns in the meaninglessness it has elevated as the only acceptable form of reality.

The impact of the entire Christian movement since its early beginnings lies partly in its fitting into a vacuum left by both ethnic and therefore non-global rigidification of Judaism at the time and dissatisfaction with the official, narrow, religion of emperor worship. It created a new, inspiring return to, and ever revitalizing tradition of, Hebrew prophecy. It also meant a resurgence of those sections of the population who were least part of, and least comfortable with the religious and political powers and establishments of the time.

To sum up: heaven in the Bible and Calvin's interpretations are a symbol of purity (Isaiah 55:9), the habitation of order (Psalm 119:89), the universal peace, perfection, spirituality of heaven (the ascension story), the undergirding, hidden, meaning provision (in the heavenly kingdom). Yet all this is not enough. Intellectual apology and deep understanding can only go so far. It has to be anchored in comprehensive commitment to God who is represented in Jesus Christ and the Holy Spirit. Calvin, true to the Bible, speaks of this 'faith' in the word of God as the strongest and safest anchor in a world which is dangerously devoid of stability and order.

Do we need a physical location of heaven? Given today's reading Calvin implies that we do not. Actually he persuades us that the more spiritual interpretation is the more accurate one. This is also expressed in our final Hymn 330 (ARB):

> The heavens declare your glory,
> Lord. In every star your wisdom shines
> But when our eyes behold your word
> We read your name in fairer lines.

ABOUT THE AUTHOR

Johannis (Hans) J. Mol was born in the Netherlands in 1922 and is professor emeritus of the Social Scientific Study of Religion at McMaster University in Canada. He studied economics at the University of Amsterdam, but was jailed by the Gestapo for 'undermining the Nazi war economy' from 1943-1945. He did his MA with Reinhold Niebuhr at Union Seminary and obtained his doctorate in sociology with Robert Merton at Columbia University, New York. He was the minister of Bethel Presbyterian Church in White Hall, Maryland from 1956-1961.

He was lecturer in sociology at the University of Canterbury in New Zealand from 1961-1963 and fellow in sociology in the Institute of Advanced Studies of The Australian National University from 1963 until he came to McMaster in 1970.

He is the author of fourteen books and monographs in the sociology of religion and the editor of two more. The best known among these works are *Religion in Australia* (1971), *Western Religion* (1972), *Identity and the Sacred* (1976), *Meaning and Place* (1983) and *Faith and Fragility* (1985). He has also published close to fifty chapters in books and articles in refereed journals. In 1978 he was invited to give the Payne Lecture at the University of Missouri and the opening address at the International Conference for the Sociology of Religion in Tokyo. In 1985 he was the keynote speaker at the Fifteenth World Congress of the International Association for the History of Religions in Sydney, Australia.

He has been very active in professional organizations. From 1963-1969 he was the secretary-treasurer of the Sociological Association of Australia and New Zealand. From 1972-1978 he was first secretary and subsequently president of the Sociology of Religion Research Committee of the International Sociological Association.

Hans Mol is married with four children and eleven grandchildren. He and his wife, Ruth, have retired on their property, Talpa, near Canberra, Australia.

Although retired Hans Mol is active in The Australian National University community and is a Visiting Fellow with the Research School of Humanities.

OTHER BOOKS BY THE AUTHOR

Churches and Immigrants (1961)
Race and Religion in New Zealand (1966)
The Breaking of Traditions (1968)
Christianity in Chains (1969)
Religion in Australia (1971)
Western Religion (Editor, 1972)
Identity and the Sacred (1976)
Religion and Identity (editor, 1978)
Wholeness and Breakdown (1978)
The Fixed and the Fickle (1982)
The Firm and the Formless (1982)
Meaning and Place (1983)
The Faith of Australians (1985)
How God Hoodwinked Hitler (1985)
Faith and Fragility (1985)
The Regulation of Physical and Mental Systems (with d'Aquili, 1990)

POSTSCRIPT

This book of sermons has been a return to my early love: theology and Biblical exegesis. It is the first one of my sixteen books that is not about sociology. Yet it is also about taking stock. It is an attempt to make sense of the intervening fifty years. For a long time now I have wanted to discover how these years have affected that early love.

In 1951 I was a final year theological student at St Andrew's College at the University of Sydney. I had just won the prize for the best student in theology and I decided to blow it all on the forty-odd volumes of Calvin's commentaries. Yet having all these books is not a major reason for finally making greater use of them.

It has been just as much an attempt to what was uppermost in Calvin's mind: to unify knowledge. He felt (and so do I) that the search for truth is a basic one and that the Christian faith gives a more comprehensive answer to that quest than the assumption that individual rationalism alone is sufficient.

It has also been an attempt on my part to persuade many of my friends and relatives who are enthralled by the latest book of Bishop Spong that there is a more sophisticated way of looking at religion generally and Christianity in particular. After all Spong has never fully understood the rich heritage of which we in the West are all part and thus suffers from having married the 'spirit of the age' which Dean Inge once observed is very likely to soon make widowers of those who espouse it.

Yet these sermons have also been the product of a typical 'mature age' problem: how to combine what hitherto has been held in two rather separate, watertight, compartments. The first one is my academic teaching and writing. This was and is an intellectually exciting study of the effect of religion on society and vice versa. Yet knowing and learning all about commitment is quite different from being committed.

The other, second, compartment is my religious activity. I wore two hats: at the university I wore the hat of the objective observer carefully weighing arguments, pro and con. At church I wore the other hat of participant in worship. But as I observed in the last sentence of the keynote address on 'Religion and Identity' opening the Fifteenth World Congress of the International Association for the History of Religions in Sydney in 1985: 'Studying identity does not necessarily lead to one, learning about salvation does not make one saved, religious scholarship does not produce religious people, in the same way as knowing all about love does not help one much to be in love.'

The intention of the sermons preached over a number of years, mainly at the national Presbyterian Church in Canberra was to marry Calvin with up-to-date research in the social scientific study of religion. Right from the beginning I wanted to do this without injustice to either and without intellectual compromise. After all, centuries separate the social sciences and Calvin. And particularly the former have recently made impressive advances.

To make the same point differently: in my sermons I assumed that my fellow worshippers shared my commitments, whereas in my lectures, seminars and academic books I observed these commitments and attempted to unravel for my students what function and social effects they had.

Calvin's view of the comprehensive intent of religion fitted like a hand in a glove with my own belief in the unity of truth. Even more important was his openness for what he called 'the works of the ungodly' and his disdain for the 'lazy believers who do not make use of those works (*Inst*. II ii 16-18).'

If anything I became more of a critic than Calvin tended to be particularly about the divinity of reason, being convinced that analytic reason tended not to be particularly helpful for the synthetic intention of all religions.

Usually, however, I shared from the outset many of Calvin's assumptions. One is that basically existence is a constant symbiosis of order and chaos. Actually Plato believed that too as do many other philosophers and historians, such as Toynbee and Bryce. Social scientists, such as Comte, Spencer and Parsons also contrasted integration with differentiation.

Another assumption I shared with the Bible and Calvin is that transcendental order is not only well documented and described, but also emotionally anchored through faith and that its social effect is impressive and for all to discern.

I learnt more and more about Calvin the more I consulted his voluminous writings while preparing the sermons. I slowly developed a sense of (1) what in the modern social sciences he certainly would agree with, (2) what he only probably would agree with, and (3) what he would out and out reject. Let us take each of these in turn.

(1) What he most certainly would agree with:

(a) In the sociology of religion values and norms are judged according to whether or not they make for greater solidarity. Always when Calvin (and the Bible!) approved of certain values and norms such as humility, understanding, love, etc. they were on the plus side of the sociological balance. And the other way round. Always when Calvin (and the Bible!) disapproved of certain values and norms, such as the ones mentioned in the Ten Commandments or the seven deadly sins, they were on the minus side of the sociological balance.

(b) In the sociology of religion beliefs are treated as shorthand summaries of what a particular culture thinks about itself. Also in Calvin (and the Bible!) the authority of Yahweh/God/Allah sums up what is expected by the citizens of a particular society.

(c) In the psychology of religion there is extensive literature on personal and social commitment as whole making. When Calvin follows both the Bible and Luther on the importance of 'salvation by faith' he is usually talking about the same thing. I say 'usually' because he sometimes includes in that phrase the rational consent to propositions which 'commitment' tends to exclude.

(d) In anthropology religion is very often identified with a charter for order. So does Calvin occasionally. Much more often he uses such concepts as 'God's sovereignty', 'predestination', 'election' which don't seem to differ much, if at all, from what is meant by 'order.' Certainly in the passages where he uses the phrase 'God's order' it is closely associated with sovereignty, predestination and election.

(e) Max Weber's views about charisma as a vitalising force in any society together with his insistence on the Calvinistic ethic possessing the Archimedean point for leveraging the development of capitalism would have Calvin's amused approval. Here as well as in Jelineks' work on the effect of Calvinism on democracy or Merton's on science, Calvin would say that all this had nothing to do with his enterprise and that the consequences were wholly unintended.

(f) Marginality, as a major explanation in the 21st chapter on St Stephen's martyrdom, is based on extensive sociological research which Calvin would certainly accept as valid.

(2) What he might agree with:

(a) Another fellow Frenchman, Emile Durkheim, suggested that the sacred tended to be contagious. I translate this to mean that organization has its own laws and principles and that religious organization and the boundaries it necessarily creates around its core beliefs tend to also become untouchable. Calvin's views about church order and ritual, for instance, would be in that category. Would he be happy to separate core beliefs and the organization necessary to protect them and perpetuate them? Some of the Biblical views (e.g. Hosea view's of sacrifice) and Calvin's own distinction between civic and heavenly order or the visible versus the invisible (less corrupted) church makes one confident that he would be inclined to take the extra step.

(b) Sigmund Freud regards the 'id' (instincts) as in conflict with the 'super-ego' (social morals and rules) with the 'ego' as a compromise. Similarly Calvin (like St Paul's remarks about the 'flesh') has a good deal to say about spirituality as bolstering whatever lifts humans beyond 'preying beasts.' Freud also has a lot to say about sexuality as the basis for the sublimation of other, socially relevant, kinds of love. Others have related this not only to the virgin birth, but also to the Pauline recommendation of sexual abstinence in order to strengthen the sublimation, its social effect and to distance it from its physical ('animal') origin. Yet Freud's ideas, analysis and rational awareness as the only means for salvation and restored integrity would be strongly rejected by Calvin.

(c) Calvin would probably be sympathetic to the stress on 'understanding' by the phenomenologists of religion. After all it fits again with the Biblical and his views of altruism. It encourages the empathetic, bird's eye view that he perceives God to have for mankind. Yet he would be rather critical of their tendency to ignore the crucial relevance of the transcendental frame of reference for motivation and action.

(d) Calvin would be sympathetic to the Marxist view of class as potentially harbouring discriminating, unfair, power abusing propensities. He would certainly have sympathy for the Marxist concern with the powerless and marginal in any society. After all the Bible in general and the New Testament in particular are full of examples of those who suffered unjustly and immensely (Jesus' crucifixion, John the Baptist's decapitation, Jeremiah's and Stephen's stoning) from displeased establishments, whether religious, political or social. Yet he would be very critical of Marxist utopianism and particularly its incapacity to think in terms of a moving equilibrium between the social need for firm authority and yet consent of the people, as is so obvious from his own writings.

(e) Calvin would be interested in the progress made about the function of dreams. There seems to be scientific agreement that all dreams are integrative and that therefore his distinction between those that are divinely inspired and others that are not may have to be revised.

(f) Calvin is convinced that the word of God (as uniquely expressed in the Bible) has come to humans via agents who were not only strongly committed to accurately communicating God's intentions but also to having it received as well as possible by those for whom it was intended. Calvin is aware that humans are invariably conditioned by the culture and society which they take for granted.

Yet to make God's message relevant, this taken for granted culture and society has to be effectively used for God's message to be heard at all. He therefore would be vitally interested in cultural, social and scientific change. This certainly would apply to changes in thinking about evolution, DNA, genetic engineering, cosmology and computer science.

His reaction, I imagine, would be twofold. He would emphasize that none of these changes have made a difference to the basic human condition of disorder, sin and propensity to make gods out of mundane concoctions and fabrications. In other words salvation is not any less urgent, he would conclude.

Yet his other reaction would be that God's world can only be vaguely understood and known and that therefore no one can presume that findings of a particular time and place should be regarded as final, however much they might be appropriate vehicles for communicating God's message.

He would also be intrigued by God's creating order out of chaos or salvation from sin being rather similar to the symbiosis between inertia and force in physics, structure and process in chemistry, heredity and variation in biology, gravity and radiation in cosmology, analysis and synthesis in philosophy and integration and differentiation in the social sciences.

(3) What Calvin would out and out reject:

(a) Calvin would condemn in the strongest of terms the attempt of Comte (the father of sociology) to trample on many biblical ideas (such as God's disapproval) which Comte barely understood. Even more would he be upset by his fellow Frenchman's embarkation on the new religion of society, in which Comte would be pontiff. He would also shake his head where Comte expressed his profound regret for not yet having found a worthy successor to his reign.

To Calvin this would be despicable heresy and would totally negate the importance, and therefore effect, of God's pure order as quite distinct from man's disorder. To Calvin this would make man's authority holy rather than God's. For very similar reasons he would also be scathingly critical of Nietzsche's 'ubermensch' or Feuerbach's elevation of the self as the source of all religious sentiment.

(b) Calvin would be just as adamant about any commitment leading to 'wholeness' or salvation. He might grudgingly admit that this might be so, but then add that all the other commitments would lead to segmental idolatries rather than the more comprehensive canopy provided by Yahweh and therefore inevitably issue in the fatal mistake of human navel-staring.

(c) Calvin would not likely be very happy with the hermeneutic enterprise in religion. Scholars interested in this approach appear to search for the key to unlock the interpretation of religion as it were from the outside. The assumptions in this search seems to be that the linear, progressive, thinking of Darwinists, the rationalist assumptions of the creationists and the cognitive positivism that has some of the sciences teetering on the brink of bankruptcy are all possible ways of interpretation, even if one totally disagrees with them. Calvin would deny this. He would strongly maintain that all religions are attempts to interpret existence from within their frame of reference and that the assumption that they could be studied otherwise would ignore what they are basically all about. Of course, Calvin would also maintain that his Christian interpretation is finely attuned to the heritage of the West and as such superior to any competing way of looking at the world.

Hans Mol, 26 February 2008

www.ingramcontent.com/pod-product-compliance
Lightning Source LLC
Chambersburg PA
CBHW060929170426
43192CB00031B/2869